ECONOMICS, GROWTH AND SUSTAINABLE ENVIRONMENTS

Also by David Collard

ALTRUISM AND ECONOMY
PRICES, MARKETS AND WELFARE
THE NEW RIGHT: A Critique
ECONOMIC THEORY AND HICKSIAN THEMES
  (*with D. R. Helm, M. Fg. Scott and A. K. Sen*)

Also by David Pearce

COST–BENEFIT ANALYSIS
COST–BENEFIT ANALYSIS: THEORY AND PRACTICE (*with A. K. Dasgupta*)
THE ECONOMICS OF NATURAL RESOURCE DEPLETION
ENVIRONMENTAL ECONOMICS
PRICE THEORY (*with W. J. L. Ryan*)
DECISION-MAKING FOR ENERGY FUTURES (*with L. Edwards and G. Beuret*)
SOCIAL PROJECTS APPRAISAL (*with C. A. Nash*)

Economics, Growth and Sustainable Environments

Essays in Memory of Richard Lecomber

Edited by

David Collard
Professor of Economics, University of Bath

David Pearce
Professor of Economics, University College, London

David Ulph
Professor of Economics, University of Bristol

MACMILLAN
PRESS

First published 1988

Published by
THE MACMILLAN PRESS LTD
Houndmills, Basingstoke, Hampshire RG21 2XS
and London
Companies and representatives
throughout the world

Printed in Hong Kong

British Library Cataloguing in Publication Data
Economics, growth and sustainable
environments: essays in memory of
Richard Lecomber.
1. Economic development—Environmental
aspects
I. Collard, David   II. Pearce, D. W.
III. Ulph, David   IV. Lecomber, Richard
330.9   HD75.6
ISBN 0–333–42187–6

The royalties, earned by sales of this book will be paid to the Council for
the Preservation of Rural England.

In memory of Richard Lecomber

Contents

Notes on the Contributors

John Bowers is Senior Lecturer in Economics at the University of Leeds.

John Broome is Reader in Economics at the University of Bristol, England.

Malcolm Clarke is Lecturer in Economics at the University of Bristol, England.

David Collard is Professor of Economics at the University of Bath, England.

Michael Common is Senior Lecturer in Economics at Stirling University, Scotland.

Herman Daly is Professor of Economics at Louisiana State University, USA.

David Pearce is Professor of Economics at University College, London, England.

Richard Pryke is Senior Lecturer in Economics at the University of Liverpool, England.

R. Kerry Turner is Lecturer in Environmental Economics, School of Environmental Sciences, University of East Anglia, England.

Alistair Ulph is Professor of Economics at the University of Southampton, England.

David Ulph is Professor of Economics at the University of Bristol, England.

1 Introduction

David Collard, David Pearce and David Ulph

These essays present some important developments in environmental economics revolving largely round the issues posed by the problems of growth and environmental sustainability.

The essays are offered in memory of Richard Lecomber. Though Richard was a talented economist who worked on many aspects of economics, he was best known for his work on environmental issues, both through his academic writing and the work he did in conservationist circles. Richard Pryke, whose family were close friends of the Lecombers for many years, provides a sketch of Richard's short life and work which will revive memories for some and serve as an introduction for others. Each of the subsequent essays relates more or less directly to themes which most interested Richard.

Pryke makes the point that Richard was committed both to the great issues involved and to rigorous analysis: there was then no retreat into either simple slogans or arid theory. This raises the following question: it is said that hard cases make bad law – do they also make bad economics? Of course, the analogy is an imperfect one for, in law, the hard cases are relatively unimportant whereas in economics they have more often than not provided the dynamic for changes in the mainstream analysis itself: Ricardo's *Principles* was stimulated by the price inflation of the Napoleonic Wars, Keynes's *General Theory* by the inter-war slump. On the other hand we have not seen, or rather have not yet seen, the 'greening' of economics. A major issue for the economics profession is therefore this: can orthodox analysis take on board the great issues of resource exhaustion, atmospheric poisoning and so on? If not, how substantial is the problem of reconstructing the analytical tools to take account of these issues? These questions lie more or less explicitly at the heart of all the essays in this volume.

Thus Michael Common (Chapter 3) examines the idea that economic development, rather than being a smooth, sustained process, is a process of solving a succession of economic problems thrown up by trying to achieve a sustainable environment in the face of technological change. This process moves the economy through a succession of

1

increasingly costly economic niches, and it is by no means clear that economic welfare improves through the process of development.

This theme is developed by Herman Daly (Chapter 4), who criticises the use of GNP as a measure of welfare on the grounds that it is 'a conflation of costs, benefits and changes in accumulation'. This is particularly so, he argues, in the context of sustainability where current actions may make it more difficult to sustain levels of activity in the future, yet this last is not reflected in GNP calculations. The question of how to reflect these considerations in national income calculations is one that bothered Richard Lecomber: Daly argues for three accounts instead of one; a services account, a throughput account and a capital account.

Some of the issues posed by sustainability are developed further by David Pearce (Chapter 5). In addition to the question raised by Daly of how one should revalue activities to take account of the intertemporal externality introduced by sustainability considerations, he asks whether the 'traditional' welfare objective in much environmental analysis has to be revised to make sustainability an explicit objective of policy if 'optimal' policies are not to lead to the ultimate destruction of the environment. He argues that the latter will be the consequence of traditional objectives which discount the future too heavily.

The question of the proper objectives of policy is taken up in a number of other essays. Thus both Malcolm Clarke (Chapter 8) and Kerry Turner (Chapter 9) examine the adequacy of 'traditional' criteria in the context of the issues thrown up by forestry and wetlands respectively. Clarke emphasises the importance of taking the long view, or, more generally, the sensitivity of policies to the discount rates employed, while Turner argues that 'traditional' objectives which give due weight to the future can provide an adequate basis for prescription for the environmental issues posed by wetlands.

More troublesome issues are raised by David Collard (Chapter 6) and John Broome (Chapter 7). In an essay written well before Chernobyl, Collard asks how adequately standard risk analysis as encapsulated in the theory of (subjective) expected utility can handle the kind of 'catastrophic' risks thrown up by major technological accidents such as the destruction of chemical plants or nuclear power stations. The problem of how to evaluate policies when the number of people who will be alive to 'enjoy' the benefits of those policies is one of the key variables, raises issues which are fundamental and as yet largely unresolved. Broome offers a penetrating analysis of a suggestion noted by Richard Lecomber, as to how one might tackle the problem.

Implicit in much of the discussion covered by the essays mentioned so far is the idea of a single government confronted by a single issue. In his essay (Chapter 10) John Bowers considers the problem of policy evaluation for a government which has the twin objectives of maintaining the environment but at the same time maintaining farmers' incomes. This raises the question of whether one can infer from the government's policy on farm subsidies its attitude to environmental policy, so that there is no need to take additional account of environmental issues in policy appraisal. Bowers offers some controversial views on this question.

Finally, Alistair and David Ulph (Chapter 11) emphasise that many environmental issues arise in the context of one government/country pursuing its best interests to the detriment of those of other countries/governments. Policy formulation in this situation will depend on the precise form of interaction and the extent to which it is recognised. This idea is illustrated in the context of an intertemporal model of trade between a resource (oil)-rich country and a resource (oil)-poor country, where the very intertemporal nature of the problem posed by exhaustibility provides the resource-poor country with some bargaining power it can exploit to 'countervail' that of the oil-rich country.

These essays illustrate the challenge that environmental questions pose not just to policy-makers but to academic economists in providing an adequate intellectual framework within which policies can be discussed and assessed.

It is precisely the thrill of this challenge that Richard Lecomber relished, and we offer these essays in tribute to his memory.

Note

1. We are very much indebted to Sue Pearce for help with editing and proof-reading.

2 Richard Lecomber: A Memoir and Tribute

Richard Pryke

Richard Lecomber was born in 1937. His father was a mathematics teacher at Kings College School, Wimbledon, in the days when it was a direct grant school. Richard was educated at Bryanston, where he became head boy, captain of rugby and an opening batsman in the first eleven. He spent his school days in a place of great beauty, for Bryanston is situated in splendid sylvan parkland and set in the midst of the hilly and upspoilt Dorset countryside. It was surely no accident that Richard was later to become involved in conservation societies and to turn his attention to environmental economics.

Richard left Bryanston with an open scholarship in mathematics to Wadham College, Oxford. However, after national service and a year of mathematics at Oxford, he switched to Philosophy, Politics and Economics. His economics tutor was Sir Donald MacDougall, who had moved back and forth between the academic world and government, and had little patience with theory for its own sake. MacDougall instilled the attitude that economics was valuable when it bore on questions of public policy.

After obtaining his degree in 1961, Richard spent another year at Oxford studying statistics and was then recruited by MacDougall to the National Economic Development Office (NEDO), of which he had just become the first Economic Director. At NEDO Richard was engaged on investigating obstacles to economic growth and on making medium-term projections of the UK economy. In 1964, when the Labour Party was elected, he transferred with MacDougall to the new Department of Economic Affairs and worked on the National Plan for 4 per cent growth. He had, during the previous year, been seconded to the Department of Applied Economics at Cambridge to look at Professor Stone's input-output model of the UK economy, and Richard had the job of using the model to produce forecasts for the Plan. He later complained that

little reliance was placed on the, admittedly crude, input-output calculations, much more credence being given to the submissions

5

from industry . . . . In some cases this may have been justified: industry may, formally or informally, have taken into account factors not known to the input-output analysts. But this was not always so; in many cases the industrial forecasting methods were known, and it was apparent, not only that no special expertise or judgement was used, but that mechanical methods were employed of far greater crudity than the input-output calculations.[1]

After the demise of the National Plan, Richard left the Department of Economic Affairs and became a full-time member of Stone's team working on developing the international trade side of the model.

In 1969 he joined the Economics Department at the University of Bristol, where he was to work for the rest of his life. This was the turning point in Richard's career. Hitherto his work had been based on the assumption that economic growth, as measured by the rise in the GDP, was desirable; although he had, as he explained in a cogent article, already become sceptical about whether it could be speeded up by means of an indicative plan drawn up in co-operation with industry. Now he began to question the desirability of growth itself. Stone's team had become inward-looking and preoccupied with their particular area. Hence Richard's move to Bristol had a liberating effect and he quickly turned his attention to new problems and to wider issues. This was the period when economists and others were becoming concerned about environmental issues and the depletion of natural resources. It was to these fields that Richard turned his considerable energies and formidable intellect.

His contribution took the form of two books – *Economic Growth Versus the Environment* (1975) and *The Economics of Natural Resources* (1979) – and numerous pamphlets and articles. This corpus was based on an extensive study of the relevant literature, which helps to explain why Richard's first publications on environmental economics did not appear until 1974. However, from then until his illness he was highly productive.

The distinctive features of his work were its clarity and balance. At a time when the growthmen and the environmentalists were fiercely attacking each other, and often generating more heat than light, Richard patiently sorted out the issues and weighed up the arguments. He was one of those rare individuals who are passionately concerned about a subject but are virtually impartial. Here is a taxonomy of the type which Richard himself sometimes employed:

	Caring and concerned	Uncaring and unconcerned
Biased	I	II
Impartial	III	IV

On any important issue, and certainly on the environment, there are a large number of individuals of type I, who care but are biased. There are also a considerable number who are uncaring and biased (box II) or uncaring and impartial (box IV). The rare group on the environment, and on any great issue, are type III individuals who care strongly but are impartial. Richard was, without a doubt, a type III man.

The fact that Richard was so concerned influenced both his mode of exposition and the content of his work. Because he wanted his works to be readily comprehensible by those with no great knowledge of economics or mathematics he almost entirely avoided algebra. This, however, was not the only reason. Richard used to complain that he found it tedious to wade through pages of mathematics, particularly as the point being made often turned out to relatively straightforward. He regarded much current economic literature as pretentious, and with pretension he had no sympathy. The absence of algebra does not mean that his own work was not thorough. He was, I think, sometimes over ready to list all his assumptions and spell out all the qualifications.

Richard's concern about the topics with which he dealt meant that he made no great effort to be original. His aim was to expound, evaluate and analyse in order that his readers might better understand the issues. It is therefore difficult to reel off a list of original ideas which he put forward and which might have been inscribed on his gravestone. This does not mean that his work lacked importance. Newly minted coins, despite their shine, are often less valuable because they are of lower denomination than those which are already in circulation. The striking point about much of Richard's work was its high denomination. Moreover, I suspect that much of what Richard said is more original than it may appear. It is easy to fall into the trap of believing that because most of the points he made were obvious –

or at least seem obvious once one has read them – they must be derivative.

It is not possible here to embark on an extended examination of what Richard had to say and, unfortunately, just because he was so fair-minded and impartial, his arguments and conclusions do not lend themselves to neat summary. However, it is possible to convey some idea of the nature and quality of his work by considering, by way of example, a little of what he had to say about the rate of discount and the welfare of future generations. As he says, the traditional view is that a reduction in the rate of discount (or interest) will benefit future generations by encouraging investment. However, environmentalists often object that an increase in capital expenditure, and hence the rate of (measured) growth, will have an adverse effect on future welfare. Moreover, conservationists regard higher investment as the root cause of increasing resource use. Richard pointed out that what the environmentalists are objecting to is not growth *per se* but its concomitant environmental ill effects and that, if this link could be broken, the rationale for a high discount rate, and other anti-growth policies, disappears. On the other hand, 'If this link cannot be broken, then the growth rate must be lowered and this implies raising the discount rate. In this context the conventional presumption that a lower discount rate favours the future is not valid.'[2]

An increase in the rate of discount was, however, very much a second best. If the rate fell, the price of depletable resources would, in accord with the Hotelling principle, rise to the point at which the enhanced rents were once again growing in line with the reduced rate of interest. What the conservationists overlooked was that the rise in prices, together with the greater attractiveness of investment, would lead to higher capital expenditure on projects designed to save resources. In Richard's own words,

we have become accustomed to the idea that a low discount rate promotes growth, which surely aggravates the resource problem. However, this idea is derived from a capital theory which takes no account of resource depletion. In fact a lowering of the discount rate will both encourage investment in man-made capital and discourage resource depletion. There will thus be two opposing effects on growth in GNP. But, more important, the structure of output will be changed, away from, for example, consumption and resource-intensive products and processes, and towards, for example, resource-saving investment and recycling.[3]

Richard noted that the effects of a fall in the discount rate would not be uniform but discriminating:

> The depletion of some resources may in fact increase if, for example, this is critical to the development of some important resource-saving project or if exhaustion is not much of a problem, say because of a renewable substitute. On the other hand, where conserving a resource is critical to future welfare, then lowering the discount rate will bring this about.[4]

It has been suggested that in the absence of government intervention the rate of interest will be excessively high and too little provision will be made for the welfare of future generations. In particular, it has been argued that people acting in isolation will bequeath less than if they were able to make a mutual contract to increase their bequests. Richard made some comments on this 'isolation paradox' which were both important and original.

The reason why isolated individuals supposedly make sub-optimal bequests can be shown by a simple example. Say that I obtain four times as much utility from the marginal £1 devoted to my own consumption as from an additional £1 which you spend on yourself. However, I only derive twice as much utility from an extra £1 left to, and presumably consumed by, my heirs as from an extra £1 left to, and presumably spent by, your heirs. Let us further assume that I have increased my bequests, and reduced my consumption to the point where I obtain the same utility from the marginal £1 which I consume and from the marginal £1 which I leave to my heirs. In this situation I can improve my welfare by making an agreement with you whereby we both increase our bequests. When we increase them by £1, I forgo £1 worth of personal consumption and lose the benefit equivalent to £0.25 that I previously obtained when you consumed the £1 which you now bequeath. But, on the other hand, I obtain £1 of extra benefit from my bequest to my heirs and make a gain equivalent to £0.50 from your bequest of £1 to your heirs. On balance I am therefore better off by £0.25.[5]

The extraordinary feature of this example, and line of argument, is that bequests made in isolation are always sub-optimal regardless of how affluent future generations are likely to be. This had already been pointed out by Professor Gordon Tullock. However, it was Richard who spotted the questionable assumption made by the proponents of the 'isolation paradox'. They assumed, as in my example, that individuals will, on the one hand, be less altruistic when they place values on their own consumption and that of their contemporaries than when, on the other hand, they judge between their heirs' consumption and that of their fellows. As Richard pointed out, this is by no means self-evident. It could be true that 'we care greatly for our descendants and for some or all of our contempories but care little for future generations in general, because they seem too distant to warrant our concern'. If so, 'Isolation serves to inflate the general level of bequests above the optimum level'.[6]

Richard went on to produce further reasons why, despite the belief that future generations would be more affluent, the level of bequests was so high.

An individual [he argued] may wish to set his heir up in the same relative position to which his upbringing has accustomed him. Moreover, a bequest may provide satisfaction to the giver . . . , and such satisfaction is likely to be relative to the general level of bequests. Such considerations would tend to push up the level of bequests and a contract to reduce them would be beneficial.[7]

Richard ended by giving the argument a conservationist twist by examining the implications of negative growth and falling consumption, due to resource depletion. He suggested that in this situation there would be an increase in concern for future generations and that there might well be a particularly large rise in generalised concern, not directed specifically to one's own heirs. Moreover, if future generations are going to be poorer, there is likely to be less concern about their relative standard of living and more about their absolute position. It therefore seems plausible to suppose that, if it were believed that consumption would go into decline, the 'isolation paradox' might operate in the direction that was originally supposed, viz sub-optimal bequests and an excessively high rate of discount.[8]

Although, as I have said, Richard's views are difficult to summarise, if only because they were so carefully qualified, he did arrive at one major conclusion. This is, fittingly, to be found in the final paragraph of his last book, where he wrote that, because government discretion is severely limited by what the public will vote for,

the conservationist must address his analysis less to the government than to the people. He must seek to dispel ignorance and facile optimism, to make the public more fully aware of the risks associated with unrestrained resource use. He must try to put these issues vividly to counteract myopia. He must appeal to the hearts of the current generation to ponder afresh the ethics of exposing future generations to substantial risk. In this way individuals may be led both to modify their own behaviour and to support appropriate collective action through the government.[9]

This passage might well serve as Richard's epitaph because it aptly describes what he was trying to achieve both through his academic writings and his conservationist and environmentalist activities. Richard did not only sit in his study writing books and articles which certainly helped to dispel ignorance and facile optimism but because of their very strengths – their theoretical nature and impartiality – are unlikely to have touched men's hearts, or even to have had a direct influence on government policy.[10] He also became active in the Society for the Protection of Rural England and the Conservation Society. He served as Chairman of the local branch of the Society for the Protection of Rural England and belonged to the Executive and various Sub-Committees of the Avon County Society. These Sub-Committees included, among others, those on the Avon Structure Plan and the Severn Barrage. In the Conservation Society Richard was a member of the Economics Working Party, where he contributed some much-needed expertise. Mention should also be made of the report *Energy to 2025* which Richard prepared on behalf of the Conservation Society and the National Centre for Alternative Technology.[11] This was Richard's last piece of written work and, because he was already ill, its completion involved considerable worry and strain.

In the concluding passage of *The Economics of Natural Resources*, which has previously been quoted, Richard declared that those who were concerned about conservation should modify their behaviour. This was not something which he preached but failed to practice. The duty to husband resources and protect the environment was for Richard a veritable religion, and one which shaped his life. Richard and his beloved wife, Maggie, whom he married in 1963, had always planned to have four children; but, after they had produced two, Richard became concerned about the pressure of population on resources. They decided that henceforth they would resort to adoption, which they duly did. Because of Richard's desire to conserve oil they purchased a minute Fiat, although this had eventually to be replaced by a larger car, and they made minimal use of their oil-fired central heating, as their guests can testify. A solar panel was installed in the roof with the hope, which proved vain, that this would produce hot water. Richard seldom went for a walk without returning with a dead branch for the fire. He collected empty bottles to deposit in bottle banks far away, used scrap paper and would not turn the dishwasher on until it was over-full. Like most religions, Richard's conservationism contained an element that was smile-provoking. However, his life was characterised by a rare unity of belief and behaviour.

I have spoken of Richard's life and work, and must come soon to his death. Before I do, I would like – however inadequately – to say something about Richard as a person and as a friend. There are many characteristics and qualities that might be mentioned: his disregard of appearance (I shall always recall him in baggy jumper and scruffy corduroy trousers); his keen sense of humour and merry laugh; the pleasure he obtained from singing; his love for the countryside and for camping; his affection for Thomas Hardy; the beautiful way in which he caught a cricket ball; his passion for china lions; his over-enthusiastic glueing of broken crockery . . . . Some of these characteristics were important whereas others were not. All in retrospect are dwarfed. What was outstanding about the man was his great patience and singular kindness. I never, for instance, remember him losing his temper and becoming angry with a recalcitrant child. Even signs of irritation were a rare occurrence and difficult to discern.

There was never any tension between us, although I was a growth-man and took a highly optimistic view about the exhaustion of depletable resources. Despite his sharper intellect and greater theoretical proficiency, Richard was never patronising and one could always admit to ignorance in the knowledge that one would not be made to feel small. In those almost continuous economic seminars which we used to conduct during family visits he always showed a lively interest in whatever work I happened to be engaged on. Moreover, when I sent him anything I had written, he always made extensive and detailed comments, which must have involved considerable labour. These may seem small points to recall, but they illustrate his kind and warmhearted nature.

In 1978 Richard was afflicted by what appeared to be epileptic fits; in 1982 he underwent brain surgery, and a malignant tumor was removed. Richard's behaviour from that time on was characterised by great courage and fortitude, for he had been told that he had only two years of life. Despite this he continued, to all outward appearance, to be almost his normal self: calm, courteous, considerate, and concerned. Not for him self-pity or 'Rage, rage against the dying of the light'. Richard's way of meeting death was to keep facing resolutely towards life and to refuse to give up hope. He was assisted here not by religion but by alternative medicine. As recommended Richard adopted a rigourously vegetarian diet and practised meditation. He did not give up teaching but went on almost to the end. Richard may have thought that by these means he would prolong his life but, since he was an eminently rational man, it is difficult to believe he expected anything more. Even this was not to be, and in July 1984 Richard died. He is buried in a quiet country churchyard. *Requiescat in pace*.

Notes

1. Richard Lecomber, 'Government Planning with and without the Cooperation of Industry: Reflections on British Experience', *Economics of Planning* (1970), p. 78.
2. Richard Lecomber, *Economic Growth Versus the Environment* (London: Macmillan, 1975) p. 34.
3. Lecomber, *Economic Growth Versus the Environment*, pp. 50, 51.
4. Richard Lecomber, *The Economics of Natural Resources* (London: Macmillan, 1979), pp. 95, 96.
5. This is my example and not Richard's. His explanation of the 'isolation paradox' was one of the few places where he resorted to algebra.
6. Lecomber, *The Economics of Natural Resources*, p. 103. See also Richard Lecomber, 'The Isolation Paradox', *Quarterly Journal of Economics* (1977), pp. 495–8.
7. Ibid.
8. Lecomber, *The Economics of Natural Resources*, p. 104; 'The Isolation Paradox', pp. 498, 499.
9. Lecomber, *The Economics of Natural Resources*, p. 215.
10. The exception here is the pamphlet *Tax Reform and Conservation* which Richard wrote with John Fisher, (London: Institute for Fiscal Studies, 1979).
11. Sadly, this document was never published. It was part of an imaginative exercise commissioned by the then Secretary of State for Energy, Tony Benn, who wanted the Energy Technology Support Unit (which is attached to the Department of Energy) to evaluate alternative future energy scenarios for the UK. Richard Lecomber was responsible for one set of scenarios and various other bodies, such as Friends of the Earth, assisted with the others. They were all compared to a 'reference scenario' which did not differ much from what was then official government energy policy. One of the current editors (David Pearce) was involved in the comparative evaluation.

3 'Poverty and Progress' Revisited

Michael Common

INTRODUCTION

The title of this essay derives from the fact that it is primarily an exposition of ideas which are either explicit or immanent in R. G. Wilkinson's *Poverty and Progress* (1973). The ideas concern an environmental approach to the understanding of the historical experience of economic development in its broad outlines. They do not appear to be widely known among economists, even among those who, as Richard Lecomber did, work on resource and environmental issues.[1] I think this is a regrettable situation, and this volume in memory of Richard seems an eminently suitable context in which to attempt to remedy it. While the 'growth versus the environment' controversy has abated somewhat in the 1980s, there remain those, including some economists, who argue for a fundamental break with past patterns of economic development. While Richard Lecomber was keenly aware of the environmental and other costs associated with growth, he was not a member of the zero growth persuasion.[2] I think that such agnosticism is the appropriate response to our current state of understanding regarding the fluid relationships between economic activity, environmental conditions and human welfare.

It is to the improvement of such understanding that this essay is addressed, in the sense of seeking to raise some pertinent questions rather than providing definitive answers. This intention should be kept in mind in reading what follows, since brevity requires that I put things in a more positive and assertive way than is properly justified. The argument being offered is that to regard economic development as a process primarily involving adaptive response to environmental change is a useful, and neglected, perspective on a very complex set of phenomena. The argument is not that all economic history can be understood, and only understood, within such a framework: the message is not ecological determinism. Again, it will not be possible explicitly to instance in what follows all of the particular qualifications that this general caveat implies.[3] I imagine that the interpretation

15

of the development process to be outlined here is sufficiently at odds with the standard economic interpretation that there is little danger of its uncritical acceptance.

PRODUCTION AND THE ENVIRONMENT IN DEVELOPMENT

The point of departure is the concept of economic development as a process which is essentially about adaptation to a changing environment, while being itself a source of environmental change. As Wilkinson (1973, p. 105) puts it:

> Looking at economic development in its ecological setting . . . we see that it is a process of solving a succession of problems which from time to time threaten the productive system and the sufficiency of our subsistence. In effect, human societies out of ecological equilibrium have to run to keep up; their development does not necessarily imply any long term improvement in the quality of human life.

I shall first use simple numerical illustrations, in the framework of input-output analysis, to expand on these summary statements.

Initially society is in a state of ecological equilibrium, in that its population size is constant and adjusted to the carrying capacity of its ecological niche. The constant population size is 100, and each individual has subsistence requirements of 0.55 units of 'food' and 0.3 units of 'clothing'. The technology by which this society exploits its environment is shown in I of Table 3.1; entries above the dashed line are intermediate input requirements per unit of output of food and clothing, entries below the dashed line are primary input coefficients. The primary input R1 is some renewable resource, for which the maximum sustainable yield is 100 units. The subsistence requirements for 100 individuals are 55 units of food and 30 units of clothing, requiring primary inputs of 260 units of labour and 100 units of R1.[4] It is in this sense that the society is in ecological equilibrium: its size is the maximum that its niche can support on a sustainable basis.

The development process is initiated by some disturbance to this state of affairs.[5] There are two possible sources of such disturbance: an increase in population following a breakdown of the cultural

Table 3.1

I	Food	Clothing
Food	0.25	0.4
Clothing	0.14	0.12
Labour	0.8	3.6
R1	0.5	1

II	Food	Clothing	Fuel
Food	0.25	0.4	0.1
Clothing	0.14	0.12	0.05
Fuel	0.1	0.2	0.1
Labour	0.8	3.6	1
R1	0.4	0.8	0
R2	0	0	1

III	Food	Clothing	Fuel 1	Fuel 2
Food	0.25	0.4	0.1	0.1
Clothing	0.14	0.12	0.05	0.05
Fuel 1	0.1	0	0.1	0
Fuel 2	0	0.2	0	0.1
Labour	0.7087	3.1889	3	1
R	0.4	0.8	0	0
R2	0	0	1	0
R3	0	0	0	1

system for controlling human numbers, or a decrease in the sustainable resource yield. Wilkinson himself emphasises the former source of disturbance to ecological equilibria, and discusses the cultural practices for population regulation at some length. He does, however, note that it appears to be fairly widely agreed that the emergence of agriculture, the point of departure for the historical experience of economic development, followed climatic change which adversely affected the yields available from hunting.[6] For present purposes, it is the fact of rupture to ecological equilibrium which matters, rather than the origin of such rupture. Assume, then, that the population size increases to 110. The technology of I in Table 3.1 cannot provide a society of this size with subsistence on a sustainable basis, since its requirement for R1 is greater than maximum sustainable yield. The society must adapt or perish. Adaptation takes the form of enlargement of the ecological niche by technological change which makes it possible to exploit new resources. By exploiting the non-renewable resource R2 and producing the commodity 'fuel', as shown in II of Table 3.1, the input requirements of R1 per unit of food and clothing output are reduced. With subsistence for 110 individuals requiring deliveries to final demand of 60.5 units of food and 33 units of clothing, primary input requirements are 91.6 units of R1, 25.4 units of R2 and 322.9 units of labour.

Now, while this adaptation clearly involves innovation, it is not necessary to assume that it involves invention or the acquisition of new knowledge. Using this R2 exploiting technology to satisfy the subsistence requirements of 100 individuals would require 293.5 units of labour input, that is, 2.935 units per capita compared with 2.6 units per capita under the technology which did not involve R2 exploitation. Given the knowledge of the means to and consequence of R2 exploitation, a society of size 100 would not rationally have exploited R2, given the objective of minimising the labour costs of providing subsistence. The available evidence on pre-agricultural societies is consistent with the hypothesis that they do have cultural systems for regulating their numbers, and do adopt technologies which minimise the costs of subsistence: see Wilkinson (1973) and references cited there, and, for example, Sahlins (1974). For any society concerned only to meet some fixed amounts of deliveries to consumption, it would presumably be irrational to do so in other than the least cost manner, given the operative constraints. The question of the fixity of the per capita required consumption levels is one I return to below.

With the population size at 110 individuals, the least cost, sustainable, method of providing subsistence requires the input of 2.935 units of labour per capita, compared with 2.6 in the original situation. The society is worse off than it formerly was. This deterioration will prompt an interest in labour-saving technological innovation. To the extent that this occurs, and population size remains constant and there are no adverse environmental changes, economic welfare improves. If, for example, labour-saving innovations can be found, which involve the use of no additional quantities of commodities or primary inputs, such that the labour input coefficients become 0.7087 for food, 3.1889 for clothing, and 0.89 for fuel, then per capita labour input requirements are restored to 2.6 units. The deterioration in economic welfare accompanying the adaptation to the rupture of the initial ecological equilibrium is, that is, conceivably reversible if the adaptation results in the achievements of a new, sustainable, ecological equilibrium. In such a situation the society can give its attention to the realisation of labour-saving technological change.

However, even in the absence of environmental disturbance exogenous to the socioeconomic system's operation, the new situation will not be a sustainable ecological equilibrium. This statement does not require the assumption that population growth resumes after the initial adaptation, though clearly such would necessitate further adaptation. Rather, the point is that, even for constant human numbers, the initial adaptive response creates a situation in which further adaptation to environmental change, arising from economic activity, will be required. The new technology gives rise to the need for further adaptation in response to resource depletion and environmental pollution. In the context of the particular illustrative example now under consideration, the emergence of pollution following adaptation is not compellingly obvious. But generally it should be apparent, via the materials balance principle, that a higher level of environmental exploitation in an extractive sense means a higher level in an assimilative sense also. Residuals discharge in excess of assimilative capacity impairs ecosystem function. In the illustrative context here, the operative case would be the use of fuel in the production of food and clothing giving rise to pollution which reduces the maximum sustainable yield from R1 below the required level for technology II to deliver subsistence to 110 individuals, creating the requirement for further technological adaptation. Such would most obviously take a form similar to that involved in the transition from I to II in Table 3.1, that is, involve the exploitation of new resources. It could, alternatively or additionally, take the form of modifying the processes by which food and clothing are produced, using fuel in such a way as to reduce the quantities of residuals discharged per unit of output. In either case, the new adaptation will involve some reversal of the improvement in economic welfare associated with the labour-saving technological change initiated after the initial adaptation and will imply the need for further adaptation.

The resource depletion part of the story has more obvious appeal in the illustrative context here. It is not necessary to assume that the society actually runs out of the non-renewable resource R2. It is only necessary to assume that R2 is exploited down a decreasing quality gradient, so that the labour input requirements per unit of fuel output rise as depletion proceeds. If, for example, the technology II in Table 3.1 is modified so that the labour input coefficients are 0.7087, 3.1889 and

3.00, the use of this technology to meet the subsistence needs of 110 individuals requires a labour input of 3.09 units per capita. Assume that 3.00 units per capita is the upper limit on tolerable labour requirements for this society, and that the possibilities for labour-saving innovation within the existing mode of production have been fully exploited, so that the problem can only be solved by a change in the mode of production. In the technology III in Table 3.1, two types of fuel are produced from two non-renewable resources R2 and R3. Fuel 2 can be used in clothing production on the same terms as fuel 1, but requires only 1 unit of labour input per unit of output. Switching from the technology II to the technology III to deliver 0.55 units of food and 0.3 units of clothing to each of 110 individuals reduces the per capita labour input required from 3.09 to 2.86 units, and 'solves' the society's problem with respect to the labour constraint.

Again, this situation cannot be a new, sustainable, ecological equilibrium on account of environmental pollution and resource depletion. This, then, is what economic development essentially is – a process of shifting through a succession of ecological niches, the shifts being necessitated by the fact that the means by which a new niche is created are such that eventually it will no longer serve. Of course, some niches may serve for longer than others. Also, it must be noted, a niche may be destroyed by means other than those inherent in a society's own development process – the intrusion of another society, for example, or an exogenous environmental shift. The course of economic welfare during the development process is not, even as a trend, monotonic. With the requirement of meeting fixed per capita subsistence needs, economic welfare is measured unequivocally by per capita labour inputs.[7] Niche shifts primarily involve welfare reductions as the price of social survival: with the mode of production stable during the occupancy of a given niche, the dominant movement is welfare improving as innovation is directed in labour-saving directions. Clearly, some niches will be more favourable contexts for labour-saving innovation than others, and different niche shifts will have different implications for labour input requirements. Consequently, this interpretation of the development process implies no particular view on the historical record in respect of economic welfare. It does, however, imply the existence of two closely related monotonic trends, that is, of two hypotheses about the historical experience of development. First, over time, the level of environmental exploitation increases, in both the extractive and assimilative senses. Second, the means by which final demand requirements are met became more indirect, the production structure becomes more roundabout. Both of these trends are illustrated in Table 3.1 in the progression I, II, III.

AGRICULTURAL DEVELOPMENT

Turning from illustrative expository examples to actual experience, I shall consider first agricultural development in relation to these two hypotheses. Norgaard (1984) considers agricultural development from what he terms a 'coevolutionary perspective', which he sees as providing 'a linkage between ecological and economic perspectives'.[8] From this perspective:

> agricultural development can be viewed as a coevolutionary process between a sociosystem and an ecosystem that, fortuitously or by design, benefits man. Indeed, if the gains from agricultural development are real, not simply this generation living at the expense of the next or one region or group living at the expense of others, it is difficult to imagine how the gains from development could arise other than by a process of positive feedbacks between the sociosystem and ecosystem, whereby these systems coevolve in a manner favourable to man. In this view, sociosystem options compatible with coevolutionary development are constrained by characteristics of the ecosystem: but development is not simply ecologically determined.

Norgaard does not claim that all coevolutionary feedback is beneficial to man, and uses the term 'coevolutionary development' to refer to coevolution that benefits man. He notes that with coevolutionary development 'maintenance feedback systems frequently shift from the ecosystem to the sociosystem', which means more roundabout production. In the same connection, Norgaard argues that the 'idea that the sociosystem frequently assumes the complementary activities and regulatory functions that were either previously endogenous to the ecosystem or maintained by the individual farmer cannot be overstressed'. Regarding the level of environmental exploitation, Norgaard recognises that this increases with much of what is conventionally known as agricultural development, and that

many scientists are persuaded that man is currently exploiting the
accumulated low entropy of his environment, through both extraction and pollution, to the detriment of future generations far faster
than he is coevolving with nature to the benefit of future generations. Georgescu-Roegen may be quite correct, most of the
technologies we associate with development may simply allow us to
utilize low entropy stocks faster.[9]

Of course, this does not necessarily mean that further coevolutionary
development, in the sense defined by Norgaard, will not occur.
However, it is Norgaard's view that since 'not only the research but
the social organisation of the developed and developing world are
being structured around the exploitation of low-entropy stocks and
the correction of related social and environmental problems', a
'coevolutionary path of progress will not easily be found or followed'.

Clearly the level of environmental exploitation cannot be expressed in a single number, since many different resources are extracted and many different residuals returned to the environment. A
system of aggregation weights derived from the economic system will
not serve to provide a single environmental exploitation index over
the course of development if development is essentially about a
changing economic system. There is, apparently, no completely
satisfactory solution to this problem. The economic system's energy
use can be used as a reasonable proxy for its level of environmental
exploitation. A full argument in support of this contention is impossible here, and I shall simply note that environmental exploitation
involves moving and transforming things, for which purpose energy
use is necessary. I shall also take it that for the purpose at hand,
aggregation across energy sources on a purely energetic basis is a
satisfactory procedure.[10] If, then, there is anything in the interpretation of the historical experience of development set out above, it
should show up in the history of the way agricultural systems use
energy. This history is far from well documented. However, over
recent years quite a lot of work has been done on the study of extant
agricultural systems, in energetic and other respects.

Table 3.2 here is taken from Leach (1975) who brought together
the results of much of this work. The figures in Table 3.2 are the
results of measuring all of the inputs, direct and indirect (other than
solar radiation, rainfall, and so on) in terms of energy equivalents.
Notwithstanding the possibilities for disagreement with some of the
conventions adopted in the accounting and the complications of local

environmental conditions, and so on, the general picture which emerges is really very clear in relation to the hypothesis that, at least in agriculture, development has been about increasing environmental exploitation.[11] In purely energetic terms, this has gone with increasing labour and land productivity. It is of some interest to note, however, that energetic efficiency, as measured by the output/input ratio in Table 3.2, does not apparently increase monotonically with development. Figure 3.1 reproduced from Leach (1975), shows that I have not in these respects used an unrepresentative sample from the full set of energy budgets that he reports.[12]

Table 3.2   Agricultural energy budgets

	1	*2*	*3*	*4*
Labour	0.37	5650	460	20
Animals		960	2180	
Machinery		230[a]	1010	18590
Fertiliser			450	11660
Pesticides			60	1090
Drying				4480
Irrigation				29620
Total Inputs	0.37	6840	4160	65460
Output	2.90	281100	22900	84120
Output/Input	7.8	41.1	5.5	1.3
Output/Labour Input	7.8	49.7	49.8	4206

Units are MJ per Hectare per annum (1 MJ $\simeq$ 0.28 kwh)

1   Pre-agricultural, !Kung Bushmen, Kalahari, Africa
2   Pre-industrial agriculture, Chinese peasant farming
3   Semi-industrial agriculture, rice growing, Philippines
4   Industrial agriculture, rice growing, USA

[a] Land tools and ploughs

Source: G. Leach (1975) Budgets 49, 64, 72, 74.

I stated above that the second hypothesis about development generated by the interpretation being offered here is that it is a process involving the increasing roundaboutness of the production structure, so that as it occurs the means by which final demands are met become more indirect. This is apparent in the agricultural

24

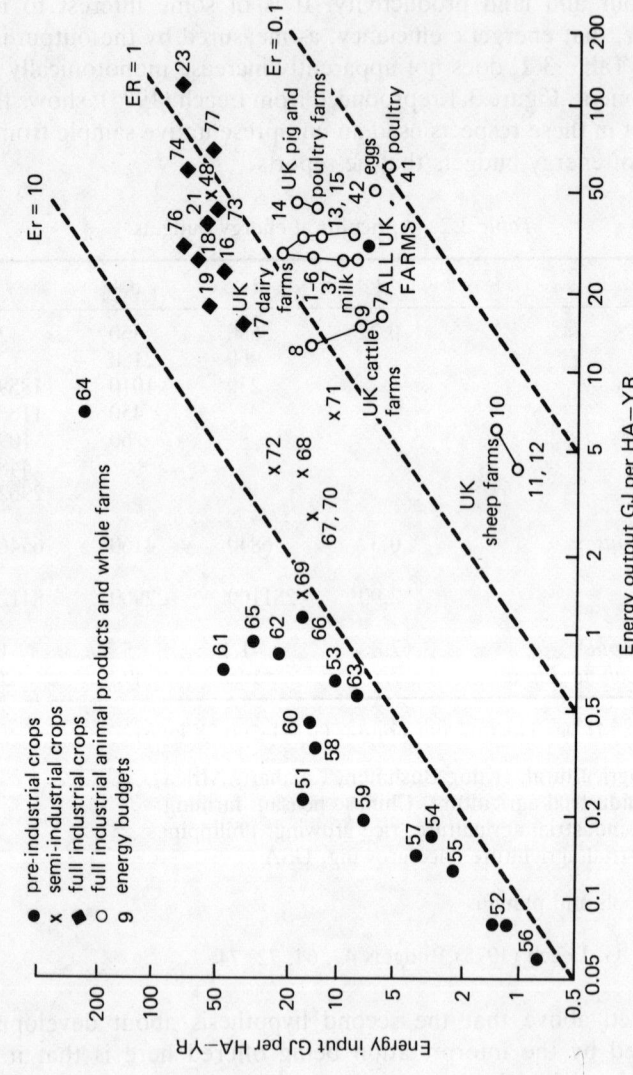

Figure 3.1 Energy inputs and outputs per unit of land area in food production (world)

Source: Gerald Leach, *Energy and Food Production*, IIED, 1975.

context, in that whereas in societies where agriculture is either not in being or in the pre-industrial stage its output is typically a direct input to consumption, in societies where agriculture is industrialised (and highly productive on conventional accounting conventions) its output is rarely a direct input to consumption. As Leach (1975) notes, the data reproduced here in Table 3.2 and Figure 3.1 concern the production of food within the agricultural system: in present-day UK terms, the inputs recorded are those arising up 'to the point where food reaches the farm gate'. Commenting on this convention, Leach says:

> This allows agriculture to be separately analysed and provides information that may be useful for developing countries, where large populations still live close to the land. For the industrial world one must look further. Urbanisation, industrialisation and other changes, largely spurred by changes in agriculture itself, have vastly increased the scale of the food chain from the farm to the mouth in every sense, including energy usage. In those societies (and increasingly in the developing world) much more energy is now used to transport, package, sell, cook, store and process (or merely titivate) foodstuffs than are used to grow it. (Leach, 1975)

Leaving aside Leach's specifically energetic approach, the point, once made, is in general terms an obvious one, and is part of many people's direct experience. Table 3.3 here gives a breakdown of the energy inputs to the production of the commodity that is a UK standard white loaf on the shelf in a shop.[13]

ECONOMIC STRUCTURE AND DEVELOPMENT

The hypothesis that one essential feature of the development process is the increasing roundaboutness of production concerns the production of all commodities, not just food commodities and agricultural output. Any attempt to test the general hypothesis faces two problems: the measurement of the roundaboutness of production, and the lack of historical data on the input-output structure of economies as they develop. While it is not apparent that either of these problems can be fully overcome, I think it is possible to make some progress by adopting as a measure of the roundaboutness of production the ratio

Table 3.3   Energy inputs to UK bread production

	MJ	(%)
Tractors, etc.	1.47	7.3
Fertilisers	2.34	11.6
Other	0.08	0.4
Total, Farming	3.89	19.3
Direct fuel use	1.49	7.4
Packaging	0.44	2.2
Transport	0.28	1.4
Other	0.40	2.0
Total, Milling	2.61	13.0
Direct fuel use	4.76	23.6
Packaging	1.67	8.3
Other	2.90	14.4
Total Baking	9.33	46.3
Heating and lighting	1.73	8.6
Transport	2.46	12.2
Total Retail Distribution	4.19	20.8

Source: Chapman, 1975, Figure 8.

of the value of total gross output to the value of deliveries to final demand.[14] If this measure is adopted, some relevant data can be found. In United Nations (1983) Table 4 gives figures, by industry, for gross output, intermediate consumption, and value added, in current and constant prices. Not all countries provide such data. Those that do are listed in the lower half of Table 3.4 here. For these countries the information available varies from figures for just one year to a complete run of annual figures from 1970 to 1980.

In Figure 3.2, I have plotted the average for each country of the available ratios of total gross output value to total value added against the corresponding per capita national income in 1976.[15] I take per capita national income as the measure of progress along the process of development. The regressions 1 and 2 reported in Table 3.4 use the data of Figure 3.2. They do not lead to the rejection of the hypothesis that the roundaboutness of production increases with development. In Figure 3.3 the horizontal axis measures energy consumption per capita in the mid 1970s (source of data: The Econ-

Table 3.4

---

1 RATIO =1.5837 + 0.0001 INC $\bar{R}^2$= 0.4492 D. W. = 1.59 26 observations
     (22.37)   (4.62)

2 RATIO =1.5913 + 0.0001 INC $\bar{R}^2$= 0.6679 D. W. = 1.67 24 observations
     (29.06)   (6.88)

3 RATIO = 1.5550 + 0.0001 EN $\bar{R}^2$= 0.6793 D. W. = 1.66 24 observations
     (26.90)   (6.83)

4 RATIO = 1.5896 + 0.0001 EN $\bar{R}^2$= 0.7310 D. W. = 1.99 22 observations
     (30.25)   (7.62)

RATIO – ratio of gross output to value added (from United Nations, 1983)
INC   – 1976 per capita national income, US $ (from *The Economist*, 1978)
EN   – 1975 per capita energy consumption, kg. of coal equivalent (from *The Economist*, 1978)

omist, 1978). Recall that the hypothesis that environmental exploitation increases with development has been advanced, and energy use suggested as a proxy for the level of environmental exploitation. The regressions 3 and 4 in Table 3.4, using the Figure 3.3 data, indicate that the level of roundaboutness of production is positively associated with the level of environmental exploitation. Also, it is clear that energy consumption and income are highly correlated.

With respect to these results, numerous caveats are, of course, in order. Perhaps the major mismatch between the story told earlier here, in terms of Table 3.1, and the data behind the regression results concerns the final demand vector. Whereas that was, in per capita terms, unchanging in the illustrative examples, it definitely does change in the actual historical experience of development. In the latter case, it changes in scale and composition. Indeed, it is only because it changes in scale that it is possible, as immediately above, to use per capita national income as an index of development. Changes in the scale and composition of the final demand vector, even on a per capita basis, are not necessarily inconsistent with the productive system always delivering subsistence requirements. There are two aspects to this. First, an unchanging subsistence requirement may be met in different ways. Second, as the productive system changes, so subsistence requirements may change. These are not mutually exclusive tendencies.

Figure 3.2

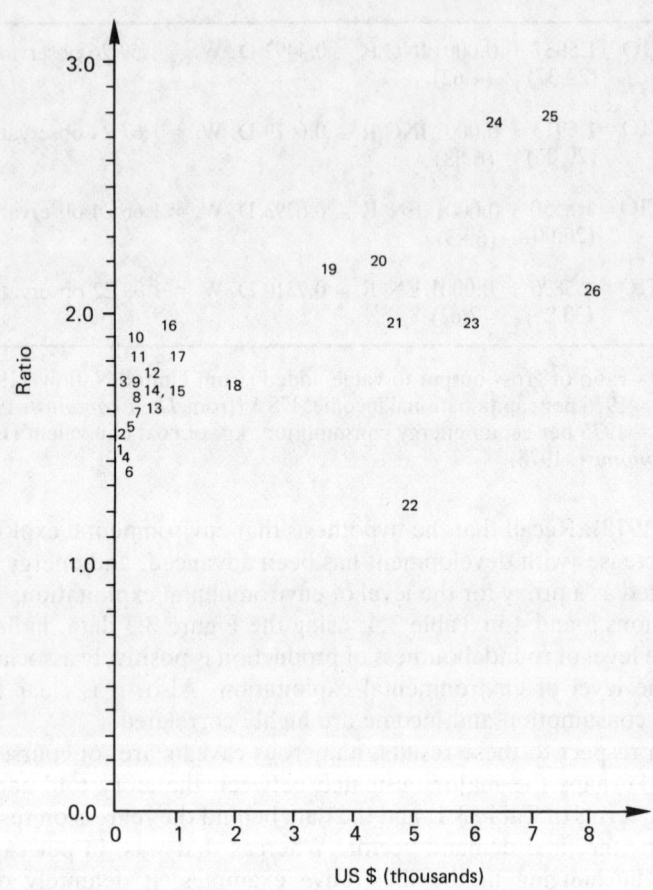

Country Coding for Figures 3.2 and 3.3:

1	Upper Volta	11	Zimbabwe
2	Rwanda	12	Ecuador
3	Burma	13	Peru
4	Benin	14	Jordan
5	Haiti	15	Algeria
6	Ghana	16	Chile
7	Bolivia	17	Fiji
8	Swaziland	18	Venezuela
9	Zambia	19	New Zealand
10	Botswana	20	Japan

21	Austria	24	W Germany
22	Libya	25	Canada
23	Netherlands	26	Sweden

Note: Countries 18 and 22 are not used in regression 2; countries 8 and 10 are not used in regression 3 (EN data n.a.); countries 8, 10, 18 and 22 are not used in regression 4.

Figure 3.3

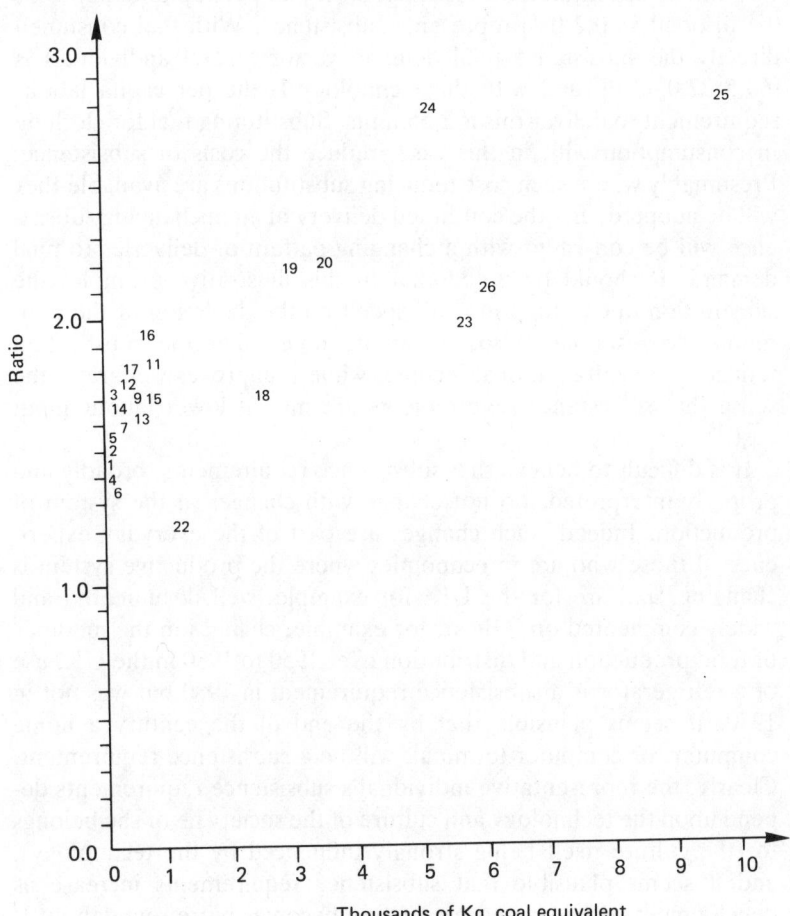

For Country Coding, see note to Figure 3.2.

CONSUMPTION AND DEVELOPMENT

The distinction here can be clarified in the context of the numerical example used above. Consider the economy at the stage of development given by the technology II in Table 3.1. Recall that with per capita subsistence requirements of 0.55 units of good and 0.3 units of clothing, and 110 individuals, labour input requirements were 2.935 units per capita. Suppose that in meeting subsistence requirements fuel can be substituted for clothing, such that per capita either [0.55 0.3 0] or [0.55 0.2 0.1] represents subsistence. With fuel consumed directly the subsistence final demand vector for 110 individuals is [60.5 22.0 11.0], and with the technology II the per capita labour requirement to deliver this is 2.55 units. Substituting fuel for clothing in consumption will, in this case, reduce the costs of subsistence. Presumably where such cost-reducing substitutions are available they will be adopted, and the continued delivery of an unchanging subsistence will be consistent with a changing pattern of deliveries to final demand. It should be noted that in this illustrative example, the substitution in consumption will speed up the depletion of the non-renewable resource. Also, it can be noted that the substitution reduces per capita national income, while it improves welfare in the sense that subsistence requirements are met at lower labour input cost.[16]

It is difficult to believe that subsistence requirements, broadly and properly interpreted, do not change with changes in the system of production. Indeed, such changes are part of the everyday experience of those who are in economies where the productive system is changing, and are for the UK, for example, well documented and widely commented on. Given, for example, changes in the methods of food production and distribution over 1950 to 1980 in the UK, use of a refrigerator is a subsistence requirement in 1980 but was not in 1950. It seems plausible that by the end of the century a home computer, or computer terminal, will be a subsistence requirement. Clearly, the representative individual's subsistence requirements depend upon the technology and culture of the society he or she belongs to (the culture itself being strongly influenced by the technology), and it seems plausible that subsistence requirements increase as development proceeds and production becomes more roundabout.[17] The possible implications of this can be seen by assuming that the use of the technology II means that individuals need to consume 0.3 units of fuel for subsistence, over and above the 0.1 units consumed to reduce clothing consumption. Then the final demand vector for 110 individuals' subsistence is [60.5 22 44] and labour input requirements are 3.05 units per capita. Recall that for the original subsistence final demand vector [60.5 33] the labour input requirements were 2.94 units per capita. The point is that while the economy is still delivering subsistence, a combination of a change in the way subsistence requirements are met and an increase in subsistence requirements has resulted in an increase in the cost of meeting subsistence, a welfare loss and an increase in per capita national income. This is, of course, in numerical terms purely illustrative. I am not arguing that, in fact, it is the case that as development proceeds so changing subsistence requirements plus changing ways of meeting those requirements must always work to increase labour input requirements. Clearly, in some circumstances things might work out otherwise. Also, I have discussed the possibilities for labour-saving technological change in the course of development.

The point that I am making is that the observation that development is, in fact, accompanied by a changing final demand vector is not itself inconsistent with the proposition that at all times the productive system, which is becoming more roundabout and more exploitative of the environment, is delivering subsistence requirements. Also, this is not inconsistent with an increasing per capita national income. If it is accepted that it is subsistence that is always delivered, then the history of economic welfare is the history of per capita labour input requirements. In the light of the earlier discussion of development and the production system, and of this discussion of changing subsistence requirements, it is not to be expected that history would show a monotonic downward trend in labour requirements, that is, an upward trend in economic welfare. One would expect different trends as particular circumstances differ.

This is not the conventional view, which regards the basic situation to be one in which economic development and progress are synonymous. I use the word 'progress' rather than the phrase 'improving economic welfare' (or some variant thereof) here deliberately, in order to make a distinction between two types of expectable reaction to the interpretation of development offered here, which I can label the 'non-economic' and the 'economic'. It is possible to reconcile the idea that all the economy ever does is to deliver subsistence with the idea of economic development as progress by taking the view that some subsistence patterns are preferable to others, on non-economic grounds, and that in development preferable succeed less preferable patterns. The criteria of preference here could be philosophical, religious or aesthetic.[18] A single example will have to serve to indicate what I think is involved here, that of education and knowledge. It might be conceded that as development proceeds, so it is the increasing complexity of the productive system required to deliver subsistence that necessitates that individuals have more education and that nature is more fully understood. Higher levels of education and knowledge are, that is, new subsistence and production needs and do not imply higher levels of economic welfare. However, it might be argued that more education and knowledge mean greater self-awareness for individuals, and that increasing self-awareness represents progress on philosophical grounds.

Economists would not, on the whole, be happy with this line of argument. They would argue that, given proper measurement (a major caveat in practice), economic welfare increases with development that results in increasing per capita national income or expenditure. Essentially, the argument here is that some representative individual would prefer his or her situation as it existed with higher per capita national income to his or her situation as it existed with lower per capita national income.[19] The problem with this argument is that it requires that the representative individual is taken to have a preference system which is independent of the situation to be evaluated. This is not, I suggest, an appealing assumption in the context of a view of development which takes it that its essential characteristic is that it is a process of adaptation to changing environmental conditions. With respect to the relevant arguments, individual preference systems cannot reasonably be regarded as genetically determined, but must rather be seen as being, at least partially, learned. If development involves changing the context in which individuals learn their preferences, it will presumably result in changing preferences. The point at issue here can be illustrated with an extreme example. In comparing the situations of an Australian aboriginal prior to European incursion and a present-day inhabitant of the Sydney suburbs, whose (revealed) preferences should be used?

CONCLUDING REMARKS

The interpretation of economic development suggested above can, I suggest, integrate many of the criticisms of the growth objective raised in recent years.[20] The limits to growth argument of, for example, Meadows *et al.* (1972) is essentially the argument that the world economy's occupancy of its current niche will be temporary, and that the transition to a new one will be painful. With respect to this issue, I suspect that recent work by theoretical and applied ecologists on the relationship between the complexity of an ecosystem and its response to shocks might be fruitfully used to examine the prospect of 'doom' at this particular niche transition.[21] The advocacy of the 'steady state economy' by, principally, Daly (1973) is essentially an argument for the deliberate selection of a new niche of a particular kind, which, it is thought, would offer the prospect of more prolonged occupancy. Another type of anti-growth argument concerns the costs associated with it, rather than its feasibility.[22] The environmental costs of growth – pollution and resource depletion – are signals that niche occupancy is transitory. The social costs of growth are manifestations of the increasing indirectness of consumption and of the increasing complexity and roundaboutness of the productive system.

One of the few attempts to study how those affected feel about economic growth is the work of Easterlin (1975).[23] He summarises his results as follows:

> The concern of this paper has been with the association of income and happiness. The basic data consist of statements by individuals on their subjective happiness, as reported in thirty surveys from 1946 through 1970, covering nineteen countries, including eleven in Asia, Africa and Latin America. Within countries there is a noticeable positive association between income and happiness – in every single survey, those in the highest status group were happier, on the average, than those in the lowest status group. However, whether any such positive association exists among countries at a given time is uncertain. Certainly, the happiness differences between rich and poor countries that one might expect on the basis of the within-country differences by economic status are not borne out by the international data. Similarly, in the one national time series studied, that for the United States since 1946, higher income was not systematically accompanied by greater happiness.

Easterlin's proposed explanation for his results is that preferences are interdependent, as in the relative income hypothesis of Duesenberry. An alternative, but related, explanation could be developed in terms of the role of positional goods, as in Hirsch (1977). Easterlin's results are also consistent with the interpretation of economic growth and development offered in this paper. While interdependent preferences and positional goods no doubt play some role, their significance need not be very great. The reason why development does not deliver what economists (in the main) expect of it is simply that it is essentially about adaptation.

Notes

1. It is of interest to note that Wilkinson's book appears in the bibliography to Richard's *Economic Growth versus the Environment* (1975) and gets a brief mention in the text (p. 45). Reviews of *Poverty and Progress* by economists were relatively few, as are references in the economics literature. It is noted in Mishan (1977) and discussed in Boulding (1974) and Flammang (1979).

2. In an essay on 'Economic Growth and Social Welfare', Richard (1979) concluded, 'Neither indiscriminate growth nor indiscriminate halting of growth are likely to be beneficial . . . . Even if for "GNP" we substitute some more complete measure of welfare and for "economic growth" the growth in this wider measure (call this "progress"), it must be recognised that "progress" involves considerable costs. The principle of these are (a) current sacrifice, including the costs of change, (b) effects on the distant future via resource depletion and progressive environmental deterioration'.

3. I make this explicit in order to avoid the sort of misunderstanding apparent in, for example, Desai's review (1975) of *Poverty and Progress*. Desai accuses Wilkinson of offering a 'unicausal explanation of a complex process', and of setting out a 'deterministic thesis' according to which 'any disturbance in equilibrium *necessitates* economic development' (italics in the original). In fact, in his preface Wilkinson states that he is concerned with 'three distinct sources of change: the breakdown of ecological equilibrium, the demands of technical consistency, and the development of new forms of need as the real costs of living are changed' and remarks that 'None of them will on its own explain all change'. Also, in Chapter 10, 'Explanations of Underdevelopment', Wilkinson discusses the question of why some societies out of ecological equilibrium do not experience economic development. See also Boulding (1974).

4. The primary input requirements are given by $L = lx$ and $RI = r_Ix$ where $x = (I - A)^{-1}f$, l is the labour input coefficient vector, r_I is the RI input coefficient vector, x the gross output vector, f the final demand vector, and A is the matrix of inter-industry coefficients.

5. More properly, some disturbance to ecological equilibrium is necessary, but not sufficient, for the initiation of the development process.

6. See also Smith (1975), for example.

7. In saying this, I am assuming that longevity, health, and so on, are maintained constant by the unchanging subsistence. As already noted, I deal with changing deliveries to final demand, and changing subsistence needs (possibly to maintain longevity and health), later. Note also that I am, implicitly, assuming away problems associated with social inequalities, whatever the basis for such.
8. See also Norgaard (1981). In both of these papers Norgaard notes the relevance of Wilkinson's work, and also that of Boserup (1965), for the coevolutionary perspective.
9. The reference is to Georgescu-Roegen (1971).
10. Ecologists find energy accounting one useful way of analysing ecosystems: see, for example, Phillipson (1966) by way of introduction. For a discussion of the laws of energy use, thermodynamics, in relation to economic activity, see Georgescu-Roegen (1971) and (1979).
11. It is of interest to quote some of Leach's notes accompanying the data for the !Kung Bushmen. Apparently these

> hunter-gatherers secure a good diet (93g protein and 8.27 MJ per day on average) but require 1040 ha land (10.4 km²) per person. Time required for food gathering is not excessive. Lee found that 156 man days were needed for 668 population days of consumption: in other words, while 65% of the population spent 2.5 days per 7 day week gathering food, the remaining 35% did no work at all.

12. It should be noted that in some of the budgets for full-industrial agriculture covered by Figure 3.1, human labour input is ignored, being negligible in energetic terms.
13. It can also be noted that some recent trends in retailing in advanced societies are tending to shift costs from what appears in the accounts as production to what appears in the accounts as consumption. An example is the growth of supermarkets and central shopping malls at the expense of small local stores.
14. With $x = (I - A)^{-1}f$ and $p = (I - A)^{-1}l'$, where p is the price vector, the value of total gross output is $x'p = f'(I - A)^{-1'}(I - A)^{-1}l'$ and the value of deliveries to final demand is $f'p = f'(I - A)^{-1}l'$. Clearly, for given A, multiplying either f or 1 by a scalar will change both $f'p$ and $x'p$ by the same scalar, so that the ratio of $x'p$ to $f'p$ will be unchanged. For given A, that is, changing the scale of the economy or changing labour productivity in the same proportion across all industries will not affect the ratio of gross output value to final demand value. It is not clear that anything can be said analytically about the effect on this ratio of non-scalar changes to the vectors f and l for given A, or of changes in the structure and/or dimensionality of A. However, it is intuitive that the ratio should increase as A increases in dimension. For the technologies of Table 3.1, the ratio of gross output value to final demand delivery value gives 1.5385 for 'I, 1.9344 under II, 2.0317 under III for scalar changes to the initial f vector. I also find it intuitive that the ratio should increase for A of constant dimension but changing so as to have fewer

zero elements. In this connection the work of Carter (1970) on structural change in the USA economy is of interest. Carter finds that the total intermediate output requirements for delivering the 1961 final demand vector are, in millions of 1947 dollars, \$324 288 using the 1939 technology, \$336 296 using the 1949 technology, \$336 941 using the 1958 technology, and \$334 160 using the 1961 technology. Carter comments, in Chapter 4, on these figures as follows:

> Note that the dollar volume of intermediate inputs (in constant prices) is quite stable, growing slightly over time – the total volume of inputs required to produce the same final product tends, if anything, to be a little greater with newer, than with older, techniques of production over this time interval. At first glance, this may appear paradoxical. If technological change is to be considered technological progress, how can more inputs have been required to produce the same deliveries to final demand at a later date? Actually, an increased volume of intermediate inputs means an increase in specialisation. . . . If, as Adam Smith suggests, division of labour depends on the extent of the market, then this tendency is to be expected as the total volume of production expands. Perhaps one should ask why apparent division of labour has not increased more.

A partial answer to this question is given in Chapter 11:

> In part, intermediate structure remains relatively stable because production is organised so that many rapidly changing 'intermediate inputs' are not reported as transactions at all. Adaptive change appears small because establishments combine those activities that are most sensitively attuned to each other. When two activities are combined in a single establishment, the statistical reporting system gives no evidence of their interdependence.

It should also be noted here that, in terms of an economy's historical experience of development, 22 years (1939 to 1961) is a small timespan.
15. In some cases there are 10 observed ratios to average, in some cases there is just one observed ratio. Where several observations existed I regressed the ratio on time with very mixed results – in some cases the time coefficient was positive and significant, in others negative and significant, in others non-significant. Bearing in mind that at most the time period here is 10 years, and the purpose at issue, and the results obtained by Carter (1970; see previous footnote), I considered it most appropriate to use the simple averages. The data on per capita incomes come from The Economist (1978).
16. Since $L = lx = l(I - A)^{-1}f$ is the total labour input requirement, and the value of deliveries to final demand is $f'p = f' (I - A)^{-1}l'$.
17. Two points can usefully be made here. First, I explicitly consider only private consumption in final demand in the text. But, deliveries to final demand are also, on conventional accounting conventions, to meet the needs of public consumption and the capital stock. These needs also

would be expected, on a per capita basis, to increase as production becomes more roundabout. Also, I am implicitly assuming that subsistence is defined to encompass certain standards with respect to longevity and health. To the extent that pollution problems increase with development, that is, that production processes are adopted which involve residuals discharges in excess of the relevant assimilative capacities, then so will subsistence needs change – the consumption of medical services will increase. Second, the idea that, culturally defined, subsistence requirements for private consumption increase with economic growth is, essentially, the motivation for the approach to the definition of poverty in advanced economies taken by, for example, Townsend (1979). This approach yields, among other things, the policy recommendation that levels of welfare payments should be increased in line with average earnings rather than inflation. Clearly, if subsistence requirements increase with growth, it is not difficult to understand why the record on poverty amelioration has been so disappointing in most advanced economies in the post-Second World War period. It is not necessary to invoke, as Hirsch (1977) does, the concept of positional goods to explain why what he terms 'the distributional compulsion' has not diminished in such economies as per capita consumption has spectacularly increased.

18. It is, of course, possible that on some philosophical, religious or aesthetic criteria earlier stages of development would be preferable to later stages. However, those adopting such criteria appear generally to be regarded as 'odd'.

19. In this context it is of some interest to note some remarks made by W. A. Lewis in an Appendix entitled 'Is Economic Growth Desirable?' to his major work on economic development (1955). These remarks are quoted in Arndt (1978) and described there as being 'still one of the best statements of the case' for economic growth. According to Lewis,

> the advantage of economic growth is not that wealth increases happiness, but that it increases the range of human choice . . . We certainly cannot say that an increase in wealth makes people happier. We cannot say, either, that an increase in wealth makes people less happy, and even if we could say this, it would not be a decisive argument against economic growth, since happiness is not the only good thing in life. We do not know what the purpose of life is, but if it were happiness, then evolution might just as well have stopped a long time ago, since there is no reason to believe that men are happier than pigs or fishes. What distinguishes men from pigs is that men have greater control over their environment: not that they are more happy. And on this test, economic growth is greatly to be desired. The case for economic growth is that it gives man greater control over his environment, and thereby increases his freedom.

This is, in my view, a non-economic argument for development as progress. What Lewis calls greater control over the environment, I interpret as an increasing level of environmental exploitation. I do not

see any meaningful connection, necessarily, between such and greater freedom.
20. For a review see Arndt (1978).
21. See especially May (1975) and also Westerman (1978) for further references.
22. For a recent contribution to this literature see Zolotas (1981), where an attempt is made to construct an 'Economic Aspects of Welfare' index for the USA. This exercise is in the spirit of Nordhaus and Tobin (1973) but allows for more sources of adjustment to the initial national accounting measure, which is for Zolotas private consumption expenditures.
23. For further references to work of this type see Zolotas (1981), ch. 4.

References

Arndt, H. W. (1978), *The Rise and Fall of Economic Growth: A Study in Contemporary Thought* (Melbourne: Longman Cheshire).

Boserup, E. (1965), *The Conditions of Agricultural Growth: the Economics of Agrarian Change under Population Pressure* (Chicago: Aldine).

Boulding, K. E. (1974), 'What Went Wrong, If Anything, Since Copernicus?', *Science and Public Affairs*, vol. XXX pp. 17–23.

Boulding, K. E. (1978), *Ecodynamics: A New Theory of Societal Evolution* (Beverley Hills: Sage).

Carter, A. P. (1970), *Structural Change in the American Economy* (Cambridge MA: Harvard University Press).

Chapman, P. (1975), *Fuel's Paradise: Energy Options for Britain* (Harmondsworth: Penguin).

Daly, H. E. (1973), 'The Steady State Economy: Toward a Political Economy of Biophysical Equilibrium and Moral Growth', in H. E. Daly (ed.), *Toward a Steady-State Economy* (San Francisco: W. H. Freeman).

Desai, M. (1975), Review of R. G. Wilkinson, *Poverty and Progress*, in *The Economic History Review*, vol. XXVIII, pp. 152–3.

Easterlin, R. A. (1975), 'Does Economic Growth Improve the Human Lot? Some Empirical Evidence', in P. A. David and M. W. Reder (eds), *Nations and Households in Economic Growth* (Stamford University Press).

Economist The (1978), *The World in Figures* (London: Macmillan).

Flammang, R. A. (1979), 'Economic Growth and Economic Development: Counterparts or Competitors?', *Economic Development and Cultural Change*, vol. 28, pp. 47–61.

Georgescu-Roegen, N. (1971), *The Entropy Law and the Economic Process* (Cambridge, MA: Harvard University Press).

Georgescu-Roegen, N. (1979), 'Energy Analysis and Economic Valuation', *Southern Economic Journal*, vol. 45, pp. 1023–58.

Hirsch, F. (1977), *Social Limits to Growth* (London: Routledge & Kegan Paul).

Leach, G. (1975), *Energy and Food Production* (London: International Institute for Environment and Development).

Lecomber, R. (1975), *'Economic Growth versus the Environment* (London: Macmillan).

Lecomber, R. (1979), 'Economic Growth and Social Welfare', in W. Beckerman (ed.), *Slow Growth in Britain: Causes and Consequences* (Oxford University Press).

Lewis, W. A. (1955), *The Theory of Economic Growth* (London: Allen & Unwin).

May, R. M. (1975), *Stability and Complexity in Model Ecosystems* (Princeton University Press).

Meadows, D. H. *et al.* (1972), *The Limits to Growth* (New York: Universe Books).

Mishan, E. J. (1977), *The Economic Growth Debate: an Assessment* (London: George Allen & Unwin).

Nordhaus, W. D. and J. Tobin (1973), 'Is Growth Obsolete?', in M. Moss, (ed.), *The Measurement of Economic and Social Performance*, Studies in Income and Wealth, vol. 38 (New York: National Bureau of Economic Research).

Norgaard, R. B. (1981), 'Sociosystem and Ecosystem Coevolution in the Amazon', *Journal of Environmental Economics and Management*, vol. 8, pp. 238–54.

Norgaard, R. B. (1984), 'Coevolutionary Agricultural Development' *Economic Development and Cultural Change*, vol. 32, pp. 525–46.

Phillipson, J. (1966), *Ecological Energetics* (London: Edward Arnold).

Sahlins, M. (1974), *Stone Age Economics* (London: Tavistock).

Smith, V. L. (1975), 'The Primitive Hunter Culture, Pleistocene Extinction and the Rise of Agriculture', *Journal of Political Economy*, vol. 83, pp. 727–55.

Townsend, P. (1979), *Poverty in the United Kingdom: A Survey of Household Resources and Standards of Living* (Harmondsworth: Penguin).

United Nations (1983), *Yearbook of National Accounts Statistics, Volume 1, Part 2, 1981* (New York: United Nations).

Westerman, W. E. (1978), 'Measuring the Inertia and Resilience of Ecosystems', *Bioscience*, vol. 28, pp. 705–10.

Wilkinson, R. G., *Poverty and Progress: an Ecological Model of Economic Development* (London: Methuen).

Zolotas, X. (1981), *Economic Growth and Declining Social Welfare* (Athens: Bank of Greece).

4 On Sustainable Development and National Accounts

Herman E. Daly

INTRODUCTION

This essay discusses an anomaly that confronts current views on economic development: namely, that economic development as currently understood and measured is neither sustainable for a long future nor generalisable to all presently living people. There follows a preliminary proposal for changes in national accounting and valuation procedures necessary to correct this fundamental anomaly in GNP-based theories of growth and development.

THE ANOMALY – AN IMPOSSIBILITY HYPOTHESIS

In the days of mercantilism economists urged nations to accumulate treasure through a favourable (surplus) balance of international trade. The policy implications of mercantilist (bullionist) orthodoxy were that nations with gold mines should invest much capital and labour in digging up metals with only minimal use value, and that all nations, especially those without mines, should strive to trade products of great use value for relatively useless yellow metal which represented the wealth and power of the state. Since trade was competitive, costs had to be kept low, and since labour was the major cost, wages had to be low. The way to keep wages low is to have an excess supply of labourers either through population growth or technological unemployment. For a country to be rich therefore, the majority of the citizens had to be poor, and to dedicate themselves to producing, either directly in mines or indirectly through trade, something which was of no use to them as individuals. Furthermore, the policy advice to strive for a surplus balance of payments was clearly not a goal that could be attained by all countries, since one country's surplus is some other country's deficit. The policy goal of a balance-of-payments surplus, even if it was really beneficial to the surplus country, is not a generalisable goal, and today is used in textbooks as a classic example of the 'fallacy of composition'.

We smile and shake our heads at the mercantilist view, so full of contradictions and impossibilities, which are easy to see from our historical vantage point. It is not so easy to see the anomalies in our own development theories, but I want to suggest that some might exist: that we may be advocating something that is impossible, somewhat analogous to urging all countries to run a surplus balance of payments, and which will only lead to conflict and disappointment. The case of mercantilism shows that such an error is not without historical precedent. Maximising GNP probably makes more sense than maximising gold stocks, but serious anomalies remain. I am not referring here to the problem of distribution, which has been widely recognised and on which economists have contributed much useful work. I refer instead to the fact that GNP, however distributed, may be more an index of cost than of benefit – a point to be developed later. The first question to be raised concerns the impossibility of generalising 'development' as it is currently understood (real GNP per capita and associated resource flows similar to US levels), to all countries in the world.

Most basic laws of science are impossibility statements: it is impossible to create or destroy matter energy, it is impossible to travel faster than the speed of light, it is impossible to make a perpetual motion machine, and so on. In today's world, however, impossibility is not a popular concept. Yet if we know that something is impossible then we can save an infinite amount of time and money by not trying to do it. Economists therefore should be very interested in impossibility theorems, and I would like to suggest one, namely: that a US-style resource consumption standard for a world of 4.8 billion people is impossible, and even if it could be attained it would be very short-lived. Even less possible then would be the dream of an ever-growing standard of resource consumption for an ever-growing world population.

This impossibility hypothesis is not a straightforward logical impossibility like that of all countries simultaneously having a surplus balance of payments. It suggests a factual rather than a logical impossibility. What evidence is there to support it? There are all sorts of studies including Meadows *et al.* (1972), the Leontief 1977 UN study, Lester Brown *et al.* (1971), and the *Global 2000 Report to the*

President (1980). The latter's major finding was that, 'If present trends continue the world in 2000 will be more crowded, more polluted, less stable ecologically, and more vulnerable to disruption than the world we live in now . . . . Despite greater material output the world's people will be poorer in many ways than they are today.' To what extent are these trends driven by our goals of growth and development as currently defined? Can we say that the cost of being 'poorer in many ways' is greater or less than the benefit of greater material output? The second question takes us into the problem of national accounts. For now let us focus on the prior question of the feasibility of economic growth and development when generalised to all people in the world.

Sometimes simple back-of-an-envelope calculations are more in-structive than voluminous studies. Consider that it requires about one-third of the current annual world extraction of non-renewable resources to support that 6 per cent (or less) of the world's population in the US at a per capita level to which it is thought that the rest of the world should aspire. This means that even if US levels of capitalisa-tion and technology could be instantaneously extended world-wide, current resources flows could at most support 18 per cent of the world's population at the US resource consumption standard, with nothing left over for the other 82 per cent. Without the labour services of the bottom 82 per cent, the top 18 per cent would of course not be so well off as this simple calculation suggests.

It may be objected that the obvious solution is to expand total world resource flows by whatever factor is necessary to generalise the US per capita standard of resource consumption. How much would that be? Returning to the back of the envelope, let M be the required factor and R be the current world annual resource extraction. For world per capita resource usage to equal US per capita resource usage requires that:

$$\frac{M \cdot R}{4.8 \times 10^9} = \frac{R/3}{2.3 \times 10^8},$$

where 4.8×10^9 = world population and 2.3×10^8 = US population. From this:

$$M \cong 7$$

Thus the annual resource flows would have to increase by roughly a factor of 7. Current rates of material and energy use are already doing serious damage to the life support capacity of our globe. Could we really get away with a sevenfold increase? And if so, for how long?

But even the sevenfold increase is a gross underestimate, because we have neglected the differences in accumulated capital stock that would be required to process and transform that larger annual flow. This capital stock would have to be accumulated out of a still larger flow in the initial years. Harrison Brown (1970) estimates that to supply the rest of the world with the average per capita 'standing crop' of the industrial metals already embodied in the existing artifacts of the ten richest nations would require more than sixty years' production of these metals at 1970 rates. But even assuming for the sake of argument instantaneous capital accumulation *ex nihilo*, the problem is still understated because of increasing costs due to depletion of mines and wells. A sevenfold increase in net, usable minerals will require a much greater than sevenfold increase in gross resource flows, since more energy and materials will be required in the extraction of energy and material from ever less accessible sources. And it is the gross flow rather than the net that produces environmental impact. The monetary and environmental costs of attempting the impossible are the more demonstrable, but the cost of instability and social conflict engendered by repeated failure to meet impossible expectations could be even more politically disruptive.

Technological optimists counter the above argument by claiming that technology can increase resource productivity without limit, and that therefore all nations can become richer. Even if true, such a claim does not counter the argument which has been in terms of per capita resource use, not per capita product or welfare. Even if technology could increase resource productivity without limit, so that the same physical resource flow would yield an ever greater value flow, we would still face the problem of keeping physical flows within ecological limits, and still could not generalise the current US industrial economy to the whole world. We might generalise some new as yet unknown system that made much more efficient use of resources, but that is more a concession to the impossibility hypothesis than a refutation of it. If the technological optimist really believes in unlimited increase in resource productivity then limitations on the volume and distribution of the physical resource flow would be seen as desirable, since this would force technological effort into increasing resource productivity (unlimited possibility) and away from the path of increasing intensity of resource usage (strictly limited possibility). In any case the impossibility hypothesis is unaffected, since even if 'development' in some sense continues indefinitely, the currently underdeveloped countries still cannot all pass through the window of the high resource consuming industrial stage of the developed countries of today. Therefore a major question becomes how high a resource consumption level should LDCs aim at?

These considerations also suggest a concept of 'overdevelopment' as correlative to 'underdevelopment': an overdeveloped country might be defined as one whose level of per capita resource consumption is such that if generalised to all countries could not be sustained indefinitely; correspondingly an underdeveloped country would be one whose per capita resource consumption is less than what could be sustained indefinitely if all the world consumed at that level. Instead of 'indefinitely' one might substitute an arbitrary time period, say 100 or 500 years, to lend greater specificity. A serious shortcoming of these definitions is that since they are in per capita terms they do not take account of the absolute size of population and its distribution among countries. This means, for example, that a currently under-developed country might be reclassified as an overdeveloped country solely as a result of population growth in *other* countries. What is generalisable to all depends on how many is 'all'! In any event, population growth must be stopped as soon as humanely possible.

Some economists have begun to express doubts about the tradi-tional notion of economic development. Economic historian Richard Wilkinson writes, 'Predictions on when the resources which modern industrial technology depends on will run out are usually within the same time scale as the predictions of when many underdeveloped countries may reach maturity' (1973). Disturbing coincidence!

A similar view was expressed by John M. Culbertson (1971), 'But elevating the present population of India to the present-day standard of living of upper-class Americans is unthinkable because of its implications for environmental destruction'.

The usual attitude, however, is that expressed by Paul W. McCracken (1975), former economic advisor to the President of the United States, 'The action most urgently needed in the world economy is for the stronger economies to be willing to accept higher levels of living. Their reluctance to do so seems to be of Calvinistic proportions.' Unless the abstemious rich make the 'sacrifice' of consuming more, the poor will not be able to sell their resources, and hence will not be able to develop.

The only problem is insufficiency of aggregate demand. Keynesian pump-priming is the paradigm within which world development is viewed. McCracken and the many economists for whom he is the distinguished spokesman obviously do not believe in any 'impossibility hypothesis'. Even many Third-World economists share this view, which is surprising only until one remembers that these Third-World economists usually get their degrees in US and British universities, studying under people who think like McCracken. Any change from McCracken's position with Reagan's economic advisors has only been for the worse. Nor is the situation much different in Western Europe. Of course, the traditional economists may be right. If so they should be able to refute the impossibility thesis, yet none has.

It may be that the coincidence of interests seen by McCracken and others is a short-run affair. Taking a longer view it is possible that by exporting their resources the less-developed countries will increase their dependence on the developed countries. The less-developed would remain dependent on the developed as export markets. In addition, as the richest and most easily available resources are extracted first, only the leaner and less accessible deposits are available for later development. The latter require more capital-intensive technologies, for which the less-developed must again depend on the developed. To make the point clearer, consider a thought experiment suggested by Harrison Brown (1970). Suppose all the physical capital stock of the US were annihilated, with everything else (knowledge, natural resources, and so on) remaining intact. Could we replace the lost physical capital, given time and effort? The answer is no, because that equipment was built with concentrated and easily available resources which are now depleted. The reconstruction could not start again with East Texas oil, but would have to start with offshore Alaskan oil to be exploited without the further natural subsidy of Mesabi range iron ore. Third-World countries that export their prime geological capital in exchange for luxury consumer goods for their elite class could end up in exactly the same fix. Are there any categories in our national accounts that would alert us to such a possibility? Kuwait, for example, has a very high GNP per capita, but is this income or capital consumption? Common sense suggests mainly the latter, but GNP accounts treat it simply as current income.

Enough has been said to indicate the seriousness of the anomalies of current economic development theory. Could it be that, like the mercantilists, we are seeking to maximise something which does not merit maximisation? Real GNP may not bear much closer relation to welfare than does gold, yet our national accounts are wedded to the concept, and our investment criteria generally are designed to increase GNP. Development may have to be reconceived in terms other than GNP if the anomalies discussed are to be avoided. It may be that our adherence to GNP has led us to a concept of development that is impossible of general attainment by all countries. To the extent that this is true it becomes imperative to redefine development in such a way that it is attainable by all (or else admit the impossibility and accept the consequences). A reformulation of the meaning of development requires a reformulation of the national accounts in terms in which development is defined. A possible alternative basis for national accounts is adumbrated below.

COST, BENEFIT AND CAPITAL ACCOUNTS: AN ALTERNATIVE TO GNP

It is worth inquiring whether our difficulty with GNP had its origin in A. C. Pigou's decision not to follow Irving Fisher's definition of the 'national dividend'. Pigou (1970) reasoned as follows,

> Professor Fisher himself takes the position that the national dividend, or income, consists solely of *services* as received by ultimate consumers whether from their material or from their human environment. Thus a piano or an overcoat made for me this year is not a part of this year's income, but an addition to capital. Only the services rendered to me during this year by these things are income . . . . This way of looking at the matter is obviously very attractive from a mathematical point of view.

Fisher's view is attractive mathematically because it does not add up unlike things: only the values of current services (psychic income) are added. We do not conflate income with capital; we do not add up the value of the service itself with the value of the item that renders the service. In his concept of capital, Fisher included the material and human environment. Human beings render services to other human beings, but we count only those services; we do not add in the capital value of the human being in the year he was born or graduated. For the material environment, Fisher had in mind artifacts mainly, not the natural material environment. Conceptually it would be easy to extend his view to cover natural ecosystem services as well, although problems of valuation are great. But in both cases we should treat services from the material environment consistently with services from the human environment. We should always count only service as income, and that which renders service as capital. In so doing we recognise that physical capital always depreciates (due to entropy) and that its continual maintenance and replacement is a cost. The cost of maintaining capital intact must not be counted as a part of the 'net national dividend'; and all physical production (except net investment) is a cost of keeping capital intact.

But national income accounting did not develop along the lines outlined above. Pigou (1970) rejected Fisher's approach because 'the wide departure which it makes from the ordinary use of language involves disadvantages which seem to outweigh the gain in logical clarity'. Although Pigou's position was quite defensible in his own time, it may be that subsequent economic evolution has been less kind to his concepts than to Fisher's, and that if Pigou could have foreseen the extent to which GNP would be relied on as the *summum bonum* of economic policy, he might have opted for logical clarity as did Fisher. Had national accounts developed in accordance with Fisher's concepts, their extension to cover environmental services and ecological and geological capital depletion would have been obvious and easy, except for valuation problems for services without markets. As it is now, incorporation of ecological services and natural capital must be very *ad hoc*, and in fact it may ultimately be necessary to adopt Fisher's approach.[1]

Why has the traditional national accounting approach of Pigou and others become so inappropriate? At least a part of the answer lies in the fact that the world has changed since 1920, and that change has been qualitative as well as quantitative. It has changed in a way that Fisher's view could have accommodated, but Pigou's could not. The qualitative change I have in mind is that from a relatively empty world to a relatively full world, from a world of 'unemployed carrying capacity' to a world of 'fully employed carrying capacity'. When the world was empty, throughput could be considered a flow from an infinite source to an infinite sink, and not regarded as a cost because not scarce. The fact that a larger stock required a larger throughput meant that throughput was an index of capital stock, and consequently an indirect index of service rendered by the capital stock. And throughput had the irresistible advantage of being more measurable than service. But in a full finite world where throughput is itself a cost, it is no longer legitimate to make it do double duty as an index of benefit. A certain sacrifice of logic for the sake of measurability and conformity to common language may have been justifiable in Pigou's time, before the cost nature of throughput had become so apparent. But in a full world throughput is cost, and current 'empty-world' accounting concepts such as GNP become inappropriate.

Since 1949, when he was still very much an orthodox economist, Kenneth Boulding (1969), has been arguing the logic of Fisher's view:

> I shall argue that it is the capital stock from which we derive satisfactions, not from the additions to it (production) or the subtractions from it (consumption): that consumption, far from being a desideratum, is a deplorable property of the capital stock which necessitates the equally deplorable activities of production: and that the objective of economic policy should not be to maxi- mize consumption or production, but rather to minimize it, i.e., to enable us to maintain our capital stock with as little consumption or production as possible.

Of course GNP is a flow measure of production or consumption. As such it is largely the maintenance cost of the capital stock, a measure of the regrettably necessary activities of depletion, pollution and labour, that are required to maintain the capital stock against physi- cal depreciation that inevitably occurs as the capital is used to satisfy wants. Remember that 'capital' is used in the broad sense of Fisher, so that it includes umbrellas, shoes, pencils, and so on. Wants are satisfied by the existing capital stock, not by the unavoidable but regrettable characteristic of the stock to become worn out or used up.

This issue can be clarified with some careful definitions of terms:

(1) *Accumulation* (or 'capital' in Irving Fisher's sense) is the total inventory of consumers' goods, producers' goods and human bodies. Accumulation takes two forms: a *fund* or a *stock*. A *stock* is an unstructured inventory of like things or of a homogeneous substance, which gets used a little at a time – that is, some gets totally used up before the rest is affected at all (for example, petrol). A *fund* is a structured organic whole, all parts of which must participate together, and which depreciates as a whole (for example, an automobile). Stocks get 'used up', funds get 'worn out'. Both require replacement.

(2) *Service* is the satisfaction experienced when wants are satisfied

(psychic income in Irving Fisher's sense). Service is yielded by accumulations (stocks and funds). The quantity and quality of the stocks and funds determine the intensity of service. Service is yielded over a period of time, and thus appears to be a flow magnitude, but unlike true flows it cannot be accumulated.

(3) *Throughput* is the entropic physical flow of matter and energy from nature's sources, through the human economy and back to nature's sinks; it is the flow that is accumulated into stocks and funds and out of which stocks and funds are replaced and maintained.

The basic relationship between these three fundamental magnitudes can be seen by an identity. Let A = accumulations (both stocks and funds), S = service; and T = throughput. Then

$$\frac{S}{T} \equiv \frac{S}{A} \times \frac{A}{T}$$

Service is the final benefit. Throughput is final cost. Accumulation is throughput 'frozen' in structured forms and inventories in shapes and amounts appropriate to our purposes and to the duration required for their satisfaction. Eventually this frozen throughput is 'melted' by entropy (either through wearing out or using up) and flows back to the environment as waste. Replacement of stocks and funds requires the accumulation of more throughput. The throughput flow begins with depletion of environmental low-entropy and ends with the pollution of the environment with high-entropy wastes, facts which underline the cost nature of the throughput. Accumulation cancels out in the identity just as it ultimately wears out in the real world. Nevertheless, accumulation must be the central concept because it is the accumulation that on the one hand yields benefits, and on the other hand imposes costs. For any given accumulation we clearly want maximum service and minimum throughput. Alternatively, for a given ecologically sustainable throughput we would want maximum stock and maximum service per unit of stock.[2]

What is the relation of these concepts to GNP? The relationship is given in the following equation:

GNP = value of some services + value of throughput + value of change in accumulated stocks and funds

GNP adds up parts of each of the three basic magnitudes. GNP counts the value of service of all assets rented during the accounting period, but not the value of services of owner-used assets, with the exception of owner-occupied houses for which a rental value is imputed and counted. Nor does it count natural ecosystem services. The value of the throughput is reflected in the production-consumption flow – the value of production required for maintenance and replacement of people and of stocks and funds, including consumer goods. The last term, value of net change in accumulated stocks and funds, represents net investment. However, it does not include changes in natural stocks and funds, such as depletion of geological stocks, or disruptions of environmental functions, or depletions of ecological funds of other species upon which we depend. The depletion of minerals and the depreciation of ecological life support 'capital' accumulated over millenia is not subtracted in calculating change in stocks and funds,[3] nor is the loss of current service of environmental functions subtracted from the value of current services supplied by produced goods. Indeed, efforts to defend ourselves against the effects of pollution lead to new demands for commodities and services and so lead to an increase in GNP.

How much sense does GNP make when translated into these more basic magnitudes? Consider that service is benefit, throughput is a cost, and net accumulation is a change in stocks and funds. What sense does it make to add these incongruous magnitudes? Is it not as if a merchant's bookkeeper added up receipts plus expenditures plus the change in inventory? Of what analytic interest could such a conflation of numbers possibly be? Should economic development be defined in terms of the increase of such a dubious sum, even when corrected for inflation, population size, and maldistribution? Clearly such questions must be of prime concern to all development economists. Economics requires the *comparison* of costs and benefits, *not their addition*. The whole thrust of microeconomics is to compare costs and benefits at the margin so as to be able to limit the activity under consideration to its optimum extent. But the macroeconomic activity of national economic growth is not conceived of as having an optimum extent. If quantitative growth in real GNP is considered a permanent norm that must never cease, then it is convenient not to compare costs and benefits lest they become equal at the margin (which is the usual tendency). One way to avoid comparing costs and benefits is to add them together and treat the sum as if it were the most unique of all good things, that for which more is always better than less. But GNP is a conflation of costs, benefits and changes in accumulation, and is no better a guide to determine the optimum level of economic activity than is the stock of gold bullion.

Some economists would object to the above argument on the grounds that every entry into GNP is based on a transaction, and for that transaction to have occurred each party had to decide that the benefits to him or her of making the deal were greater than the costs to him or her. Therefore any increase in GNP is already based on a micro-level comparison of costs and benefits and an additional macro-level comparison would be redundant at best, and at worst destructive of individual freedom. But the macro-level comparison is not redundant for two related reasons. First, costs and benefits to the individuals making the transaction do not exhaust all costs and benefits. Private costs and benefits do not fully reflect social costs and benefits. Externalities are pervasive, and become more so as we move from a relatively empty to a relatively full world. Second, arguing from the part to the whole commits the fallacy of composition. Micro rationality often leads to macro irrationality, as evidenced by the paradox of thrift, the tragedy of the commons, the prisoner's dilemma, the tyranny of small decisions and the arms race. Macro-level comparison of costs and benefits is necessary. Furthermore this point is accepted by standard economists when they argue in favour of stimulating aggregate growth beyond the individualistically market-determined level. Public policy to stimulate aggregate growth must be based on an implicit comparison of costs and benefits at the macro level and the perception that the social benefits of growth are greater than the social cost. The issue is whether that perception is right or wrong, not the legitimacy of the macro cost-benefit comparison. The three-accounts approach would provide more relevant information and increase the accuracy of our perceptions of social costs and benefits.

Instead of one account, GNP, we should keep three accounts, one for each basic magnitude. We need:

(1) a *Benefit Account* which would seek to measure the value of the services yielded by all accumulations (not just those rented during the accounting period, and not just those used by consumers, but also those used in production that is enjoyable and self-fulfilling);

(2) a *Cost Account* which would seek to measure the value of depletion, pollution, and disutility of those kinds of labour that

are irksome (and of 'waiting' in Alfred Marshall's sense). With separate accounts for costs and benefits we could occasionally ask if the extra benefits of further accumulation were worth the extra costs. In addition we need

(3) a *Capital Account*, an inventory of the accumulation of stocks and funds and their ownership distribution. Included in the capital account would be not only produced stocks and funds, but also natural capital such as mines, wells and ecosystem infrastructure.

Currently we count present consumption financed by geological and ecological decapitalisation no differently from present consumption financed by sustainable production. Kuwait, for example, has a per capita GNP of some $17 000 of which a significant fraction is royalties based on geological decapitalisation. The three-accounts approach would make this decapitalisation obvious. It would invite the question of the extent to which petroleum earnings should be tied to compensating capital investments and the extent to which they should be used to finance current consumption.

Ideally one could argue that accumulation should continue up to the point where the marginal benefit of services rendered by the extra stocks and funds is equal to the marginal cost of the extra throughput required to maintain the extra stocks and funds. Once the optimal accumulation was reached further growth would cease, at least until such time as the underlying conditions of taste and technology changed.

Such optimisation is an ideal case. In the real world we are likely to resort to 'satisficing' rather than optimising, that is seeking a sufficient or satisfactory level of accumulation rather than the optimum level. A separate behaviour mode would be associated with each of the three basic magnitudes:

(1) the accumulation of stocks and funds would be *satisficed*;
(2) service would be *maximised*, given the sufficient accumulation; and
(3) throughput would be *minimised*, given the sufficient accumulation.

Behaviour modes (1) and (3) are in direct conflict with the current goal of maximising GNP. Indeed, optimising as well as satisficing would be in conflict with fostering growth in GNP.

The problem with an optimising approach lies not only in the requirement for accurate measures of cost and benefits of further stock accumulation, but also in the requirement that marginal cost and benefit functions be 'well-behaved'. This means that the marginal benefit curve should be monotonically decreasing and the marginal cost curve monotonically increasing. The former would not be unreasonable to expect since rational people satisfy their most pressing wants first. Thus each additional stock or fund would on average be devoted to a less pressing need. But the marginal cost curve reflects depletion of geological capital and loss of current environmental service functions. There is no reason to expect that loss of environmental function will be incurred in an ordered sequence from less to more important under the pressure of increasing throughput. The wisest course may be to try to set the level of accumulation at an ecologically sustainable amount. Population times per capita resource consumption would be set equal to or, for safety's sake, less than carry capacity. Sufficiency and sustainability would be the criteria for choosing a level of accumulation. Efficiency would be achieved by maximising service yielded per unit of accumulated stocks and funds, and by minimising throughput per unit of stock or fund required for maintenance and replacement. In terms of the identity, maximising S/A means maximising S with A given. The ratio S/A reflects the intensity of service yielded per unit of time by the accumulated stocks and funds. That intensity in turn depends on the allocation and distribution of the total accumulation among alternative artifact uses and among different people. Maximising A/T means, in effect, minimising T given A. The ratio A/T reflects the durability of stocks and funds, the number of units of time over which they continue to render service.

It seems to me that Irving Fisher's way of looking at things is eminently sensible, coherent and logical. It has the advantage of clearly separating costs and benefits and of measuring each more inclusively. Benefits include not only the service of rented assets, but also the service of owner-used assets which are currently omitted. Costs include depletion of natural capital, loss of current environmental service and disutility of labour, all currently neglected in GNP, or, worse, implicitly treated as benefits. Might this not be a more sensible approach than maximising GNP, which is nearly equivalent to maximising throughput and consequently maximising the costs of depletion and pollution?

Even if it is admitted that the three-accounts approach is theoretically much superior to GNP, there remains the admittedly enormous problem of making these accounts operational. But is not even the poorest approximation to the correct concept always better than an accurate approximation to an irrelevant or erroneous concept? Indeed, it could be reasonably argued that we might be better off to abandon GNP as a criterion even if we had nothing better to put in its place. G. K. Chesterton tells the story of the English pub that served poisoned beer. People were dropping dead. Some alert citizens had the beer analysed, discovered it was poisonous and petitioned the local magistrate to close the pub forthwith. The magistrate said 'the house you mention is one in which people are systematically murdered by means of poison. But before you demand so drastic a course as that of pulling it down or even shutting it up, you have to consider a problem of no little difficulty. Have you considered precisely what building you would Put In Its Place, whether a. . . . ' The point is of course that when something is found bad enough you do not have to put anything in its place, just remove it and be glad to be rid of it. It is admittedly an exaggeration to say that GNP is worse than nothing, but I suspect that the world could get along well enough without it, as it did before 1940. We must face the question of what would you Put In Its Place, but without letting its operational difficulty be converted into an argument for staying with the 'poisoned beer' of GNP.

Notes

1. For a recent critique of GNP see Roefie Hueting (1980). Hueting does not adopt Fisher's concepts, but offers many insightful comments on the shortcomings of GNP.
2. In the language of benefit-cost analysis, S becomes benefit and T becomes cost. Hence, S/T is the same thing as the benefit-cost ratio. The objective function is then to maximise the benefit-cost ratio, a familiar enough mechanical welfare function, but not, of course, expressed in the same units we are using here.
3. It is ironic that when Keynes introduced the concept of user cost applied to man-made capital, he appealed to the analalogous case of 'raw materials (where) the necessity for allowing for user cost is obvious' (Keynes, 1936, p. 73). Nowadays, in trying to introduce user cost on raw materials into national accounts, we appeal to the analogous case of man-made capital where allowing for user cost is obvious! I am indebted to Mr Salah El Serafy for this observation.

References

Boulding, Kenneth (1969), 'Income or Welfare', *Review of Economic Studies*, vol. 17, p. 79.

Brown, Harrison (1970), 'Human Materials Production as a Process in the Biosphere', *Scientific American*, September, pp. 194–208.

Brown, Lester *et al.* (1971), *State of the World* (New York: W. W. Norton).

Culbertson, John M. (1971), *Economic Development: An Ecological Approach* (New York: Alfred A. Knopf).

Global 2000 Report to the President (1980) (Washington DC: US Government Printing Office).

Hueting, Roefie (1980), *New Scarcity and Economic Growth* (North Holland: Netherlands Central Bureau of Statistics).

Keynes, J. M. (1936), *The General Theory of Employment, Interest and Money* (New York: Harcourt Brace & Co.).

Leontief, Wassily W. (1977), *The Future of the World Economy* (New York: Oxford University Press).

McCracken, Paul W. (1975), *Wall Street Journal*, 17 September, p. 16.

Meadows, D. H. *et al.* (1972), *The Limits to Growth* (New York: Potomac Associates).

Pigou, A. C. (1970), *The Economics of Welfare* (London: Macmillan) p. 35.

Wilkinson, Richard (1973), *Poverty and Progress: An Ecological Perspective on Economic Development* (New York: Praeger).

5 Optimal Prices for Sustainable Development

David Pearce

INTRODUCTION

In the 1960s and 1970s the thrust of the environmentalist argument was that economic growth was *inconsistent* with environmental preservation. There are few better surveys of these arguments than Richard Lecomber's own monograph (Lecomber, 1975). In the 1980s, however, the emphasis has shifted to the argument that growth is consistent with environmental preservation and that both must be sold as a 'package'. It seems fair to say that this duality of sustainable development and sustainable use of the environment has been only lightly analysed. This paper offers one small input into what I hope is a deeper analysis of 'sustainability'. Its starting point is a set of (as always) provocative remarks by Herman Daly in a recent essay. Daly (1986) has drawn attention to a generally unacknowledged externality relevant to the pricing of environmental services.[1] Daly was commenting on the relevance of the Laws of Thermodynamics for welfare optimisation. In particular he notes that

> In the light of the entropy law a previously neglected aggregate constraint on the physical scale of the economy relative to the ecosystem is seen to exist. The market is, by itself, unable to reflect this constraint because Pareto optimality of allocation is independent of *whether or not the scale of physical throughput is ecologically sustainable.* (Daly, 1986, my italics)

This paper sets out to

(1) expand on Daly's observation with reference to a naïve 'bioeconomic' model of economy-ecosystem interaction;
(2) establish the basis for a theory of 'sustainable' ecological prices which incorporate the externality that Daly claims (correctly in our view) is omitted in traditional shadow pricing of environmental services.

57

In many respects, the paper offers a simple exposition of some of the features of dynamic optimisation models.

SUSTAINABILITY

The concept of 'sustainable development' has become a catch-phrase for the new environmentalism of the 1980s. In simple terms it argues for: (a) development subject to a set of constraints which set resource 'harvest' rates at levels no higher than managed or natural regeneration rates; and (b) use of the environment as a 'waste sink' on the basis that waste disposal rates should not exceed rates of (natural or managed) assimilation by the counterpart ecosystems. General though such propositions are, they capture the essence of the unsystematic statements of the new environmentalism (IUCN, 1980). There are self-evident problems in advocating sustainable rates for exhaustible resources, so that 'sustainabilists' tend to think in terms of a resource set encompassing substitution between renewables and exhaustibles. Equally self-evident is the implicit assumption that sustainability is a 'good thing' – that is, that optimising *within* sustainable use rates is a desirable objective. On these terms, sustainability could imply use of environmental services at rates which can hold over very long time periods and, in theory, indefinitely. The moral appeal of indefinite or quasi-indefinite survival is not obvious since it begs the question of the *quality* of the survival (see the essay by Broome in this volume). However, we do not pursue the issue here. Suffice it to say that policies pursued now which are inconsistent with sustainability logically imply externality for future consumers of environmental services. This externality is directly analogous to a *user cost* element in current use of resources and the environment, but extends beyond what is encompassed in the usual definition of user cost. We shall term this the 'sustainability user cost' (SUC) and will show how it arises. Clearly, if the time horizon over which SUC occurs is very long, it will be open to anyone to neglect it in optimal pricing of resources/environment now. It may be, for example, that we cannot demonstrate significant impacts on ecosystem function through neglect of SUC until time periods very distant from now. Given non-zero discount rates, SUC will then tend to zero. Against this rationale for neglecting SUC we offer two arguments:

(1) value systems are not invariant with time. Setting SUC = 0 now could imply irreversibility for future generations in a much wider

sense than usually envisaged – for example, not being able to adopt *entire lifestyles* of their choosing;

(2) perhaps more telling because of its immediacy, neglect of sustainable resource use practice largely explains the dramatic and rapid loss of life-support systems in low-income countries – for example, in the sub-Sahara regions (Pearce and Markandya, forthcoming).

There is an additional and important observation of relevance here also. Traditionally, economic incentives for resource and environmental management have been directed at perceived or anticipated damage. The problem for sustainabilists is that they must justify the case for taking action now in anticipation of *undemonstrated* damage. Incentives for the restitution of environments already damaged are quite different to incentives for damage avoided: both may take the same form (a Pigovian style tax, say), but one operates in a world of perceived and largely known effects while the other operates in a shadow world of damage yet to come. A combination of myopia, faith in technological progress and a form of the 'isolation syndrome' ('it cannot happen to me') make the whole issue of protection of future generations, and of the future in general, different in scale and concept.[2]

NEOCLASSICAL OPTIMISATION AND NON-SUSTAINABILITY

In the context of the use of ecosystems as waste receptors the neoclassical static welfare economics prescription for the setting of environmental standards of product price/output levels requires that the marginal net gain function $(b'(q))$ of a polluter be equated with the marginal external cost $(e'(q))$ imposed, that is

$$b'(q) = e'(q) \tag{1}$$

where q is product output, $b(q)$, $e(q)$ are benefit and external cost functions and b' and e' are first derivatives. By the First Law of Thermodynamics, q generates an equal amount of waste, w, which, in the absence of recycling, r, enters the environment.[3] By the second law, entropy assures us that recycling is limited such that $r < w$. These are the physical and unavoidable constraints to which Daly (1986) refers.

Now, externality will arise in two ways. When waste is disposed of to ecosystems there will often be a counterpart degrader population which degrades the waste and converts it to nutrients. The rate at which those degrader populations function gives us the rate of waste *assimilation*, a, of the ecosystem. In turn there will be some limit to a, a_{max}, beyond which the ecosystem fails to cope with waste w. In such circumstances, a_{max} itself declines – that is, the act of 'excessive' pollution produces a negative feedback, making the ecosystem even less capable of dealing with waste. This much we understand from elementary ecological science.[4]

The two ways in which externality arises are then:

(1) at $w < a_{max}$ the assimilative process takes place, but over a given time period a will return to a_{max};
(2) at $w > a_{max}$ the assimilative process is impaired and a_{max} itself declines.

Type (1) externality is the 'ecologically irrelevant' externality since a returns to a_{max}: the environment is not permanently impaired. An example would be 'oxygen sag' due to waste disposed to a watercourse. Type (2) externality is ecologically relevant since a itself is impaired. Stylistic ecological relationships are shown in Figure 5.1.

We concentrate on type (2) – ecologically relevant – externality because it is this which explains the failure of markets – unregulated or statically Pareto-optimised – to account for sustainability. The essence of the difference between the two types of externality is that type (1) does not result in shifts in a_{max} whereas type (2) does.

We now demonstrate that type (2) externality can cause false signals to regulatory authorities in such a way that sustainability conditions are not fulfilled. Figure 5.2 repeats a construction used in an earlier paper (Pearce, 1976). The functions shown have already been described.

The marginal *ecological* externality function cannot begin until $w(q) > a_{max}$ (and indeed could begin at any point between q_e and q_n where q_n is the net private benefit maximisation point for the polluter). The only non-trivial case therefore arises where $e'(q)$ intersects $b'(q)$ in the region $q_e - q_n$. An intersection at Y gives an apparent social optimum of q_s.[5] But q_s is associated with $w(q) > a_{max}$ (by reference to the upper half of the diagram). Hence a_{max} moves to a^2_{max}. If q_s is produced in the *next* period then $w(q) > a^2_{max}$ so that

Figure 5.1

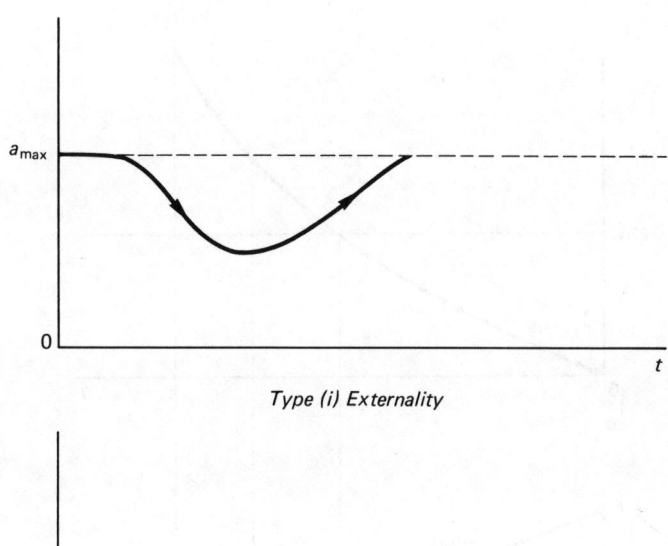

Type (i) Externality

Type (ii) Externality

a_{max} moves downward at a *faster* rate. *Continual* production at q_s sends a towards zero: the ecosystem is destroyed.

Various reactive responses to such non-sustainability can be postulated. Consider just one. As a_{max} goes to a^2_{max}, q_e moves to q^2_e. Sufferers of the externality perceive this and $e'(q)$ shifts to $e'(q)$. By observation, however, $w(q) > a^2_{max}$ for the new Pareto optimum Z. The ecosystem degradation proceeds as before, albeit at a slower rate. It is the cost of degradation process that 'sustainabilists' such as Daly refer to when they argue that even the conventionally Pareto-optimised system somehow fails us.

Figure 5.2

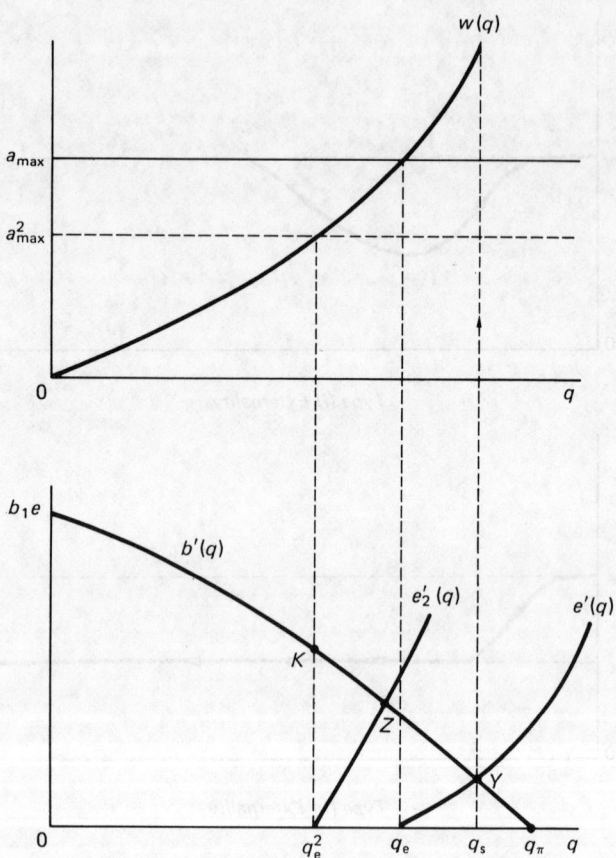

CONDITIONS FOR SUSTAINABILITY

In fact, in the naïve model presented, it is quite simple to set out the conditions which provide sustainability. Observation of Figure 5.2 shows that if planners opt immediately for q_e in the first period, the q_e can be sustained 'indefinitely'. If we have an objective of maximising net social surplus over an infinite time horizon at a zero discount rate,[6] the area Oq_eKB can be sustained for ever. But persistent production at q_s – or at sequence of apparent optima Y, Z and so on – must, at zero discount rates, result in less time-aggregated social surplus since the ecosystem has a finite life due to the failure to honour the sustainability conditions.

Once non-zero discount rates are introduced the attractions of q_e as a planning output may well disappear. If the process of ecosystem degradation is long, the *present value* of Oq_eKB each time period may well be *less* than the *present value* of a sequence of Pareto optimal outputs.[7] What this tells us is that non-zero discount rates play a contributory role in resource extinction, a well known result in the bioeconomic literature (see for example, Clark, 1976).

If substainability is part of a social objective function, q_e is the only optimum.[8] In an ideal world planners maximising long-run welfare ought to choose q_e since they ought not knowingly to seek to maximise profits (or social profits) without regard to the existence of the resource producing the profits. Sadly, we have all too many examples of just such myopic failure. If sustainability is not 'for ever' then positive discount rates are consistent with ecosystem destruction.

PRICING FOR SUSTAINABILITY

We began with Daly's observation that the Laws of Thermodynamics imply a different configuration of prices to those typically encompassed in neo-classical welfare economics. We can now see that this is true *provided* we accept some goal of sustainability. But it is as well to note that we have no guarantee that the thermodynamic laws will not bring an end to critical ecosystems even in a world where discounted future welfare is maximised: we have nothing to tell us the *speed* at which destruction occurs. We simply issue the reminder that it has taken only decades in some parts of the Sahel.

Daly goes on to argue that the 'constraint' on the operation of the economic system must be set 'according to criteria of sustainability'. Moreover,

> Operating under this newly instituted biophysical constraint the market . . . will come up with a different set of prices which now reflect the social value of sustainability. . . . (Daly, 1986)

We can use our simple model to find the relevant prices and, indeed, to measure the SUC component of such prices. This we do in the completely conventional profit-maximising model familiar in undergraduate

Figure 5.3

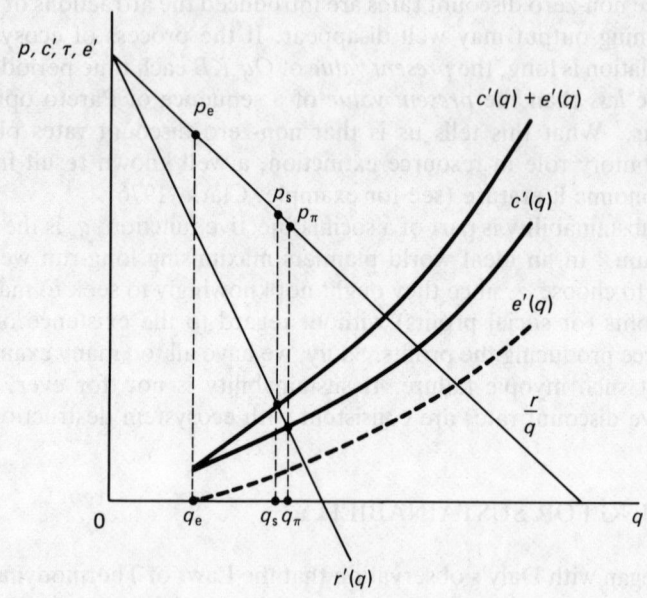

texts, this time for imperfect competition. Figure 5.3 shows the usual cost, revenue and profit functions but the marginal external cost function $e'(q)$ is seen to start at q_e and not at the origin as is conventionally assumed. This simply reflects the fact that there is a range of output Oq_e where $W(q) < a_{\max}$.

In Figure 5.3 the profit-maximising price is p_π. The Pareto-optimal price is p_s. But, as we saw in Figure 5.2, sustainability is consistent only with q_e and the corresponding price is now seen to be p_e. p_e is then the 'sustainable optimal price', or, more correctly, the *lowest* price consistent with sustainability. The 'sustainability use cost' SUC can be measured as $p_e - p_s$ or $p_e - p_\pi$ depending on the reference point taken (Pareto optimality or profit maximisation).

CONCLUSION

There is, we argue, a surcharge on conventionally optimised prices which can arise if sustainability criteria are used. This arises in the pollution context. In the renewable resource context it is well known that sustainability can be made consistent with profit maximisation, private or social (Clark, 1976).

Notes

1. An exception is Bruce Forster's paper, 'Optimal Pollution Control, with a non-constant Exponential Rate of Decay', *Journal of Environmental Economics and Management*, vol. 2, 1975.
2. While most people would acknowledge this point in passing, its central importance in actual control policies, notably in low-income, resource-poor countries, has not been emphasised. I am grateful to Gunther Schramm of the World Bank for a discussion on this point.
3. We have also abstracted from the embodiment of material flows in capital.
4. Self-evidently, *w* is a multi-characteristic variable – for example, the *quality* of waste may matter more than its quantity. We abstract from this problem here.
5. The conditions are well known. If the polluter is a firm with a revenue function $r(q)$ and a private cost function $c(q)$, then,

$$b(q) = r(q) - c(q) \tag{1}$$

Social surplus is maximised when $b(q) - e(q)$ is maximised, that is,

$$b'(q) = e'(q) \tag{2}$$

Under perfect competition, $r'(q) = p$, the ruling market price. From (1) and (2), then, $p = c'(q) + e'(q)$, that is, marginal social cost.
6. It is not clear if sustainabilists are committed to zero discount rates. If they believe in the 'survival imperative' one is tempted to say they must subscribe to zero rates. But in turn this is likely to imply optimal current consumption levels at or near subsistence levels – see Olson and Bailey (1976). See also the thought-provoking discussion in Lecomber (1975), pp. 95–104. As long as the focus is on renewable resources, sustainability is assured if discount rates are below or equal to resource regeneration rates.
7. In terms of Figure 5.2 for just two periods

$$\sum_{t=1}^{t=2} \frac{[Oq_eKB]\,t}{(1+s)^t} \begin{array}{c} < \\ > \end{array} \left[\frac{Oq_eYB}{1+s} + \frac{Oq_e^2ZB}{(1+s)^2} \right]$$

depending on the magnitude of the shift in $e'(q)$. s is the social discount rate.
8. Abstracting from safety margins. Indeed, q_e has parallels with the Ciriacy–Wantrup–Bishop concept of a 'safe minimum standard'. (See Bishop, 1978.)

References

Bishop, R. (1978), 'Endangered Species and Uncertainty: the Economics of a Safe Minimum Standard', *American Journal of Agricultural Economics*, vol. 60, no. 1. (February).

Clark, C. (1976), *Mathematical Bioeconomics* (Wiley, New York).

Daly, H. (1986), 'A Comment on Burness, *et al.*, 'Thermodynamic, and Economic Concepts as Related to Resource-Use Policies', *Land Economics*, February 1986.

IUCN (International Union for the Conservation of Nature) (1980), *World Conservation Strategy* (Geneva: IUCN).

Lecomber, R. (1975), *The Economics of Natural Resources* (London: Macmillan).

Lecomber, R. (1975), *Economic Growth versus the Environment* (London: Macmillan).

Olson, M. and M. Bailey (1976), 'Positive Time Preference', *Journal of Political Economy*, vol. 89, no. 1.

Pearce, D. W. (1976), 'The Limits of Cost–Benefit Analysis as a Guide to Environmental Policy', *Kyklos* Fasc., 1.

Pearce, D. W. and A. Markandya (forthcoming), 'The Costs of Natural Resource Depletion in Low Income Developing Countries', in D. Bromley and R. Bishop (eds), *Natural Resources and Development*, (Madison: University of Wisconsin Press).

6 Catastrophic Risk: or the Economics of Being Scared[1]

David Collard

INTRODUCTION

A catastrophic risk exists when there is a chance (albeit a small chance) of a project going very badly wrong, with extremely severe human and environmental consequences. Should such projects be undertaken? The issue is related to those which Richard Lecomber explored in his *Economic Growth Versus the Environment* (1975). The empirical analogues of my discussion here are nuclear power stations and certain types of chemical plant.

There are two underlying attitudes to this sort of risk, an optimistic one ('hard', technical) and a pessimistic one ('soft', environmental). The optimist points to the extremely low probability of catastrophe, perhaps so low as to be below our thresholds of perception. He or she emphasises the role of advancing technology in helping to deal with any (highly improbable) catastrophe that might occur. The pessimist points to the ghastly and perhaps irreversible nature of such catastrophes which should be avoided at all costs: he or she mistrusts the assurances of the experts about probability. One cannot expect easy answers from economics to these great questions. However, one might reasonably look for help, in the first instance, from a standard approach to decision-making under uncertainty, subjective expected utility theory (SEU).

Under SEU the expected utility of an outcome is equal to *the utility of the outcome multiplied by its probability*. The rule was first devised to deal with probabilities and outcomes within the normal range of human experience. Yet the extreme cases are clearly important and we ought to be able to say something useful about them. The present paper is very much in the spirit of this statement from Bailey (1982):

> The extreme uncertainties represent a bigger potential threat than do the 'most probable' outcomes, with the severity of the threat

increasing with the degree of uncertainty. It is therefore prudent to consider the extremes with some care, even though it is impractical to translate them into costs and benefits.

In a similar vein, Dasgupta (1982) writes:

> It makes great sense to fear [increases in collective risk] if [probability] is small and the loss is 'large'. But this is the case of a small risk of a mammoth social loss – precisely the kind of example over which people express their greatest anxieties.

The next section rehearses some well-known reasons why there may be large catastrophic, 'external' costs. Later sections discuss how these costs might plausibly be captured in a 'disutility function'; the calculation of subjective probabilities; the putting together of the utility and probability aspects; and the implications for policy.

COSTS

There are many reasons for believing that agents will tend to underestimate the 'external' costs of projects involving catastrophic risk.

Imperfect compensation

The social costs of a project of the sort being considered here are normally larger than the private costs, that is, those actually paid by the agency responsible for the project. This is asymmetrically true of costs (rather than benefits) and arises mainly because people lack 'property rights' in a clean environment and safety. Litigation can never therefore be entirely satisfactory in the case of nuclear or chemical plants: for example, Smets (1985) shows that the industries concerned are insured for nothing like the sorts of third-party claim that could arise from a major leak of toxic gas from a European plant (see also AEI, 1984). Indeed, there are limits to the amount of insurance that may be purchased in a market economy, and firms may choose to risk bankruptcy rather than seek heavy insurance cover. Where catastrophic damage is possible, compensation has to be organised nationally, or even supra-nationally: this already happens on an industry-wide basis for nuclear or oil spillage accidents (for example, the US Price–Waterson Act of 1957). When a whole industry is unable to meet potential claims for compensation there is a prima-facie case for suggesting that the externalities are in some sense too large.

Discounting

Though catastrophic risk exists immediately, much of it will fall on future generations: we cannot be certain that they will have the technology to deal with it at a reasonable cost. For example, nuclear waste may be dangerous for *at least thousands* of years (Fyfe *et al.*, 1984). The practice of discounting effectively gives less weight to costs in future years, particularly those falling on future generations. Some, including the present writer (1979), have suggested that each future generation be allowed to do its own discounting and then be allocated a 'weight' by the present generation of decision-makers. This is much more favourable to them than being given a weight of near zero simply because of the arithmetic of discounting. The effect would be to reduce, though not eliminate, the effective discount rate.

Free-riding

When economic agents (including governments) find themselves locked into a prisoners' dilemma they tend to adopt Pareto-inferior solutions (over-fishing, polluting) which make things worse for everyone. Collective action is then usually required and sometimes comes about. River systems are a good paradigmatic case of this: the Thames Authority has much improved the Thames; President Rajhiv Ghandi has recently set up a Ganga Authority to deal with pollution of the Ganges; West Germany is leading collaborative action in Northern Europe on North Sea pollution; the United Nations is making efforts (so far largely ineffectual) to coax the Meditraenean countries into co-operation. Most of the important pollution and resource depletion problems (from the ozone layer to the sea bed) require concerted international action which has so far been woefully inadequate. (See Downing and Kates, 1982.)

Exhaustion

A very special kind of catastrophe occurs when the assimilative power of the environment begins to decay: this can occur as a result of a gradual or creeping build-up of pollution which can no longer be absorbed by the soil, the sea or the atmosphere. A catastrophe is suddenly revealed: the disutility function has a sudden break, a discontinuity at the point of catastrophe. This sequence is the nearest that one gets, in the present paper, to the 'catastrophe theory' of mathematicians. The dynamics of the process then require, for example, the sort of super-pricing policy (over and above the normal externality tax) described by Pearce in Chapter 5.

A particularly good example of 'exhaustion' is acidification of water and soil in the Elbe basin caused by deposition of dry sulphur dioxide and the application of industrial fertilisers; die-back of trees occurs once the buffering capacity of soils is exhausted. The exhaustion phenomenon is essentially a dramatic example of externalities and free-riding in a series of self-interested, but ultimately self-defeating, moves. Here I shall be assuming a disutility function which does not break sharply but rises very steeply in its upper ranges.

Distributional weighting

We saw above that discounting gives less weight to future generations: companies and governments will 'weight' costs in space as well as time – probably giving a lower weight to foreigners, especially poor foreigners. Further, if compensation has to be awarded for catastrophic damage it tends to be based upon loss of earning power: it will then be cheaper for a company to run risks in a low-income country than in a high-income one. There was some suspicion at Bhopal that Union Carbide had been less strict about its safety standards in India than at home in the USA (though a major toxic gas leak has since occurred at Union Carbide's other methyl isocynate plant near Charleston).

Even a 'responsible' decision-taking agency will be tempted to consider only those external costs which legally concern it. Taking into account imperfect compensation, discounting, free-riding, exhaustion and distributional weighting there are sound reasons for expecting that such agencies will ignore social costs or repeatedly postpone consideration of them until forced to take action. By the time a potential catastrophe has become a political issue social cost may well be very large and increasing quite rapidly.

DISUTILITY

Catastrophic risks are no ordinary risks: they involve loss of life, destruction of trees, soil and wildlife, poisoning of the atmosphere and of drinking water and mass evacuation and disruption. What can be the appropriate compensation principle? The maximum which individuals would be prepared to pay to avoid such catastrophes or the minimum amount which they would be prepared to accept to endure them? These two alternative principles require opposite changes in the distribution of income, in the former case from the sufferers to the rest of the community, in the latter case vice versa. In the former case individuals cannot possibly offer more than their entire wealth, including borrowings: in the latter there is strictly no limit – that is the assumption I shall be making. Knetsch and Sinden (1984) have argued that compensation required can greatly exceed willingness to pay, even when wealth effects are negligible.

Cost-benefit analysts have never been very happy about using this version of the principle because it produces results that seem too strong. In answering questions about dislocation, noise, and so on, some respondents state that they would not have it *at any price*. This is embarrassing, for it implies an infinitely high cost and abandonment of the project, so analysts are tempted to 'cheat' by imposing some arbitrary upper limit. Equivalently, the decision-taker may wish simply to override the preferences of these respondents. It is clear, however, that sharply increasing damage functions are not merely the whim of recalcitrant protesters: Lowe *et al.* (1982) show, using a modified 'Delphi' technique, a marked non-linear relationship between quantity of pollutant and harmful effect as assessed by experts – for example, in the case of cyanides, damage would vary roughly with the *square* of quantity over the range considered.

The polar case considered in the economic literature is the loss of life. Except in special cases which will not be considered here, there is no sum that the individual would be prepared to accept in exchange for his or her life. We may say that the compensation required would be infinitely great. But as we never know for any project exactly who will die (though we know for certain that some will die), we may base our valuation on the probability of death, rather than upon death itself. People frequently make such (unarticulated) valuations in everyday life.

Much usually depends (Broome, 1978; Jones-Lee, 1979; Ulph,

1982) on whether the decision is *ex ante*, when it is not known who is to die, or *ex post*. In the most extreme case of catastrophic risk, where the whole community would perish, it makes no difference. The community might still decide to take the risk in view of the low probability of catastrophe but it would do so (as the individual does) in the full knowledge of who would die if things were to go wrong. For the present discussion the relevant point is that as widespread damage *to the community* would occur in the event of a disaster it is appropriate to conceive of the *community* having a loss or disutility which tends to become very large as the externality becomes large.

At the risk of providing superfluity of detail I shall now cite examples, some of them well-known, of catastrophic or potentially catastrophic effects. These make the point that we are concerned not with small-scale nuisances like dirty smoke from a factory chimney but with extreme cases.

(1) The escape of methyl isocyanate (MIC) from a factory owned by Union Carbide at Bhopal in India led to the deaths of over 2500 and the injury of many more.
(2) The dumping of chemical waste in the disused Love Canal at Nicaragua led to mass evacuation and litigation.
(3) In the mere two months following Bhopal there were evacuations and hospital admissions in Lima (Peru), Jabalpur and Trichur (India), Matamoros (Mexico), Cabatao (Brazil), Little Rock (USA) and Karls Koga (Sweden), due to chemical emissions.
(4) The Krakov area of Poland has suffered an ecological calamity due to industrial waste.
(5) Phosphorous and nitrogen effluent in Lake Bawa, Japan, has polluted underground drinking water.
(6) The massive release of fission products from a nuclear reactor would do enormous and widespread damage, the typical large reactor having a potential release of 1500 Hiroshimas. (The *probability* of this happening is a separate issue to be discussed in the next section.)
(7) The safe disposal of nuclear waste is a major problem and the Nuclear Industry Radioactive Waste Executive has had great difficulty in finding suitable sites: one has to ensure that radionuclides will not permeate through their encasing concrete blocks for at least 300 years. Press reports indicate regular concern about the disposal of waste at the Sellafield reprocessing plant in Cumbria.

David Collard

(8) Miscellaneous mini-catastrophes are regularly reported in *Nature*. A quick search reveals mercury dumping from batteries in Japan, depletion of wild plant varieties leading to genetic difficulties in stock-breeding, the need to replace phosphates drained off farmland by mining, lake and forest acidification in Central Europe, and so on.

To model these dramatic possibilities I propose an environmental *disutility function* which increases at an increasing rate and without limit.[2] It is anchored on current wealth, the disutility of no change being zero. So we have

$$u = u(x)$$

where u is disutility
    x is externality
and

$$u(o) = 0$$
$$u'(x) > 0$$
$$u''(x) > 0$$
$$\lim_{x \to \infty} u(x) = \infty$$

$$(1)$$

Generally economists have preferred to work with utility functions rather than disutility functions, although it makes no difference in principle. Thus Cropper (1976) has utility falling to zero if a catastrophe reduces consumption to zero. This would be acceptable in the present context if consumption were to be defined *extremely* broadly to include consumption from all types of human and environmental capital. Large and unlimited losses make the point much more clearly. Several sorts of functions satisfy condition (1), including those based on x^n, e^x and $e^{\log^2 x}$,[3] but in what follows I shall consider only the simple exponential form as it adequately covers the main point I wish to make.

PROBABILITY

For most of the catastrophes we speak of there is not, fortunately, an established frequency distribution of historical occurrences – as is available, for example, for flood damage. A 'subjective' assessment of probability is then necessary, in which case some sort of logical model has to be constructed. In practice, the prior probabilities thus concocted need to be revised as further information comes along, in a Bayesian fashion. There is nothing wrong with this in principle, though it does imply a judgement about the adequacy of the model used and hence the weight placed upon it or the degree of belief in it.

Thus one might devise a probability based upon the fault tree analysis below and then revise it upwards following, say, a Three Mile Island (TMI) incident. The well-known Rasmussen Report (1973) recommended the use of 'fault trees' (or their inverses, 'event trees'). Essentially these trees model the probability of particular kinds of failure by utilising evidence on the probability of the constituent elements of the failure. In nuclear power stations there is a mechanism, known as SCRAM, for stopping a chain reaction. Suppose it could go wrong at one or more of five stages: a pipe break, an electric power failure, an emergency cooling system failure, a fission product removal system failure and a containment system failure. If the probability of failure at each stage is known, it is an easy matter to calculate the probability of system failure.

None of these early analyses, including Rasmussen, foresaw the TMI incident: in part because analyses never go more than a few steps down the sequence. Hence after a fairly short time the operators were dealing with a situation that had not been foreseen and for which they had no relevant training (Lewis, 1980). As far as is now known the detailed sequence of events of Bhopal was not so different from that at TMI. The Company had initially laid most of the blame at the feet of relatively inexperienced Indian workers. But it now appears (*New Scientist*, 1 January 1985) that the methyl isocyanate (MIC) had been driven out under pressure caused by a water leak into the tank: 'water alone caused the Bhopal disaster, and the factory could not contain a runaway reaction'. The plant had not been built to withstand a 'worst case' outcome.

Since TMI it has become impossible to rely solely upon fault trees: they make insufficient allowance for human error, they do not admit of grey areas, they ignore common cause failure, and so on; nor can they easily take into account the probability of espionage or of theft of weapons grade material. In short, they are a scientistic device for giving respectability to educated guesses. Some sorts of failure, for example gross failure of the pressure vessel, are described as 'incredible', which presumably means they should be directly assigned a probability of zero. Other sorts of failure were indirectly assigned a zero probability on the argument that one chance in a million is a risk acceptable to the public whilst the probability of a large uncontrolled radiation release to the environment (using fault trees) was one in ten million reactor years of operation. This figure is itself contentious: the UK Nuclear Installations Inspectorate has suggested that it could be increased a thousand-fold. Somewhat less serious incidents were assigned higher acceptance levels; for example, a radiation dose requiring the evacuation of the area around the station should be less than once in ten thousand reactor years. I shall return to this point about 'comparables' in the next section.

The notion of acceptable risk is somewhat imprecise. In *Acceptable Risk*, Fischhoff *et al.* (1981) show it has no meaning outside of a specific context. May we use risk compendia? There is certainly a great deal of evidence that people are prepared, quite voluntarily, to undertake far greater risk than is implied by fault tree analysis for nuclear power stations. (Risk compendia show the loss of life expectancy due to motor vehicles accidents to be 207 days, due to all catastrophes combined 3.5 days, and due to reactor accidents between 0.02 and 2.0 days.) But the authors comment that 'risk compendia are superficial and misleading in that they ignore benefits, equity, catastrophic potential and uncertainty'.

Revealed preference for risk is an attractive complementary approach. Starr, in a much cited article (1969) concluded that:

(1) the acceptable level of risk is proportional to the third power of the benefit;
(2) the public is willing to accept a 1000 times greater risk for voluntary than it is for involuntary activities that provide the same level of benefit;
(3) acceptable risk decreases as the number of people exposed increases. These conclusions together imply a lower tolerance or acceptance of risk in the catastrophic case than in other cases.

Detaching, as we should do, the probabilities from the outcomes how do people view small probabilities *per se*? Kahneman and Tversky (1979) showed that people 'overweigh' small probabilities. But Starr

and Whipple (1982) assert that this tendency does *not* extend to very
tiny probabilities. Indeed they postulate that probabilities of less than
10^{-6} are counted as zero. It is difficult to accept this as a valid
procedure, for consider its implications.

(1) As expected disutility is disutility times probability, it would have
    to be counted as zero even for quite horrendous outcomes.
(2) A horrendous but unlikely outcome would have to count not
    merely for less than a moderately bad (but more likely) outcome,
    but for *nothing at all*.
(3) *Ceteris paribus*, society would be indifferent between project A
    which has a horrendous but unlikely outcome and project B
    which does not. The approach seems to be at least as unattractive
    as the opposite 'Murphy's Law' (if anything *can* go wrong, it *will*
    go wrong) which implies giving all bad outcomes a probability of
    one!

I therefore wish to retreat to subjective probabilities, bearing in mind
that they will be held with some *degree of belief*. In the catastrophic
risk case we may think of the probability density function as being
skewed with a tail of potentially large disasters carrying very small
probabilities. It is therefore plausible that probability itself should
decay as the scale of damage increases. As in the case of the disutility
function it is convenient to assume as exponential form.

EXPECTED DISUTILITY

It is now a simple matter to multiply exponentially increasing disutili-
ties and decreasing probabilities so as to obtain the *expected disutility*
arising from any one hypothetical level of externality. In particular
we wish to know what happens when x becomes very large. Should
expected disutility from catastrophes be very large because of their
disastrous outcomes or very small because of their low probabilities?
As I am assuming exponentially increasing and decreasing functions,
the analysis is particularly easy. For this part of the exercise, we write
a disutility function:

$$u = a\,(e^{\alpha x} - 1) \qquad\qquad\qquad (2)$$

and a probability decay function:

$$p = be^{-\beta\alpha} \tag{3}$$

These functions are illustrated in Figure 6.1. Multiplying these together we have the expected disutility function:

$$v = c\left[e^{(\alpha-\beta)x} - e^{-\beta x}\right] \tag{4}$$

where $c = ab$. The final term clearly goes to zero as x becomes large so we have:

$v \rightarrow \infty$ as $x \rightarrow \infty$ when $\alpha > \beta$

$v \rightarrow 0$ as $x \rightarrow \infty$ when $\beta > \alpha$

$v \rightarrow c$ as $x \rightarrow \infty$ when $\alpha = \beta$

There is no wishy-washy compromise here, except in the fluke case of $\alpha = \beta$: the prospect of catastrophe counts for nothing or it counts for everything. This is a very satisfying, though perhaps not terribly helpful outcome. Everything hinges on whether probability is decaying at a faster rate (β) than disutility is increasing (α): if $\alpha > \beta$ the environmentalists are right; if $\alpha < \beta$ the technological optimists are right. I propose to call these the *strong* and *weak* cases of catastrophic risk respectively.

Though my main concern is with extreme values, it is instructive to plot some more modest, though also more probable, mishaps. For illustrative purposes it is assumed that,

$a = 100$

$b = 0.1$

$\beta = 0.115$

Resulting plots are shown in Figure 6.2.

The assumed value for β is chosen so as to ensure that the probability of a catastrophe of the scale $x = 100$ is 10^{-6}. Various values of α are then inserted . Notice that for weak catastrophic risk the expected disutility function reaches a maximum at a relatively small catastrophe.[4] This means that for every major catastrophe there will be a *disutility equivalent* small catastrophe: in this sense the community may be said to be indifferent between matching pairs of

Figure 6.1

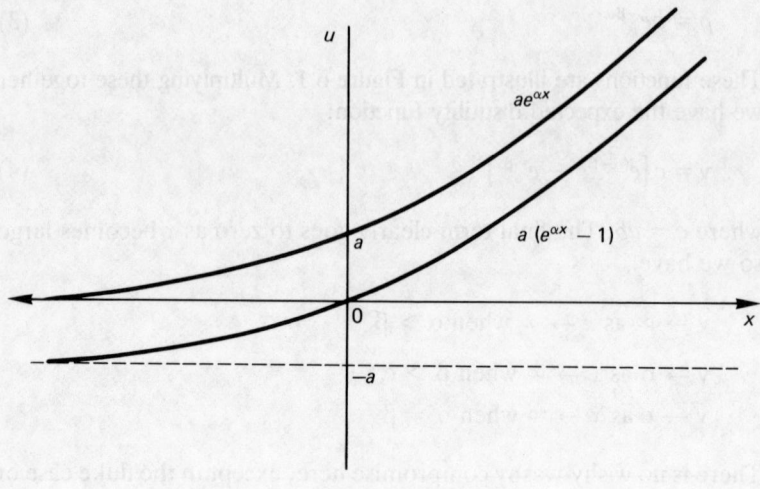

(i) *The disutility function*

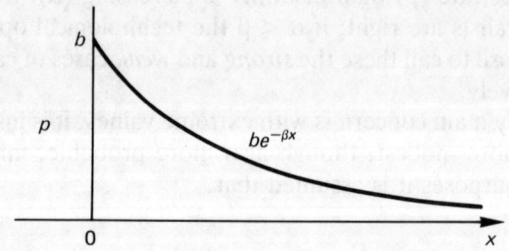

(ii) *The probability decay function*

Notes:

(i) $-\alpha$ may be interpreted as bliss or maximum positive utility. The utility
function corresponding to $e^{\alpha x} - 1$ is the exponential, $1 - e^{\alpha x}$. This dis-
plays constant absolute risk aversion, α, and increasing relative risk
aversion αx.

(ii) Probability decays at the rate β and tends to zero.

small and large incidents. Slightly more formally we may say that for
every $\bar{x}$ there exists a disutility equivalent but more probable $\underset{\sim}{x}$. Such
an analogy may have heuristic value. No such analogy is possible in

Figure 6.2

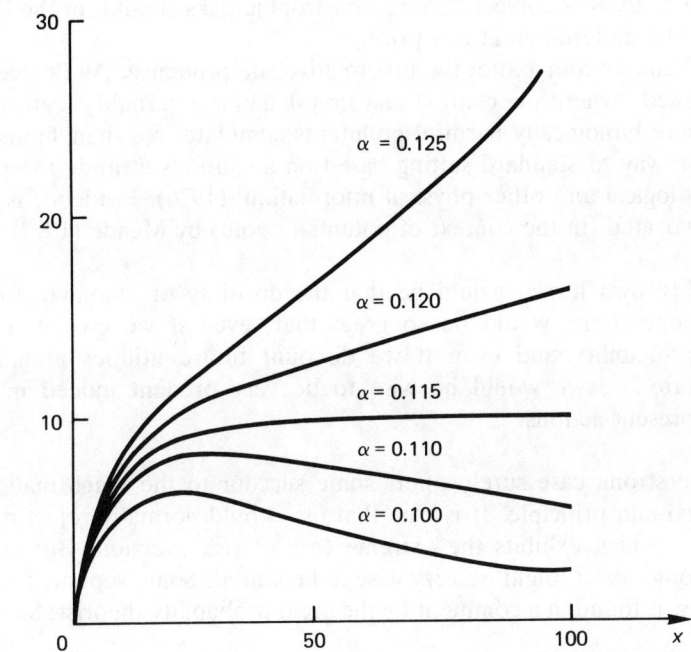

Note:

$v = up$ where

$u = 100 \, (e^{\alpha x} - 1)$

$p = 0.1 \, e^{-\beta x}$

$\beta = .115$

α as illustrated.

the case of strong catastrophic risk: it has to be understood on its own terms.

IMPLICATIONS

We have isolated the case of 'strong' catastrophic risk: it occurs when the probability of catastrophe decays less rapidly than its prospective disutility increases. Expected disutility therefore becomes very large indeed *even though* the probability of disaster is extremely small. If the analysis is correct, strong catastrophic risks should, in the limit, not be undertaken at any price.

I am, of course, not the first to advocate prudence. As Pearce has argued: 'where the context takes on dynamic externality features or where biologically harmful pollutants cumulate, cost-benefit should give way to standard setting based on a cautious attitude to epidemiological and other physical information' (1976). Prudence is also advocated (in the context of potential doom) by Meade (1973):

> My own hunch would be that the disutility of Doom to future generations would be so great that, even if we give it a low probability and even if we discount future utilities at a high rate . . . we would be wise to be very prudent indeed in our present actions.

The strong case surely offers some succour to the much maligned maxi-min principle. It is true that one would normally reject maximin, which exhibits the extreme case of risk aversion. But in the strong case it might be very wise to be scared. Some support for this view is found in a comment by the great probability theorist, Savage:

> Personal probability is imperfect: I could be wrong – I am not confident enough about it – but I am confident that one choice cannot give me a loss of more than L^* (the maximin loss) – so it is chosen.   (Savage, 1954)

What would 'prudence' imply? If there is absolutely no way of modifying the catastrophic risk so as to turn it into a 'weak' case, the whole project should be rejected. Otherwise one has to consider whether α might be reduced or β increased. All three of the following are sensible procedures when faced with a strong case.

(1) Postpone the final decision. Keep options open by choosing an interim, relatively harmless, solution in the hope that a safer technology will eventually turn up. A sophisticated analysis of this response is provided by Viscusi and Zeckhauser (1976). They argue (illustratively) that where there is technological uncertainty it might be better to store nuclear waste at ground level – for easy access and safe future disposal – rather than bury it in salt mines. Their technical device is the Markov process with

known transition probabilities but they recognise that 'even a small probability of entering a state that will be forever inferior may render unacceptable a strategy that risks irreversibility'.

(2) Adopt a series of 'low-tech' solutions which give lower benefits but avoid catastrophic risk altogether (reduce α).

(3) Take safety measures so as to prevent the worst-case scenario (raise β). If these costs are 'excessively' costly, so much the worse for the project.

How much support is there, in the analysis of this paper, for one or other of the protagonists mentioned at the beginning? The possibility of the strong case is, of course, discomforting for the 'hard' technocrat and comforting for the 'soft' environmentalist. The environmentalist will be reluctant, however, to admit the weak case, for in this case horrendous outcomes are contemplated *provided that* $\alpha < \beta$. As mankind does seem to have become used to taking some kinds of catastrophic risk, it is as difficult to get rid of this case in practice as it is in theory.

A final point to be made concerns the uncertainty surrounding both α and β. Given this, 'prudence' would dictate that catastrophic risks should be taken if and only if α is not merely less than β but *very much* less.

SUMMARY

(1) Catastrophic risk can be analysed using subjective expected environmental disutility.

(2) In the limit probability approaches zero and disutility approaches infinity.

(3) In the exponential cases considered, the 'strong' case of catastrophic risk emerges where disutility is increasing at a faster rate than probability is decaying. There is a presumption that such projects should be rejected out of hand.

(4) In less strong cases a catastrophic risk may be considered as in some sense 'equivalent to' a less catastrophic but more probable risk.

(5) One is more likely to find strong cases where damage and disutility functions are increasing very rapidly over some range – for example, as absorptive capacity of part of the environment becomes exhausted or as other irreversibilities are encountered.

(6) While it may or may not be possible to neglect tiny probabilities, it is not permissible to *assume* that they may be safely ignored.

(7) Though the issue is not discussed in this paper, the strong case would seem to be eminently applicable to the catastrophic risk of nuclear war.

Notes

1. For helpful comments and/or discussion, I am grateful to Roger Bowles, Stella Collard, Stephen Jenkins, David Pearce, Richard Pryke, David Ulph and Andy Whittingham. The responsibility for any remaining errors is mine.

2.   'And in the lowest deep, a lower deep,
                   still threatening to devour me opens wide,
                   to which the Hell I suffer seems a Heaven.'

                                       (Milton, *Paradise Lost*, I)

3. *For* $u = e^{\log^2 x}$
   u' is positive so long as $x > 1$
   u'' is positive so long as $x > e^{1/2}$

4. $e^{-\beta x} (e^{\alpha x} - 1)$ is maximised when

$$e^{\alpha x} = \frac{\beta}{\beta - \alpha}$$

so, where $\beta > \alpha$ we have

$$\underline{x} = \frac{1}{\alpha} \log \frac{\beta}{\beta - \alpha}$$

For example, for one of the cases illustrated in Figure 6.2

$$\beta = \cdot 115, \; \alpha = \cdot 110 \text{ so } x_{max} \text{ is } 28.50$$

(For this value to be a maximum it is required that

$$\beta^2 > e^{\alpha x} (\alpha - \beta)^2$$

at the above value for x, or

$$\beta^2 > \beta (\beta - \alpha)$$

which is clearly so for all positive values of α and β_2).

References

American Enterprise Institute (AEI) (1984), *Toxic Torts: Proposals for Compensating Victims of Hazardous Substances* (Washington DC: American Enterprise Institute).

Bailey, M. J. (1982), 'Risks, Costs and Benefits of Fluorocarbon Regulations', *American Economic Review, Papers and Proceedings* (May).

Broome, J. (1978), 'Trying to Value a Life', *Journal of Public Economics*.

Collard, D. (1979), 'Faustian Projects and the Social Rate of Discount', *Bath Papers in Political Economy*, no. 1.

Cropper, M. L. (1976), 'Regulating Activities with Catastrophic Environmental Effects', *Journal of Environmental Economics and Management*.

Dasgupta, P. (1982), *The Control of Resources* (Oxford: Blackwell).

Downing, T. E. and R. W. Kates (1982), 'The International Response to the Threat of Hydrocarbons to the Atmosphere Zone', *American Economic Review Papers and Proceedings* (May).

Fischoff, B. *et al.* (1981), *Acceptable Risk*, (Cambridge University Press).

Fyfe, W. F. *et al.* (1984), 'The Geology of Nuclear Waste Disposal', *Nature* (August).

Hohenemser, C. and J. X. Kasperson (1982), *Risk in the Technological Society*, AAAS Symposia Series, (Boulder, Colorado).

Jones-Lee, M. W. (1979), 'Trying to Value a Life: Why Broome does not sweep clean', *Journal of Public Economics*.

Kahneman, D. and A. Tversky (1979), 'Prospect Theory: An Analysis of Decision under Risk', *Econometrica*.

Knetsch, J. L. and J. A. Sinden (1984), 'Willingness to Pay and Compensation Demanded: Experimental Evidence of an Unexpected Disparity in Measures of Value', *Quarterly Journal of Economics*, vol. 99.

Lecomber, R. (1975), *Economic Growth versus the Environment*, (London: Macmillan).

Lewis, H. W. (1980), 'The Safety of Fission Reactors', *Scientific American* (March).

Lowe, J., D. Lewis and M. Atkins (1982), *Total Environmental Control*, (Oxford: Pergamon).

Meade, J. E. (1973), 'Economic Policy and the Threat of Doom', in B. Benjamin *et al.* (eds), *Resources and Population*, (Academic Press).

Pearce, D. W. (1976), 'The Limits of Cost-Benefit to Environmental Policy', *Kyklos*, 1.

Rasmussen Report (1973), *The Reactor Safety Study*, NUREG – 75/014.

Savage, L. J. (1954), *Foundations of Statistics*, (New York: Wiley).

Smets, H. (1985), 'Environment: Major Risks and Compensation', *OECD Observer*, no. 134 (May).

Starr, C. (1969), 'Social Benefit versus Technological Risk: What is our Society willing to pay for Safety?', *Science*, vol. 165.

Starr, C. and C. Whipple (1982), 'Risks of Risk Decisions', in C. Hohenemser and J. X. Kasperson, *Risk in the Technological Society*, AAAS Symposia Series (Boulder, Colorado).

Ulph, A. (1982), 'The Role of Ex-Ante and Ex-Post Decisions in the Valuation of Life', *Journal of Public Economics*.

Viscusi, W. K. and R. Zeckhauser (1976), 'Environmental Policy Choice Under Uncertainty', *Journal of Environmental Economics and Management*.

7 Some Principles of Population[1]

John Broome

Richard Lecomber had a special interest in economic policies that will have profound effects far in the future. He was, for instance, concerned with protecting natural resources, and with the use of nuclear power. Assessing policies like these raises many questions that economists have not yet learnt to answer. In this paper I shall concentrate on just one of them. These policies are bound to affect the world's future population. They will affect how many people are born and how long they live for. How should we take account of these effects in judging the policies?

I want to follow up what Lecomber himself wrote about this problem (Lecomber, 1979, pp. 69–71). He posed the problem in the form that is, perhaps, traditional in economics. Each year in the future will bring to people a quantity of good; there will be a stream of future good ('utility'). Different policies will bring about different streams. How should alternative streams be compared? Lecomber mentions three possible ways. One is simply to look for the greatest total of utility: to maximise

$$\int n(t)u(t)dt \qquad (1)$$

where $n(t)$ is the population at any time and $u(t)$ is utility per head. Another is to be concerned only with utility per head and maximise

$$\int u(t)dt. \qquad (2)$$

The third I shall mention later.

Of these principles, the first is what has come to be known as the 'classical' or 'total' utilitarian principle. It was recommended by Henry Sidgwick (1907, pp. 415–16), and since then it has been so thoroughly discussed that I do not need to spend time on it here. The main difficulty with it is well recognised, and was mentioned by Lecomber (1979, p. 70). Imagine a world where everyone is very well off. It will always be possible to imagine another world where everyone leads a dreary life that is scarcely good at all, but where there are so many people that the total of good is actually greater. Total utilitarianism prefers this second world. This is a conclusion that Derek Parfit (1984, p. 388) calls 'repugnant'.

Lecomber's second principle looks superficially like the 'average' utilitarian principle, the best established rival to the total principle. The average principle has received some support in the literature. Most notably, it has been endorsed, in a qualified way, by John Rawls (1972, pp. 161–6). But actually Lecomber's is not really the average principle at all. Since Lecomber's principle is quite commonly applied in economics, it is worth pointing out the differences. The average principle would require one to maximise

$$\frac{1}{N} \int n(t)u(t)dt \tag{3}$$

where N is the total number of people who live. (I am being deliberately vague here about the time period, for a reason that will appear.) And this is not at all the same.

There are really two differences between the average principle and Lecomber's. The first is that in Lecomber's the averaging is done only at each particular time and never between two different times. This is peculiar. Compare two policies. For each date in the future, both bring about the same living standards at that date. And both policies bring it about that the same number of people are born altogether. But one brings it about that more are born and live at times when living standards are high, the other when they are low. Lecomber's principle values both of these policies equally. But one policy gives more people better lives, and surely it ought to be preferred. If we are to use a criterion that concerns itself with the average of people's good, the averaging operation must cross time at least to some extent. To be sure, it is very hard to know just how wide the scope of the averaging should be (see McMahan, 1981). Is it right, for instance, to include in the average people whose lives are already ended? (This makes a difference, because the average principle favours bringing into existence a person whose life will be better than average but not one whose life will be worse.) This doubt is one difficulty with the average principle itself. But it is clearly intolerable not to average at all across different times. I can think of no defence for this aspect of Lecomber's principle. A variant principle, which does not have this fault, is to maximise

$\int n(t)u(t)dt \,/\, \int n(t)dt.$ (4)

The second difference between the average principle and Lecomber's is this. The aim of the average principle is to make sure that the average person's life is as good as possible. But how good a life is depends on its length as well as on the person's standard of living. It is commonly assumed that one life is better than another if it contains more good in total. But in any case, whether or not this is so, it is hard to doubt that a longer life, at a particular standard of living, is better than a shorter one. Lecomber's second principle (or the variant represented by (4)), however, pays attention to the standard of living only, and not to the length of lives. It is indifferent between a world where lives are short and one where they are long, provided only that the quality of life is the same. Conceivably, one might take the view (the analogue of average utilitarianism applied within a life) that one life is better than another, not if it contains a greater total of good, but if it has a higher average flow of good over time. In this case a long life at a particular standard of living would be no better than a short one. But even if this were so, (4) would still not be a formula for the average goodness of lives. Twist it how you may, then, Lecomber's is very different from the average principle.

No support for this principle, therefore, can be drawn from the arguments (such as Rawls's) for average utilitarianism. Can any independent rationale be found for it? The total utilitarian principle, of course, pays no attention to lengths of lives. It cares only about good, without any concern for whose life it occurs in. It fits Rawls's dictum (1972, p. 27) that 'utilitarianism does not take seriously the distinction between persons'. The average principle, on the other hand, does not fit it so well. It does care about how good is divided between lives. The principle embodies in (4) is a sort of compromise. On the one hand, it has the averaging spirit in that it is concerned with the level at which people live and not with the number of people who live at that level. On the other hand, it is not concerned with how good is distributed amongst different people's lives. It is concerned only with the quality of living of the moment, and not with how the qualities of different moments add together to make up a good life. It is a formula, therefore, that might appeal to someone who does not think that the continuity of a life is morally significant, that it does not matter morally whether two good periods of life occur in the same life or in different lives. This certainly seems like a defensible moral attitude; it has been thoroughly explored by Derek Parfit (1984, pp. 321–47). That, together with the 'averaging spirit' as I called it, might give some basis to a formula like (4).

Now I come to Lecomber's third suggested principle (1979, p. 70). He says:

> What is the effect on welfare of an addition to the population? To highlight the source of difficulty, ignore birth-control costs, parental satisfactions and all other impacts on the rest of the population . . . . Interestingly the same question arises in the cost-benefit analysis of birth control where yet a third assumption is (implicitly) adopted, namely that this impact on welfare is zero. This is also the assumption generally adopted in everyday life: when deciding not to have a child, one does not generally consider the lost satisfactions which the hypothetical child misses through not being born. Thus, of the three assumptions, the last seems the least unsatisfactory, though its application as a macro context is fraught with difficulty.

There is in this really not much more than a hint at a principle for assessing policies. And working it out in detail is, as Lecomber says and as I shall be explaining, fraught with difficulties. But the idea is certainly attractive. Take an example. Suppose it is proposed to reduce old age pensions and spend the money instead on increased family allowances. One effect will probably be to increase the number of children born. Most of them will enjoy good lives. Is the good they enjoy to be counted as a benefit of the proposal, to be set against the loss to the elderly? It is natural to think not. I shall call this 'Lecomber's third principle', rough though it is: do not count as a benefit of a policy the good of people who, but for the policy, would not exist.

This way of thinking was first given philosophical expression by Jan Narveson (1967). Narveson's claim was that a benefit has to be a benefit *to* somebody. But being brought into existence and enjoying a good life is not a benefit to anyone. To be benefited you must be made better off than you would otherwise have been. And being brought into existence does not make you better off than you would otherwise have been; had you not been brought into existence it would not have been the case that you were worse off, because there would have been no you.

This claim about benefit has been disputed. McMahan (1981) and

Parfit (1984, pp. 487–90) suggest that bringing a person into existence may be said to benefit her 'non-comparatively'. I am not going to participate in this dispute; it is really only about the meaning of 'benefit'. What is important is whether the fact that a person would, if brought into existence, have a good life, is a reason in favour of bringing her into existence. Narveson's idea is that a reason always has to be 'person-based' as I shall put it. A reason always has to be a benefit to a person. And since, he says, the goodness of the person's life is not a person-based reason for bringing her into existence, it is not a reason at all.

I am not myself going to assume that reasons have to be person-based. The idea that they do is certainly attractive. But I think that at least a part of its attraction comes from confusing it with a different idea. The different idea is that all good is personal, there is no sort of good other than the good of a person. There is, for instance, no such thing as the good of 'society' apart from the good of its members. Now, all the good considered in this paper is personal good. Suppose a person, if brought into existence, would have a good life. The good in her life would all belong to her, the person. But if Narveson is right, bringing this person into existence, though it creates good belonging to this person is not actually good *for* her or a benefit to her. So one might accept that every reason for acting must stem from personal good, without accepting that every reason must be a benefit to a person. In this paper I shall accept the former but not the latter.

Whatever the cogency of Narveson's argument, there are some serious difficulties about the conclusions it leads to. One is Parfit's 'non-identity problem' (1984, pp. 351–79). Suppose there is a choice between two courses of action A and B. Both will bring it about that the same number of people exist in the future. But they will not all of them be the same people. Amongst Parfit's examples is the case of a woman who might conceive a child now or else postpone conception by a month and so have a different child. Another example is perhaps a choice of economic policies, say of taxation policies. Both bring about the same size of population in the future. But under the different policies different people meet each other, marry and have children, so that within a generation or two the people who would exist under one policy are quite different from the people who would exist under the other. Call the people who exist under both courses of action the AB people, the people who exist only under A the A people, and those who exist only under B the B people. Suppose now that the AB people are equally well off under A or B. But the A

people are better off under *A* than the *B* people are under *B*. It seems clear that *A* is a better course of action than *B*. But according to Narveson's way of thinking there is no reason to prefer one to the other. Doing *A* rather than *B* benefits nobody.

That is one paradox. A simple extension of it leads to another. Suppose there are now three courses of action available, *A*, *B* and *C*. Suppose they each lead to the same total size of the future population, but again they do not all lead to the very same people coming into existence. Let there be, extending my notation, *ABC* people, *AB* people, *BC* people, and *CA* people. Suppose the *ABC* people are equally well off under all of *A*, *B* and *C*. Suppose the *AB* people are better off under *A* than *B*. Suppose the *BC* people are better off under *B* than *C*, and the *CA* people are better off under *C* than *A*. According to Narveson's way of thinking, *A* is better than *B*, *B* than *C* and *C* than *A*.

This intransitivity is a second paradox. We shall see later that intransitivities can also be generated in another way when there is a question of comparing actions that lead to the existence of different numbers of people.

A third paradox is the so-called 'asymmetry'. If a person is going to have a good life, according to Narveson creating this person is no benefit to her. If a person is going to have a bad life, then, creating her can do her no harm. If the fact that a person's life will be good is not a reason for bringing her into existence, the fact that her life will be bad is not a reason against bringing her into existence. This, however, offends intuition. We may grant that a couple who refrain from having a child they know will be happy are doing nothing morally wrong. But we will not grant that a couple who do have a child they know will be unhappy are doing nothing morally wrong.

I want to throw a new idea into the ring. It is intended to support Lecomber's third principle by a different argument from Narveson's. I do not pretend that this idea can overcome all the difficulties and paradoxes in this area. It cannot, and in the end it may have to be rejected as incoherent. But this problem of population is riddled throughout with paradoxes. No principle that has yet been found for assessing population policies – any of Lecomber's three or any other – is free from paradoxes. My idea is, I think, at least intuitively attractive. For that reason it seems worth trying out.

The idea, put roughly, is that what makes a life good is not necessarily the same as what makes it worth living. An assumption that implicitly pervades virtually all of the literature is that when lives are arranged on a scale from bad to good, a life worth living is one that lies above a certain point on this scale. I want to question this assumption.

To explain this and make it more precise I shall start by considering a life that is already in progress. What makes it worth continuing? Why should a person want to continue to live? An interesting distinction has been made in this context by Bernard Williams (1973). Williams was writing in answer to Lucretius (1951, pp. 121–9), whose opinion was that death is not an evil, and we have no reason to avoid it. Williams argues that our desires can give us a reason to avoid death and continue living.

He distinguishes two sorts of desires: 'categorical' and 'conditional'. A categorical desire is simply a desire. It has the form 'I want X'. Williams believes that such a desire gives one a reason to prevent anything that will prevent the desire from being satisfied. If, therefore, I have a categorical desire than cannot be satisfied if I die, it gives me a reason to avoid dying.

A conditional desire has the form 'If I remain alive I want X'. The form is not 'I want that if I remain alive I get X', because this desire would be satisfied by my death, it is equivalent to 'I want that either I die or I get X', and it gives me a reason to bring about my death at least if I cannot get X. A conditional desire, however, gives me no reason to bring about my death, but evidently it gives me no reason to avoid death either.

Now, if we accept the common theory that it is good for a person that her desires should be satisfied, the satisfaction of any desire contributes to making life good. But only the satisfaction of categorical desires makes it worth living; only the satisfaction of categorical desires gives one a reason for continuing to live one's life (indeed, only the satisfaction of those categorical desires that require one to continue living if they are to be satisfied). So if there really are desires that are only conditional, then there is a difference between what makes life good and what makes it worth living.

I do not wish to be committed to the theory that good consists only in the satisfaction of desires. So I shall generalise the distinction. I shall distinguish categorical goods and conditional goods. Achieving a good gives one a reason for acting in any way that achieves it. A categorical good gives one a reason for acting in any way that achieves it, and if this requires one to remain alive it gives one a reason to do so. A conditional good gives one a reason for achieving it if one is to remain alive. Both sorts of good make life good, but only categorical goods make life worth living.

Achieving a good of mine gives me a reason to act in a way that achieves it. But it also gives any benevolent agent a reason to act in a way that achieves it. It gives a reason, for instance, to a government. So it is a person's categorical goods that give any agent a reason to preserve the person's life, that amount to the value of saving her life. And if some goods are conditional, the value of saving a life will not be the whole of the good the life subsequently contains.

But are there conditional goods? And are there categorical goods? Opinions vary from one extreme to the other. Lucretius's view, evidently, was that all goods are conditional; there is no good that gives one a reason for remaining alive. Death is no loss. On the other hand, the most typical modern view in the literature of economics is that the value of saving a person's life amounts to the whole of the good she goes on to enjoy. This implies that all goods are categorical. Williams is vague about which desires are categorical and which conditional. I have no arguments to offer here. But I shall make some suggestions that strike me as intuitively plausible. It is plausible to me that some goods are conditional. Pleasure, for instance, is perhaps a conditional good. If I am going to continue to live it is good for me if my life is pleasant. But I doubt that pleasure gives me a reason for continuing to live, simply to enjoy it. On the other hand, an obvious candidate for a categorical good is the completion of some task or project that I am embarked on, such as bringing up children, or a career. In fact, I think it plausible that all categorical goods are of this sort. I am suggesting that what gives me a *reason* for remaining alive, what gives a value to my life, is the carrying on of activities I am engaged in. I think it is at least worth considering the consequences of this view.

So let us consider now a life that has not yet begun, a person who might or might not be brought into existence. The value of creating this person will be the total of the categorical goods her life will contain. If some of the goods in her life are conditional, the value will be less than the total of her good. And if it is right that the only categorical goods are the carrying on of activities the person is engaged in, all the goods in a life considered before it has started will be conditional. In that case the value of creating the person will be nothing. The good that the person will enjoy, because it is all conditional, will not be a reason for, or count as a benefit of, creating her.

I offer this as a possible basis for Lecomber's third principle. It is a different basis from Narveson's, because it does not assume that a reason has to be person-based. Conditional goods do not constitute a reason for creating a person, not because they are no benefit to the person, but because of the sort of goods they are. Saving the life of an existing person and creating a new person are both beneficial to the extent of the categorical goods contained in the person's subsequent life. In the first case the benefit can be identified as a benefit to the person saved; in the second (if Narveson is right) it is a benefit to nobody. But it could still be counted as a benefit none the less. Only it happens that this benefit is nought because a life not yet created contains no categorical goods.

If we do not insist that reasons be person-based we can also overcome the non-identity problem. Take as an example the case of the woman who can conceive a child either now or later. Suppose a child conceived later would have a better life. Then this seems to be a reason for the woman to delay conception. No one, however, would be benefited by her delaying. So if reasons have to be person-based, there cannot actually be a reason for her to do so. That is the non-identity problem. But if we drop the requirement that reasons must be person-based, we can see a good reason for delaying conception. It maximises the total good. This good is, to be sure, conditional. So it gives no reason to have either child rather than none at all. But actually, whether the child is conceived now or later there is going to be a child. It is right, therefore, to achieve the greatest total of good conditional on that. And this is achieved by having the child later. For this argument to work it is evidently necessary to conceive of conditional good as conditional on the existence of a person, rather than on the existence of any particular person. We should say, for instance, that if a life is to be led it is good that the life, whoever it might belong to, should be pleasant. And if there is to be a particular number of lives the good in those lives should be as great as possible.

I mentioned a second difficulty with Narveson's argument. It leads to intransitivities. The intransitivity I described above was a case where all three alternatives contained the same number of people. It resulted, in essence, from the non-identity problem. Since my idea overcomes the non-identity problem, it overcomes this particular intransitivity. Since there is to be a particular number of lives, the good in those lives should be as great as possible. So the alternatives are ordered according to total good. Unfortunately, though, my idea does not do so well when there are alternatives containing different numbers of people.

Consider again the woman who might conceive a child either now or later, and suppose that a child conceived later will have a happier life. But now suppose it is also an alternative that she has no child at all. Let us ignore 'side effects' such as benefits to the woman herself. Then according to my idea, having no child and having a child conceived now are morally indifferent, and so are having no child and having one conceived later. But having a child conceived later is preferable to having one conceived now. So the relation of moral indifference is intransitive.

Intransitivity of indifference, however, is not fatal. Given a set of alternatives to choose between, my argument tells you what to do. More precisely, from the alternatives available it picks out a group that are all indifferent and all at least as good as any of the others, and says that you should choose one of this group but it does not matter which. If, for instance, the woman has a choice between conceiving a child now and having no child, it does not matter which she does. But if she has a choice between all three alternatives she should either have no child or conceive one later. To speak technically, given any range of alternatives to choose from, our argument picks out a 'choice set' (Sen, 1970, ch. 1). The argument does not set up a transitive ordering of the alternatives but it does set up a 'quasi-transitive' relation (Sen, 1970, p. 15). Strict moral preference is transitive even though indifference is not, and this is enough to ensure the existence of a choice set.

This example, then, does not constitute a serious objection to my idea. But now consider an example that presses it further. Suppose there is a question whether to have one or two children. Suppose the possible alternatives, expressed schematically, are these three: (5), (4,4) and (6,1). The numbers in the brackets represent the children's wellbeing: the first child's and then the second child's, if there is one. According to the idea (5) is preferable to (4,4) because it is better for the first child and there are no reasons (ignoring side effects) for or against having the second one. Then (4,4) is preferable to (6,1) because both children will exist under either of these alternatives and the reasons for preferring (4,4) on behalf of the second child outweigh the reasons for preferring (6,1) on behalf of the first. Finally, (6,1) is preferable to (5) because it is better for the first child and there are no reasons either for or against having the second.

Here, then, is an intransitivity of strict preference. It is a fatal incoherence because if we were faced with a choice of three alternatives like the ones I described, we should not know what to do. This is a serious difficulty for my use of the distinction between categorical and conditional goods, and I do not know how to overcome it. One attempt at overcoming it is a two-stage decision rule proposed by Partha Dasgupta (1986). First, this rule says, compare all the alternatives with a population of a given size. Then having picked the best for each given size, compare these best so as to find the best of all. In the example, first compare (4,4) with (6,1). The best of these two is (4,4). Then compare (4,4) with (5). Since (5) is preferable to (4,4), it is the one this two-stage process finally picks. This is certainly a way of reaching a result. But the trouble is that there is no reason to think it will reach the right result. The two-stage procedure needs some moral justification, which Dasgupta does not provide. In the example, it picks (5) when (6,1) is available, and this is very odd. (See also Parfit's discussion of the 'mere addition paradox' [1984, pp. 419–40].)

How does my idea fare with the 'asymmetry'? Can it explain why it should be wrong to have a child one knows will be unhappy, but not wrong to refrain from having a child one knows will be happy? It seems natural to say here that, whereas a good, like pleasure, may only be conditional, a bad, like pain, must be categorical. The fact that a life will be pleasant may not be a reason for living it, but the fact that a life will be painful is a reason for not living it. So at first it looks as though the distinction between conditional and categorical good can account for the asymmetry. But things are not so simple. Suppose a couple could have a child whose life, they know, would contain a lot of pleasure and, like most people's lives, some pain. According to our idea, the pain would be a reason against having the child, but the pleasure no reason in favour. So (if there are no other categorical goods or bads to consider) the couple would be wrong to have the child. This cannot be the right conclusion. Pleasure must be allowed to weigh against pain in some way or other. Even if pleasure does not give a reason for living it must weigh against a reason for not living. But I cannot see how to set up a moral calculus that satisfies this requirement.

The distinction, then, between conditional and categorical goods runs into difficulties that I cannot overcome. And they are difficulties, too, with Lecomber's third principle in general, however it is supported. I do not see how it can deal with the asymmetry or with the intransitivity I have described. In the end this principle, despite its attractions, may have to be rejected.

Note

1. I should like to thank David Ulph for helpful comments.

References

Dasgupta, P. (1986), 'The Ethical Foundations of Population Policies', in D. Gale Johnson and R. Lee (eds), *Population Growth and Economic Development* (Washington D.C.: National Academy of Sciences).
Lecomber, R. (1979), *The Economics of Natural Resources* (London: Macmillan).
Lucretius (1951), *On the Nature of the Universe*, translated by R. E. Latham (Harmondsworth: Penguin).
McMahan, J. (1981), 'Problems of Population Theory', *Ethics*, 92.
Narveson, J. (1967), 'Utilitarianism and New Generations', *Mind*, 76.
Parfit, D. (1984), *Reasons and Persons* (Oxford University Press).
Rawls, J. (1972), *A Theory of Justice* (Oxford University Press).
Sen, A. (1970), *Collective Choice and Social Welfare* (Amsterdam: North Holland).
Sidgwick, H. (1907), *The Methods of Ethics*, 7th edn (London: Macmillan).
Williams, B. (1973), 'The Makropulos Case: Reflections on the Tedium of Immortality', in his *Problems of the Self* (Cambridge University Press) pp. 82–100.

8 Forestry Development in Upland Britain

Malcolm Clarke

INTRODUCTION

A happy collaboration with Richard Lecomber on courses in Environmental Economics which we gave jointly to undergraduates in their final year at Bristol helped me to crystallise many of the ideas in this paper. I owe a considerable debt to him and to the students who attended our seminars.

Forestry is an activity which, if undertaken at all, requires long time horizons, though these are sometimes exaggerated in popular discussion. Some countries possessing long-established forests with an ancient forestry tradition use management systems that combine selection felling with continuous regeneration. Many of the alpine regions of Europe have adopted variants of such systems. It is easy to think of forestry activities there falling into annual patterns of maintenance, thinning and harvesting with little occasion to alter the balance of these activities. Such a view is misleading. Even though much of the forests' regeneration is natural, in most areas additional efforts must be made to maintain the growing stock of timber. Planting improved strains is an option to be considered. Increases or decreases in the forests' area as alternative land uses become less or more attractive have to be weighed. These are some of the more obvious decisions that can only be made rationally if a continually updated view is taken of the balance between the present and future costs and benefits of forestry. Some costs and most benefits fall in the future long after the decisions are made.

In Britain selection felling is comparatively uncommon. The Forestry Commission and most of the larger private forestry enterprises prefer even-aged blocks in their plantations which are clear-felled at the end of each rotation. There are critics of and disadvantages to clear-felling, which produces a smaller proportion of saw logs and a larger share of less valuable small roundwood in the total cut. However, there are some countervailing advantages in lower costs and economies of scale in harvesting and in some other operations. In

97

British conditions, most afforestation this century has been on bare land and perforce the pioneer planting has produced even-aged stands.

THE INVESTMENT DECISION

It might appear that the decision to create a plantation can be made much like any other investment decision. The standard discounting formula could then be applied:

$$P = \sum_{i}^{n} (R_j - C_j) \left(\frac{1}{1 + i} \right)^{j}$$

where P is the present value of the discounted stream of revenues less costs produced by the plantation over a rotation of n years. If i is taken to be the target rate of return then a positive value for P indicates a profitable outcome. A judgement must still be made about whether or not the estimated return is sufficient compensation for the risks associated with the project. Most of the benefit from timber sales is heavily concentrated in the final year, when about half the volume and a larger proportion of the revenue from the entire rotation is harvested. The rest is obtained from thinnings which begin about halfway through the rotation period, possibly earlier in the higher yielding plantations. The cost of harvesting is of course closely synchronised with the revenues derived, but the cost of establishing a plantation must be met soon after the decision is taken and necessarily falls decades before the revenues can be enjoyed.

TIME HORIZONS

The themes in this paper are twofold. First, forestry requires decisions that are more complex than the simple application of the discounting formula as a decision rule would reveal. Secondly, decisions are required in a sequence over the time horizon set by each crop rotation. Those made early in the period limit later options by locking resources into the project in a particular way. Nevertheless there will be recurring opportunities to make some choices right up to the point where all that remains for decision is whether or not to fell this year or next. For example, foresters must choose a thinning regime and whether or not to prune selected trees some time before the middle of the rotation. These are not simply technical matters but will be affected by economic calculations about their effects on the cash flows and worth of the crops so treated. It is therefore not sufficient, having established a plantation, to let the foresters apply a standard routine of maintenance and stewardship until a predetermined felling date is reached.

The length of the planning horizon ensures that future costs and receipts are subject to uncertainty. Technical progress has been rapid and offsets the increases in real wage rates experienced until recently in the post-war period. It has reduced the cost of establishing plantations, improved the quality of planting stock and the probability of survival. This reduces the need for and cost of 'beating up', the task of replacing failed plants in the few years after the initial planting. The reduction of costs early in the rotation is important for the balance of profitability, the more so the longer the period before felling. Hazards remain. In the early years fire is an ever present danger and precautions are not costless. Older plantations can be vulnerable to wind-throw. Although the timber is usually recovered, the harvest is less than would be obtained had the trees grown to the planned felling dates. The likelihood of wind-throw is increased by a regime of heavy thinnings at infrequent intervals and must be balanced against the greater cost of thinning lightly and more frequently. The projected time-path of a plantation's growth and output can be set back by unexpectedly severe competition from weed species in the years immediately after planting and later by checks to growth from insect attack or disease. In most cases counter-measures are available, sometimes inexpensively, but possibly at a cost which had not been budgeted.

THE SOCIAL RATE OF DISCOUNT

When time horizons are so long it is essential to consider the rate of discount very carefully. A good proportion of the beneficiaries of today's investments in forestry are not yet born. The consumption forgone today when translated to output in half a century (or even twenty-five years in the case of thinnings) is to a very substantial degree an intergenerational transfer. Individual time horizons are normally restricted to our own life expectancies unless we are atypically altruistic. '*Après-moi la deluge*' is not an uncommon sentiment. Those charged with decisions in the public interest must remember that societies, unlike individuals, are almost immortal unless over-taken by catastrophe. Forestry more than most activities is one that demands long-term planning if sensible decisions are to be made. Where market interest rates are deemed to reflect the aggregation of individual agents' time preferences weighted according to the current distribution of wealth, then we can expect a degree of myopia affecting investment decisions. This is only partly because many of the future beneficiaries are not yet born. Wealth is mostly held by the old. Inheritance transfers private wealth mainly to the succeeding generation which, given the life expectancies of the populations in advanced, capital-rich countries, means transfer from the very aged to the slightly less aged. The latter will typically be in late middle age. These wealth-holders have limited personal time-horizons, and even when investment decisions are taken by large corporate bodies this tends to colour the view of many senior managers who themselves may be well advanced in years. Tobin (1964) has considered a number of other reasons for thinking that capital markets and the interest rates that rule in them bias consumption towards the present at the expense of the future. A modest degree of subsidy for forestry, whether through grants in aid of planting in the private sector or by the reduced target rate of return in the Forestry Commission's enterprise, could be defended on these grounds, but not in prefer-ence to other long period projects.

The Treasury's Interdepartmental Cost/Benefit Study (1972) re-ferred to the 10 per cent target rate of return for public sector investments, but it was not always clear whether this was a 'real' rate or intended to cover the 3 per cent to 5 per cent inflation rate experienced in the 1960s and piously projected as a component in a nominal rate of return. Losses in several nationalised industries encouraged ministers to fudge the issue. The reduction in private sector rates of return in the 1970s and greater appreciation of the distinction between nominal and real rates led to a revision in the test rate of discount to 5 per cent 'real'. For forestry a lower and con-cessionary rate of 3 per cent is applied. The difference can be construed as a subsidy or as an insurance premium necessary to secure domestic supplies against the possibility of interrupted imports of wood products from abroad or a sharp rise in their price. Long-dated index-linked exchequer funds yield between 3.5 per cent and 4.0 per cent at the time of writing. If this is taken as a reasonable indicator of the long-run, market, real rate of interest, the subsidy element of a 3 per cent target for forestry seems less favourable than when compared with the 5 per cent for public sector investments in general. The latter rate is in any case rather arbitrary and the case for setting it above the market rate needs to be made. The interdepartmental study conceded that 'a rate of 3 per cent might represent the lower limit of the range of personal time preference of large estate owners or others of substantial means'.

DEPLETION

Centuries of asset-stripping and *laissez-faire* broken only by intermittant but unsustained efforts at reafforestation left Britain in 1914 with the lowest proportion of forest cover in Europe apart from Iceland and Ireland. There would have been even less had not some of the aristocratic land-owners in the eighteenth and nineteenth centuries taken a very long and possibly uncommercial view in their forestry operations. About 90 per cent of the country's wood requirements were imported at that date while per capita consumption had grown rapidly in the preceding quarter century. In effect, the market had operated to deplete the growing stock over a long period in which the volume of timber cut exceeded the yield. Output could not be sustained on this basis, but it is not self-evident that in a relatively small country a sustainable yield should never be exceeded by the cut. Land was transferred from trees to other uses. After the Napoleonic wars, Britain had access to external supplies and the means to pay. Increasing dependence on imported timber and wood products was therefore regarded only as the operation of comparative advantage through external trade. While the world enjoyed a plentiful supply of virgin timber there seemed little point in devoting resources to afforestation projects whose returns would be modest, long delayed and limited by the price of competitive imports.

The U-boat blockade during the First World War and the low priority given to a bulky commodity like timber in the allocation of shipping space reduced the external supply to a trickle, as happened again in the Second World War. Among its many uses timber was required then for pit-props in the coal-mines and so became a key input in the war economy. Shortages were only partly met by ruthless felling of domestic stands including many immature plantations. The pattern was repeated a generation later in the second war, if anything on a larger scale.

THE BIRTH OF STATE FORESTRY IN BRITAIN

The revelation of Britain's extreme dependence on external timber sources, which far exceeded that of other major economies, resulted in remedial action. The Forestry Commission, established in 1919, marked not only the creation of a state forest service in Great Britain but also the search for criteria on which to base forestry policy. The (Acland) Forestry Sub-Committee of the Ministry of Reconstruction, established in July 1916 by Asquith, whose report led to the Commission's formation, also recommended an afforestation programme of almost 1.8 million acres in the eighty years to the end of the century. This was in addition to the restocking of the felled and devastated area of existing woodlands then estimated at approximately 2 million acres. The planting programme of 150 000 acres set out for the first decade, 1920 to 1929, of the Commission's operations was modest enough when measured against the devastation of war-time felling, even allowing for further planting in excess of 100 000 acres expected to be undertaken by private owners with the assistance of advances administered by the Forestry Commission from its budget. The first task of the new body was to acquire land, and 310 000 acres were secured in the period even though this was less than proposed by the Acland plan. The planting programme at 138 000 acres fell a little short of the plan largely through the effect of unanticipated Treasury cuts in funds budgeted for the purpose. The main objects of the programme were to replace the stock prematurely felled in the war and to increase the growing stock as a strategic reserve for insurance against subsequent interruptions of supply. Substitution of home-grown timber for imports was intended to be only partial and a secondary aim.

Progress between the wars was slow compared with developments from 1948 onwards, but the Commission's field officers gained experience, learned new techniques and tried a variety of exotic species on sites and in conditions which were then still novel. Not all experiments were successful, but many of the lessons learned then paved the way for the confident expansion of the planting programme to more than 50 000 acres per year after the Second World War. Over 20 000 acres per year were planted in the 1930s, giving more than 400 000 acres under plantations by the outbreak of war in 1939. This included the Crown Woods taken over in 1924, of which the New Forest and Forest of Dean were the best known.

At that stage afforestation was not so concentrated on the uplands as it later became. Marginal agricultural land, such as the Breckland estates in East Anglia, was acquired at low prices. However, most acquisitions were hill land in Wales, the North of England and Scotland. The greater part of land bought and planted since 1950 has been in Scotland. The shift of the Forestry Commission's headquarters to Edinburgh from Savile Row recognised that the centre of gravity had moved north. In the rest of this paper I refer to Scottish data not only because most of the estates there can be categorised as 'upland' but because it represents the largest segment of British forestry. Moreover, conditions there mirror the circumstances of Wales and northern England more closely than the well-known but now atypical woodland of southern and midland England. The soils are usually thin and infertile or peaty. In some areas, iron pan in the subsoil would prevent root penetration unless mechanical means could be found to break through it. The development of appropriate heavy ploughs was required before much otherwise suitable land could be planted. One advantage enjoyed by the Forestry Commission is that its scale of operations is sufficient to make research programmes tailored to its own particular problems worthwhile. The results are seen in the post-war development and introduction of specialist machinery as well as in silvicultural practice in the plantations and horticultural practice in its nurseries. The benefits are partly in lower costs of operations, higher yields and partly in better informed decision-making. Despite the growth of its estate since the war and the rapid development of harvesting activities in the 1970s, the Commission now employs a significantly smaller labour force than it did in 1950. Equally, the results achieved by the early plantations are an inadequate guide to those in prospect for contemporary planting.

YIELD CLASSES

When most of the plantations recently harvested or soon due for harvesting were planted there was comparatively little knowledge of the likely yields from the chosen crop or of the best alternatives. The Forestry Commission's research includes investigation of site yields according to species, provenance of seed, soil group, elevation zone and various other factors. In the 1960s and 1970s the data collected were analysed and published in a series of 'Forest Records' giving estimated data on yield classes for the major and some minor species on a variety of sites. Busby (1974) gives a summary and further references. Yield classes reveal the maximum average rates of volume (usually measured in cubic metres per hectare) for a species on a site of defined characteristics (soil type, aspect and elevation). The average is assessed when felling is delayed until it reaches a maximum. This occurs after the marginal annual increment has passed its peak and is falling. The volume yield is determined at the intercept of the falling marginal increment curve with the average increment at the latter's peak (see Figure 8.1). A metric yield class for a stand of timber can then be stated by a single number, for example, 10, which signifies that the total yield (felling plus thinnings) average about 10 cubic metres per hectare per annum over the whole rotation period up to the final felling.

Figure 8.1   Patterns of volume increment in an even-aged stand

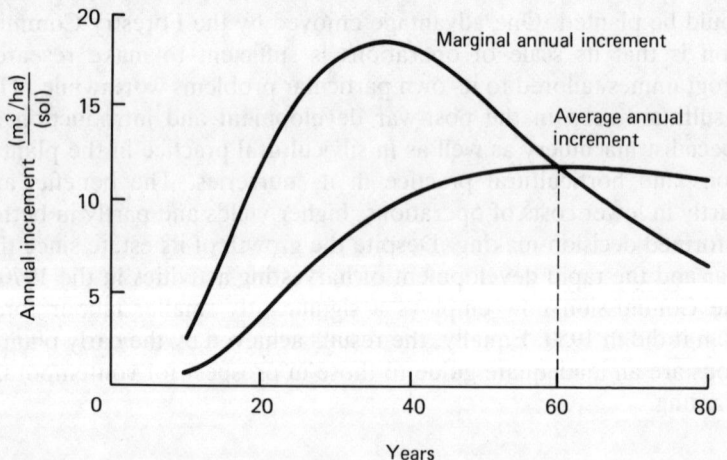

PRICES AND OUTPUT MIX

If the object was merely to maximise volume yield, then it would be sufficient to fell all plantations at the age when the average yield matched the (falling) marginal increment. In general this is sooner in the highest yield classes, possibly at about 40 years, and later in lower yield classes. There are also differences between species in the same yield class. However timber prices vary within a wide range according to the dimensions of individual trees. Helliwell (1984) records £2 per cubic metre for standing spruce averaging 0.05m³ in volume to £20 for trees exceeding 3m³. The smallest category derived from the earliest thinnings of the least desirable size and form are worth very little, while the saw logs obtained from the selected survivors at the end of the rotation are much more valuable. The question arises whether delay in felling will increase the value of the crop sufficiently to compensate not only the delay in obtaining receipts (represented by an implicit interest charge) but also the reduction in average volume. Helliwell's figures should not be taken as definitive but only representative. This decision can be left until the end of the rotation approaches.

The relative prices of saw logs (from large trees) and pulpwood are not constant. The Forestry Commission reported increases in the former of 3 per cent in 1984 against an average rise of 12 per cent for pulpwood and chipwood. The latter rise was a recovery from falling prices in 1983. Given that they supply different markets this should not be surprising. Market shocks such as the unprecedented fall in demand for sawn mining timber during the coal strike in 1984 are reflected in prices. Similarly in previous years, uncertainties about the future of certain domestic paper mills, culminating in the closure of the plant at Fort William, profoundly affected the pulp market. However, the versatile range of uses for timber and pulpwood sets floors to prices. The curtailment of domestic demand by paper makers was largely made good by exports, mainly to Scandinavia. This was a deliberate marketing tactic to work up the harvesting capacity needed to supply the demand created by the new mill at Shotton.

There is considerable scope for variation in the output mix between small roundwood for use in the pulp and chipboard markets and saw logs. For most of its history the Forestry Commission's harvesting programme was very small. Most of its efforts were devoted to planting and the maintenance of young plantations. Small roundwood from thinnings was the major product and only within the last decade have saw logs become available in quantity. Catering for the pulp and board markets brings earlier returns than those obtained from saw logs, but this must be set against a lower value product. Clearly the higher the required rate of return on the sum invested the more likely the decision will be in favour of pulp, and the more the date of clear-felling will be brought forward. This point was emphasised by the Interdepartmental Cost/Benefit Study – 'Forestry in

Great Britain', published for HM Treasury in 1972. On the basis of a 10 per cent target rate of return it was recommended that shorter rotations, of about 40 years, should be considered seriously.

The authors also assumed that global supplies would remain plentiful from 'the vast areas of virgin forest in the northern hemisphere which could more than meet the world's need for decades, if not centuries to come, without any need for restocking'. The study relied on the Food and Agriculture Organisation's forecasts of a broadly constant price, rising in nominal terms at 3 per cent compound per annum until 1985. Both assumptions were risky. The first does not accord with the fact that the Scandinavian countries have been producing close to their maximum sustainable yield for some time and that the virgin reserves in the remote parts of European Russia, Siberia and Canada are both costly to extract and slow to regenerate. The other major countries of Western Europe had emerged by 1972 as net importers of temperate wood products, and now are much stronger competing buyers on world markets. In short, the Treasury's 1972 view now seems wildly optimistic. The price assumption was shattered within a year of the study's publication. According to the Forestry Commission's Annual Report 1973/4 the average price for new sales of coniferous saw logs was 112 per cent *higher* than in the preceding year and rises of 75 per cent and 103 per cent were achieved for small roundwood and coniferous trees respectively sold standing. Of course, that was an exceptional increase, and subsequently the relative price of timber fell back, but not to the levels projected by the interdepartmental study. If nothing else, that episode should teach us how volatile timber prices can be and remind us that in the long term the relative price is likely to rise. On that basis the difference between the normal target rate of return and the special Forestry rate of 3 per cent could be treated as an 'insurance premium'.

The insurance argument for valuing future forest outputs more highly than current commercial decision-makers is reinforced by the approach taken by Brookshire *et al.* (1983). They argue that option prices in contingent markets should be used as indicators if not rules for decision. They focus on supply uncertainties and show a procedure for estimating willingness to pay (the compensating measure of value) for programmes that reduce those uncertainties.

Large-sized saw logs already command premium prices. These are held in check by the availability of large-sized mature timber from previously uncut forests, but Russian, Scandinavian and Canadian climatic conditions prevent rapid regrowth. In Britain growth giving annual increments of 10 or more cubic metres per hectare are commonplace and are commonly two or three times higher than the growth obtained in the major producing countries. Planting now for the large-sized log market in the middle of the twenty-first century could prove to be a fruitful speculation. When added to the arguments for insurance against higher prices and the low opportunity costs of the resources used, an increase in the area planted to trees seems rather more attractive.

In the past forestry has been devastated by the disappearance of markets for specialised products in the interval between planting and harvesting. The demise a century ago of lowland oak with coppice as a commercially viable system in England is associated with the replacement of the Navy's wooden walls with iron dreadnoughts and the substitution of cheap wire fencing for hazelwood hurdles in farming. The floor prices offered by the market for firewood was too low to provide a safety net. In the case of modern conifer plantations the price floor is set by the pulp and board mills. Admittedly the electronic revolution may pose a threat to a part of the long-term paper market, but the uncomfortable reliance of the chemical industry on fossil fuel feedstocks has created interest in cellulose feedstocks from timber if it can be obtained cheaply enough. Despite short-term variations in oil prices, it is difficult to project lower rather than higher prices for fossil fuels half a century hence, in which case the floor price for timber may be much higher then than now.

People in Germany and central Europe have been greatly disturbed in the last few years by trees dying back and attribute the problem to air pollution. In some areas the damage is almost catastrophic. In Scandinavia too there seems to be a similar problem. The Forestry Commission has not reported such damage in Britain, but it would be prudent not to embark on large programmes committing substantial resources until more is known about the causes and prevention of the trouble afflicting our European neighbours. This situation requires speedy and careful evaluation of research into the causes of the problem and close monitoring of the health of British forests. As soon as risks are perceived to be unexceptional, a larger planting programme would be indicated to take account of the reduction in European supplies. Their tragedy will of course increase their demand for alternative supplies on world markets and influence the prices paid by domestic users of paper, board and other wood products.

CHOICE OF SPECIES

The exposed and hilly sites of the Forestry Commission's own enterprise, and the similar character of most recent private plantations limits choice to a few species of conifers. Apart from some poplar hybrids on a limited range of wet but sheltered sites, broadleaved species would fail on these uplands. Some North American species of oak, *Quercus coccinea* and *Quercus borealis*, and Southern Beeches, genus *Nothofagus*, have been tried, and although less demanding than native species can compete with conifers on only a limited range of sites. The spruces, especially Sitka Spruce, and more recently Lodgepole Pine, also from Western North America, have dominated afforestation on bare land. The choice has been determined by their relatively high yields on difficult, peaty and poor sites and their characteristics as 'pioneer' species on erstwhile moorland. The range of useful trees is wider on more sheltered and fertile sites. Moreover, the establishment of forest conditions by the pioneer species opens the way for others to be considered in subsequent rotations. The only native conifer of commercial value is Scots Pine. Of the 766 000 hectares under conifers in Scotland, this species accounted for 144 000 hectares (19 per cent) at the 1980 Census of Woodlands, mainly in the Northern and Eastern conservancies where climatic conditions tend to be in its favour. Because about one-third of this area was occupied by trees planted before 1941 holding three-quarters of the standing volume of Scots Pine, the species was estimated at approximately 30 per cent of the volume of standing coniferous timber in Scotland. However its growth rate is slow compared with other species, which are therefore preferred in new planting. The shift away from Scots Pine is revealed in the proportion of the area planted to this species in Scotland during the decade starting in 1971 at little more than 4 per cent compared with 68 per cent to Sitka Spruce and 18 per cent to Lodgepole Pine. Table 8.1 summarises data in the 1980 census for the four Scottish conservancies on the species composition of existing plantations analysed by decades of planting.

Scots Pine dominates the surviving area planted before the end of the nineteenth century. Most of this is either natural or semi-natural woodland or plantations that are managed, if at all, for purposes other than, or in addition to, timber production. Until the First World War it was the first choice among the planting lairds in Scotland, followed by European Larch as a poor second. The timber

Table 8.1   Conifer plantations in Scotland by species and decade of planting (thousand hectares)

Species	Total	1971–80	1961–70	1951–60	1941–50	1931–40	1921–30	1911–20	1901–10	1861–1900	Pre-1861
Scots Pine	144.4	10.3	29.0	44.7	14.3	10.7	12.2	3.9	4.5	9.9	4.9
Lodgepole Pine	103.9	45.1	39.7	17.5	0.6	0.6	0.3	—	—	—	—
Sitka Spruce	364.6	169.3	108.7	49.8	21.2	11.3	3.9	0.2	0.1	0.1	—
Norway Spruce	54.7	5.3	12.4	15.6	9.3	7.8	3.4	0.6	0.3	0.1	—
Douglas Fir	11.6	1.7	3.8	3.4	0.6	0.5	1.0	0.2	0.1	0.2	0.1
European Larch	16.0	1.0	2.4	3.2	1.4	2.7	1.5	0.8	1.5	1.1	0.2
Japanese and Hybrid Larch	52.1	11.1	10.7	21.6	4.2	2.6	1.5	0.3	0.1	—	—
Other and mixed species	18.3	3.4	5.7	4.6	0.9	1.2	1.3	0.3	0.2	0.6	0.3
All conifers	765.6	247.2	212.4	160.4	52.5	37.4	25.1	6.3	6.8	12.0	5.5
All broadleaves	76.6	3.2	5.3	6.1	8.8	6.1	6.5	3.0	6.5	19.2	12.1
All woods	842.2	250.4	217.6	166.4	61.4	43.5	31.6	9.2	13.3	31.2	17.6
A (%) in each decade											
Scots Pine	18.9	4.2	13.7	27.9	27.3	28.5	48.6	62.2	65.2	82.5	88.6
Lodgepole Pine	13.6	18.3	18.7	10.9	1.2	1.7	1.1	—	—	—	—
Sitka Spruce	47.6	68.5	51.2	31.0	40.4	30.2	15.6	3.1	1.4	1.0	0.8

continued on page 110

Species	Total	1971–80	1961–70	1951–60	1941–50	1931–40	1921–30	1911,–20	1901–10	1861–1900	Pre-1861
Norway Spruce	7.1	2.1	5.6	9.7	17.6	20.9	13.4	9.0	4.2	1.1	0.7
Douglas Fir	1.5	0.7	1.8	2.1	1.1	1.4	4.2	3.1	1.7	1.4	2.3
European Larch	2.1	0.4	1.1	2.0	2.7	7.3	6.1	12.9	22.1	9.2	3.2
Japanese and Hybrid Larch	6.8	4.5	5.8	13.4	8.0	7.1	6.1	4.9	1.4	0.3	—
Other and mixed species	2.4	1.3	2.1	3.0	1.7	2.9	4.9	4.8	4.0	4.5	4.4
All conifers	100.0	100.0	100.0	100.0	100.0	100.0	100.0	100.0	100.0	100.0	100.0
B (%) of each species by decade											
Scots Pine	100	7.1	20.1	31.0	9.9	7.4	8.4	2.7	3.1	6.9	3.4
Lodgepole Pine	100	43.4	38.2	16.9	0.6	0.6	0.3	—	—	—	—
Sitka Spruce	100	46.4	29.8	13.6	5.8	3.1	1.1	—	—	—	—
Norway Spruce	100	9.6	22.7	28.4	16.9	14.3	6.2	1.0	0.5	0.3	0.1
Douglas Fir	100	14.5	32.6	29.1	4.9	4.6	9.0	1.7	1.0	1.4	1.1
European Larch	100	6.5	14.8	20.3	9.0	17.1	9.6	5.1	9.5	6.9	1.1
Japanese and Hybrid Larch	100	21.2	20.5	41.3	8.1	5.1	3.0	0.6	0.2	0.1	—
All conifers	100	32.3	27.7	20.9	6.9	4.9	3.3	0.8	0.9	1.6	0.7

Source: Compiled from Census of Woodlands and Trees 1979–82 for Conservancies in East, West, North and South Scotland. Published by the Forestry Commission.

of both species is well suited for construction purposes and saw logs command a premium over spruce and most other soft woods. But because their rates of growth are slower than spruce and demand rose for pulpwood to make paper, chip and particle board, the Forestry Commission switched its planting programme between the wars towards spruce. Sitka Spruce was found to be particularly suited to the cloudy, high rainfall sites on the western side of the country where land was cheap. By the 1930s this spruce was being planted more than Scots Pine, while Norway Spruce, which had been established on a small scale for a couple of centuries, was not much less popular.

In the great expansion of planting from 1947, Scots Pine maintained a share of a little over one-quarter of the total for a decade, while Lodgepole Pine was selected for the first time as a major component of the programme. However, in the 1960s and 1970s Scots Pine was progressively relegated to a much reduced role, and in many areas existing plantations seem likely to be replaced with higher-yielding species when felled. Norway Spruce is also being used much more selectively and is now confined to the modest range of sites where it compares favourably with alternative choices. In the west and north of Scotland it is now rarely planted and only in some parts of the east and south is it preferred to Sitka Spruce. In the 1970s the latter was selected for nearly 70 per cent of the area planted.

Larch was important until the 1960s, since when it has accounted for only about 5 per cent of the area newly planted. Moreover Japanese Larch and hybrid trees have supplanted the European species. Between the wars they were planted in equal proportions, but European Larch has proved relatively disappointing. Nevertheless, some Larch is likely to remain in the programme for the contribution it makes to landscape values. The changing colours it presents in different seasons have been exploited by Sylvia Crowe (1978) and other landscape consultants employed by the Commission to vary the appearance and increase the visual appeal of its plantations. The high yield and desirable characteristics of Douglas Fir logs will be enough to preserve a place for this handsome species but its role will be limited by its liking for comparatively fertile, well-drained sites. A number of other minor species, Western Hemlock, Western Red Cedar, Grand Fir, Noble Fir and Lawson's Cypress, are all possible contenders for more widespread use when plantations enter the second rotation. It is worth noting that like Sitka Spruce and Lodgepole Pine all these species come from western North America and so are well adapted to a climate similar to that offered in the British Isles. A study by Aldhous and Low (1974) of the economic potential of four of these suggests that they show some advantages over the major species on the more fertile sites but not on the less productive land, but each has a range of properties and requirements which make the selection of species for a particular site very exacting.

Comparisons in the performance between species (or management regime or sites) depend on the balance between costs and revenues. Abstracting for the moment from differences in costs by making a simplifying assumption that the same pattern of costs applies to all species, we can concentrate on differences in revenue arising from either premia or discounts applicable to different types of timber or variations in their volume yield. There are in fact differences in the cost of delivering plants from the nurseries to the planting site according to species and location. Harvesting costs vary more with terrain and location than with species.

EXTERNALITIES AND JOINT PRODUCTS

Forestry generates benefits in addition to saleable timber. In some areas forest scenery is an important adjunct of the tourist industry where the latter is a major source of revenue. Camping and caravanning grounds, picnic sites, forest drives, bicycle routes, information centres, observation towers and holiday cabins can now be found in British forests. In their Annual Report for 1984–5 the Forestry Commissioners refer to some 50 different recreational activities in their forests. Orienteering, cyclocross, and various types of horse-riding have increased rapidly in recent years. Walking and rambling remain the most popular activities. The valuation of these benefits is much more difficult than simply recording their existence. The consumers' surplus enjoyed by visitors exceeds the revenue obtainable by any practicable system of charges. A number of proxies can be devised to estimate this surplus. Visitors spend time which might be employed in alternative activities. Many come from a distance at some expense. Estimates could be made from data on the number of visitors with information on the lengths and costs of their time and journeys expended on the visit. Such estimates would be close to a lower bound for the recreational benefits, as some visitors would have been prepared to pay more or travel further if it were necessary.

In practice this procedure is too simple. Many visitors may have travelled to the locality with more than one purpose in mind. The main object of the journey might be to visit friends or relatives or go on holiday. The trip to the forest could be incidental to that purpose. Even so, some readers might find the Department of the Environment's estimate of 35p per head at 1972 prices a low assessment for a whole-day trip of 50 miles which was cited by the interdepartmental study. The issue is discussed by Freeman (1979) and Smith *et al.* (1983).

Weisbrod (1964) discussed the value of the options offered by natural environments, using arguments that also apply to certain man-made resources including forests. Krutilla (1967) suggested that some environments, and by extension resources such as forests, contribute to the welfare of many but admittedly not all individuals by their mere existence. We may feel better from knowing that Sherwood Forest exists and is more than a romantic legend, even when we have never visited it.

The recreational values of forests vary enormously. In some favoured locations it may even dominate timber production. The English New Forest has less than half its area under trees. Much of the woodland is left in a semi-natural state and the plantations are left for a longer rotation than normal in order to increase the proportion of mature woodland in the forest. Thetford Forest, though occupying a somewhat similar type of land and smaller in total size, has nearly twice the area under trees and produces more than four times the volume of timber. In Scotland some forests close to centres of population or popular tourist areas are important recreational resources, but many recent forestry developments are in quiet, remote districts. The recreational value of these is low, at least for the present. The same might be said for most afforestation projects on bare land, but sometimes they can make a valuable contribution to otherwise desolate or uninteresting landscapes, though it takes time for effects to mature. When a forest has matured and fellings have begun giving a varied age structure, it becomes much more attractive for many visitors. The Forestry Commission, to its credit, has taken pains to plan its felling and replanting programmes with an eye to their scenic impact. The trend towards a few dominant species in its plantations makes it desirable to avoid the monotony of large tracts of even-aged woodland and to break them into a mosaic of different age classes. It has become common practice to shield large felling coups in prominent positions or close to main tourist routes with a screen of trees saved from the chain-saw. Although this appears to impose a direct cost in terms of output forgone or delayed, the mature trees reserved for their landscape value can also provide valuable shelter, assisting the establishment and rapid growth of the succeeding rotation. By the second or later rotations forests have usually demonstrated their recreational potential, even if it is not always realised. A cost-benefit assessment of recreational and scenic benefits is therefore an essential ingredient of decision-making on the future of existing woodlands at the end of the current crop's rotation. It is, in general, less significant for afforestation on bare land.

Shooting and fishing rights generate revenue for the Commission and other forest land-owners. Not all the revenue would be lost if the plantations were felled and not replanted. In other cases, fishing rights would be improved by restricting conifer plantations close to rivers – indicating a trade-off between timber and licence revenue. The expansion of forestry this century has produced a marked growth in deer populations, who find shelter and food in the plantations. Roe deer are now much more widespread and numerous than at the turn of the century and in the Scottish highlands red deer are no longer condemned solely to a treeless moorland habitat. If numbers were not controlled they would cause an unacceptable degree of damage to young plantations. Owners have found that sportsmen are willing to pay substantial sums for shooting rights. The Forestry Commission retains the right to venison and successfully markets it in Germany and other European countries as well as at home. They employ rangers who mark out the particular animals for slaughter with the aims of maintaining herds with an optimal age and sex composition and to improve the stock.

FORESTRY AND CONSERVATION

The effects of afforestation on wildlife are a source of externalities which has provoked a wide range of sometimes acrimonious debate. In the early days of the Forestry Commission's operations most comment was hostile. The preference for conifer species over broad-leaves was singled out for special opprobrium even where soil and exposure gave no hope of the survival of the latter. A. G. Tansley (1949) the father of ecological studies in Britain and first Chairman of the Nature Conservancy, wrote that

The Forestry Commission makes dense plantations of these conifers, sometimes on the sites of old deciduous woods, sometimes on
grassland formerly used as sheep pasture, sometimes on healthland
or partially drained wet moorland. The general result is to alter
entirely the face of the landscape, destroying the old natural and
semi-natural vegetation which has been gradually moulded
through the centuries, and substituting artificial woods which are a
new, and to many people inharmonious, addition to the British
scene . . . . Most of these [conifers] are evergreen and cast so deep
a shade when closely planted that little or no vegetation can exist
beneath them. Their fallen leaves or branchlets form an acid raw
humus which also tends to make the soil unsuitable for most
woodland plants, and often leads to definite deterioration. It is too
early to say what will be the fate of most of these plantations.

It is significant that his collaborator, M. C. F. Proctor, in revising
Tansley's posthumous second edition of *Britain's Green Mantle*
(1968), felt bound to qualify this extremely critical view.

Mistakes have certainly been made in the past but, especially since
the [1939–45] war, the Commission has increasingly been able to
draw on its experience in the development of patterns of silvicul-
ture appropriate to British conditions, and in attempting to reconcile competing economic, ecological and amenity considerations in
the use of land; many criticisms of the Commission's work which
were valid twenty years ago no longer have the same force.

The criticism about the deep shade of conifer plantations applies
most forcefully for a fifteen to twenty year period, the 'pole stage'
between the closing of a young plantation's canopy at, say, ten years
and the first thinning or two. In a forest with a varied range of age
classes it would affect 30 per cent to 40 per cent of the area at any one
time. Undoubtedly there will be marked changes in plant cover of the
ground and shrub layers, but not all changes are malign. One immediate effect of afforestation is to reduce grazing pressure. Much of the
land newly offorested has been impoverished by centuries of grazing,
especially on former sheep-walks. Before canopy closes the young
plantations provide food and cover for a wide variety of animals and
insects. Increased numbers of voles and other rodents in plantations
have provided support for thriving populations of previously rare

birds of prey such as hen harriers and short-eared owls. The new forests of Southern Scotland have been described as a 'sparrow-hawk factory' from which this species throughout the country has benefited and recovered from the population crash produced by dieldrin and other organo-chlorine compounds used as seed dressings in the late 1950s.

In the later stages of the rotation new ground cover appears after thinning, which allows more light to penetrate. Rides and the edges of forest roads offer permanent refuges for a much wider range of plant species than bare land under grazing pressure could support. Sharrock for the British Trust for Ornithology (1976) organised a survey of breeding birds in all the 10 kilometre squares of the British Isles in the period 1968–72. An assessment was provided of changes in the status of each species and the factors, as far as they were known, that brought about the changes. The benign effect of afforestation is mentioned in about thirty cases. Undoubtedly, the new forests have brought a greater variety of habitat to many upland areas.

As part of a programme to make its plantations more visually attractive, the Forestry Commission, and many enlightened private owners, have taken to permitting or planting native broadleaves and shrubs around the edges of plantations or in mixture with the commercial species along roads or other prominent places. The slow growth and limited value of these broadleaves cannot justify their use as timber producers, but their appearance and contribution to wildlife permits some sacrifice of output through limited substitution for conifers. This practice removes many of the ecological objections to forestry and the balance of advantage for conservation of wildlife could now be with forestry compared with alternative land-uses. Nevertheless, general statements of this kind are of little help, but need to be tested for particular sites against the ecological conditions of the locality.

THE OPPORTUNITY COSTS OF LAND AND LABOUR

In the final analysis, the case for or against forestry expansion or contraction in particular localities depends on the opportunity cost of committing land, labour and capital to this use compared with alternative uses. As this paper argues, the comparisons are not clear-cut or simply made. Forestry is an activity with a wide range of joint-products, timber, recreation, conservation, and so on. There are externalities to be assessed. Costs and benefits span long time horizons. Moreover, the current cash costs of land and labour may be poor proxies for their opportunity costs.

The Forestry Commission and private forestry concerns compete for estates in the open market between themselves and other users, notably in agriculture. Undoubtedly forestry has attracted private investment because the annual increment of timber growth is not subject to immediate taxes on income. Income and capital transfer taxes can be delayed until timber is felled, and the liability then incurred can be offset in part by replanting grants under the Dedication and other schemes administered by the Commission. Land prices are also raised by the expectation of continuing support for lamb and the prices of other products of hill farmers under the Common Agricultural Policy. Capital charges arising from the cost of acquiring land then overstate the true opportunity cost of users.

It is also argued that in upland areas there has been a long experience of population decline as the labour demands of agriculture have fallen, and that many communities are on the margin of economic viability. The 1972 cost-benefit study considered possible savings in social capital costs from reduced outward migration, and allowed that projects that increased labour demands, such as afforestation, bring some external benefits with them on this account. The force of the argument has weakened somewhat with the substantial improvements in labour productivity (more through technical progress than by capital substitution) but as long as labour demands per 1000 acres are higher in forestry than in the best alternative land use it will still apply.

The 1972 study concluded that the shadow cost of labour was less in forestry and in agriculture in Scotland than the nominal wage; but the difference was somewhat greater in forestry. Where the shadow cost is less than the wage paid we would expect to see variations in the ratio over the trade cycle. Certainly the demand for relatively unskilled labour in the Scottish oil industry in the mid to late 1970s reduced the availability of labour in forestry in the Northern and Eastern conservancies at that period. The shadow price was then if anything greater than the wage paid in forestry. In recession the opposite is true, and forestry could again be a beneficiary as it was in the 1930s of schemes to subsidise the use of unemployed people with a subsidy related to the difference between the wage and the estimated shadow price of labour. This is unlikely to be greater than unemployment benefit scales and would provide an incentive to managers to concentrate labour-intensive activities such as planting, fencing, brashing and pruning in recession periods. At the margin projects and activities that would otherwise not be done would become worthwhile. Future benefits would accrue in terms of more and better quality output.

CONCLUSIONS AND POLICY IMPLICATIONS

The arguments above suggest some policy implications. The original purpose of the Acland Committee to establish a strategic reserve of timber has been achieved. Nationally the annual cut is substantially less than the annual increment from new growth, and the latter continues to rise. There has been a decline in the Forestry Commission's own planting programme in recent years from 21 500 hectares in 1979/80 to barely 11 000 hectares in 1984/5. All of this reduction is in the afforestation of bare land, while restocking of felled areas has increased. The decline reflects the depletion of the Commission's 'bank' of plantable land and an unwillingness to replenish it by purchases on the open market at current land prices. However, there has been a compensating increase in the private sector, where the area planted rose from 11 000 to 19 000 hectares over the same period, under the influence of grants and favourable tax treatment which has attracted institutional as well as personal investment. Planting need continue only for another decade at these rates for the national forest estate in both sectors to be capable of sustaining felling with only replacement planting to produce some 20–25 per cent of Britain's softwood requirements in perpetuity at current rates of consumption. These levels of output will be reached by the end of the century. Although a large proportion of the woods are immature, each year that passes improves the age structure of the plantations.

The question remains whether to expand or contract this estate. The original aims were confirmed by the renewal of shortages in the Second World War. The post-war planting programme was envisaged to procure 5 million acres (2 million hectares) of productive woodland by the year 2000. This implies continued dependence on imports for the foreseeable future. Past experience shows that wood prices are volatile, but the trend for more than a century has been upwards relative to other goods and services. The prospect of world-wide exhaustion of virgin timber resources next century and the slow rate of regeneration and growth in the main timber producers of the northern hemisphere suggest that the prices of coniferous softwood are likely to rise ever higher in future. The main exception has been rapid expansion and growth of Slash Pine on former cotton lands which now supplies a large part of the pulp market in the USA. My judgement is that the probability of future price increases outweighs the risk of decrease over the next half century. While the real opportunity costs of using hill lands and rural labour are low there is a case for further expansion rather than contraction in British forestry. There is certainly no shortage of relatively unproductive hill land in Scotland or in northern England.

It is beyond the scope of this paper to consider the alternative merits of private and public ownership, but the Forestry Commission has earned recognition as an efficient producer and pioneer of technical progress in its work. It has also benefited from economies derived from its scale of operations. So far it has used its new powers to sell plantations to private buyers to consolidate its estates into more efficient economic units by disposing of properties that have presented problems for management. However, it is to be hoped that it will not be forced into asset sales simply to meet the short-term financial goals of governments. Forestry works to long time horizons and, although it takes a mixture of short, medium and long-term decisions throughout the rotation period, sudden drastic changes in its financial constraints or targets are disruptive and can be unduly expensive in the long-run. Sadly, the history of forestry in Britain is a recurring saga of folly produced by policy shifts made for the sake of short-term ends.

References

Aldhous, J. R. and A. J. Low (1974), *The Potential of Western Hemlock, Western Red Cedar, Grand Fir and Noble Fir in Britain*, Forestry Commission Bulletin, 49 (London: HMSO).

Blatchford, O. N. (ed.) (1978), *Forestry Practice*, 9th edn, Forestry Commission Bulletin, 14 (London: HMSO).

Brookshire, D. S., L. S. Eubanks and A. Randall (1983), 'Estimating Option Prices and Existence Values for Wildlife Resources', *Land Economics*, no. 59, February.

Busby, R. J. N. (1974), *Forest Site Yield Guide to Upland Britain*, Forest Record 97, Forestry Commission (London: HMSO).

Census of Woodlands (1980) (1983), Northern, Eastern, Southern and Western conservancies of Scotland, Forestry Commission (Edinburgh).

Crowe, S. (1978) *The Landscape of Forests and Woods*, Forestry Commission Booklet 44 (London: HMSO).

Forestry Commission (various years), *Annual Reports and Accounts*.

Freeman, A. M. (1979), *The Benefits of Environmental Improvement* (Baltimore: Johns Hopkins University Press) ch. 8.

Helliwell, D. R. (1984), *Economics of Woodland Management* (Chichester: Packard Publishing).

Krutilla, J. V. (1967), 'Conservation Reconsidered', *American Economic Review*, 57 (September).

Sharrock, J. T. R. (1976), *The Atlas of Breeding Birds in Britain and Ireland*, (Berkhamsted: T. and A. D. Poyser).

Smith, V. K., W. H. Desvousges and M. P. McGivney (1983), 'The Opportunity Cost of Travel Time in Recreation Demand Models', *Land Economics*, 59 (August).

Tansley, A. G. (1949; 1968), *Britain's Green Mantle* (1st edn, 1949; 2nd edn, revised M. C. F. Proctor, London: Allen & Unwin, 1968).

Tobin, J. (1964), 'Economic Growth as an Objective of Policy', *American Economic Review: Papers and Proceedings*, vol. 54, no. 3.

H. M. Treasury (1972), *Forestry in Great Britain: an Interdepartmental Cost/Benefit Study* (London: HMSO).

Weisbrod, B. A. (1964), 'Collective-consumption services of individual-consumption goods', *Quarterly Journal of Economics*, 78 (August).

Wood, R. F. (1974), *Fifty Years of Forestry Research; a Review of Work Conducted and Supported by the Forestry Commission, 1920–1970*, Forestry Commission Bulletin, 50 (London: HMSO).

Cmd 6647 (1943), *Post-War Forest Policy* (London: HMSO).

9 Wetland Conservation: Economics and Ethics

R. Kerry Turner

INTRODUCTION AND OVERVIEW

Richard Lecomber (1975, 1978) was one of a number of writers who have questioned the unidimensional economic efficiency approach to welfare measurement and economic growth so characteristic of the conventional (essentially neoclassical) economic doctrine. He supported the argument that welfare is a multidimensional concept which encompasses, among other variables, per capita gross domestic product, distributional equity and environmental quality. Social welfare (economic plus non-economic welfare) is, in principle, better represented by a vector profile and not a scalar. Nevertheless, in the absence of an unambiguous measure for welfare, the integration of environmental criteria (often unpriced) into the conventional planning and decision-making processes has proved to be a somewhat intractable politico-economic problem.

Multi-criteria, extended cost-benefit analysis has been criticised as 'politico-revisionist' by Mishan (1982). His argument contains the implicit belief that efficiency is a meta-value that comprehends all others, rather than being one value among many. But if, as many other analysts believe, value conflict is a pervasive characteristic of social decision-making, then a 'proper' balancing of costs and values must (among other factors) include an identification of the distributional implications of projects, programmes or courses of action (Clawson, 1980; Sagoff, 1981).

Ecocentrists as opposed to technocentrists (this taxonomy of environmental worldviews is surveyed in O'Riordan and Turner, 1983) have been warning society for some time that the biospherical capacity constraints are, or will soon become, binding. So far the impact of the ecocentric worldview(s) on social and economic policy has been limited. However, a recent internal shift from outright rejection of the economic growth ethic to variants of the 'sustainability' concept perhaps heralds a new era of 'green' or 'semi-green' politics and economic policy (International Union for the Conservation of Nature, 1980).

The purpose of this essay is to explore the issue of wetlands conservation utilising economic analysis but also incorporating some investigation of the importance of the underlying value systems that can influence social decision-making and policy. It will be argued that the natural and social uncertainties surrounding wetland function and structure values are such that the adoption of a conservation-biased safety margin approach to policy is the most rational course of action. Despite the uncertainties there is enough evidence available to suggest strongly that wetlands are very valuable assets, though not all wetlands are of equal value. Further, the majority of wetland sites are not completely substitutable or reproducable. Many wetlands represent unique and irreplaceable assets. In total, wetlands may represent important biospherical stabilisation control mechanisms and other more localised but vital physical and biological mechanisms; as well as storehouses of extensive genetic, recreational, aesthetic and spiritual values. Higher order wetlands offer unique combinations of interrelated functional and structural values. Development of such resources would effectively represent an irreversible policy decision.

Wetland conservation rather than development seems to be the most socially beneficial option in a majority of conflict situations. For some more common, lower order, or already degraded, wetlands outright development or modified development might, in principle, prove to be socially optional. Such development may in any case not be irreversible since for this subset of wetlands substitution possibilities are positive and limited restoration practicable. Nevertheless, even in these cases the limited empirical research that has been undertaken on both sides of the Atlantic suggests that, in practice, conservation (which can mean controlled usage and management of the resource) and restoration rather than outright development is the socially optimal course of action. Many of the wetland development options analysed, in particular agricultural conversion and recreational housing schemes, have turned out to yield low or negative economic benefits.

The environmental economics literature now contains two general approaches to resource allocation and valuation problems within which uncertainty and irreversibility can be explicitly incorporated. Some analysts, all supportive to varying degrees of the neoclassical doctrine, have argued for the adoption of as determinate a cost-benefit analysis as is possible (Porter, 1982). Others, particularly those supportive of the institutional economics doctrine, urge the adoption of a fixed standard approach, either in selected cases or as a way of implementing a general 'macroenvironmental policy' (Bishop, 1978; Ciriacy-Wantrup, 1968). Macroenvironmental standards could encompass land-use zoning policy and ambient environmental quality standards. In extreme form such standards would operate as binding constraints, and although perhaps flexible over time (as knowledge increases) would limit the scope of cost-benefit analysis to cost-effectiveness analysis.

Both approaches recognise the potential importance of the concept of option value (interpreted as the effect of uncertainty on value, that is, an adjustment to convert the expected value of consumer surplus to an *ex ante* value to allow for uncertainty) and would have it included in the analysis of a given environmental resource allocation issue. What evidence there is suggests that option values are positive for resources such as wetlands. Contingent valuation studies have also uncovered, albeit tentatively, positive existence values concerning various unique and non-reproductive environmental resources. Bequest value may also exist for irreplaceable resources. Since an analysis of any policy relevant to human and environmental well-being would be incomplete without some investigation of the value systems that may underpin such policy, an important question that deserves attention is, what 'values' are being glimpsed via the contingent valuation studies?

Equally important, many analysts would argue, is a further question about the appropriateness of economic value measures as the sole value measures for public resource allocation. Ecocentrists have been arguing for some time that conventional economic value measures and related ethical values and reasoning are an inadequate basis for a policy of sustained environmental protection and should be buttressed or replaced by a new environmental ethic. However, both the content of, and the rational and theoretical support for, such an ethic are as yet unresolved problems. The position advocated in this essay indicates that conventional ethics, contrary to many of the ecocentric arguments, can provide the basis for an adequate and ongoing environmental protection strategy. With suitable modifications, both utilitarianism and contractualist egalitarianism can offer a rational ethical basis for economic resource conservation policies and protect the rights of future generations to an adequate resource endownment. It is not necessary to adopt any of the more radical 'deep ecology' viewpoints in order to be able to offer sufficient protection to exhaustible resources such as wetlands. This is important because such eco-imperative positions require the acceptance of a number of diffuse and somewhat impracticable notions, such as intrinsic value in nature, a non-sentience criterion for moral rights or systemic rights.

GLOBAL WETLAND RESOURCES

Wetland ecosystems, which comprise about 6 per cent of the global land area, are considered by many authorities to be among the most threatened (because of a range of development pressures, industrial, residential and agricultural) of all environmental resources (Maltby and Turner, 1983; US Office of Technology Assessment, 1984). The general wetland development pressures have been tempered in recent decades in at least the Western industrialised economies by the rise of environmental ideologies and pressure groups which have succeeded, to some extent, in altering the social perception of wetlands as 'wastelands'. Instead wetlands are now portrayed as valuable resources possessing a range of structural and functional benefits and in need of conservation not development. They have been identified as areas of conservation priority in the World Conservation Strategy (International Union for the Conservation of Nature, 1980). In common with most other 'resource depletion' debates, precise, quantified data on resource loss rates are somewhat scarce and therefore the exact size of the remaining and sustainable wetlands heritage is a contentious issue.

Environmentalists have claimed that in recent years the UK, for example, has been losing some 150 000 acres of wetlands per annum due to agricultural drainage and land conversion schemes. Since the 1950s, some 15 per cent of the salt marshes (including 4000 ha. of sites of scientific interest) in England and Wales have been developed and a further 20 per cent are at risk (Long and Mason, 1983). In the USA, some sources put wetland loss rates at 400 000 to 500 000 acres per annum for the period 1950 to mid 1970s (US Office of Technology Assessment, 1984). About 80 per cent of these losses resulted from the process of agricultural intensification. The national loss rate for the USA in the 1980s seems to have declined quite substantially to around 250 000 acres per annum. But it should be recognised that conversion rates differ for different types of wetland and for different geographical regions. Freshwater emergent wetlands, for example, are still under severe pressure and areas such as the Lower Mississippi River Valley are still experiencing major wetland losses. Recent (1985) changes in land drainage grant aid policy in the UK may also substantially reduce the wetland conversion rate (in terms of pasture to arable cropping regimes). Medium-term soil deterioration problems (deflocculation) on clay marshes may also provide an effective development constraint. In any case, analysts supportive of the 'cornucopian technocentrist' worldview have argued that specific wetland protection policy and legislation (or for that matter any stringent resource conservation legislation) is not required because the threat has been much exaggerated (Simon and Kahn, 1984). Simon (1982) has argued in the US context that wetland conversion rates were only around 0.5 per cent per annum over the period 1950 to the mid 1970s and declined further after that. He believes that now the annual creation of new wetlands probably exceeds the loss of traditional wetlands and by implication that such substitutions are to all intents and purposes equivalent. This represents a rather critical assumption as far as current and future wetland conservation policies are concerned. The scientific evidence concerning wetland functions and structure will be reviewed in the next section in order to test the proposition that all wetlands are essentially equal in ecological and socioeconomic value and/or infinitely substitutable.

Economists would stress that every effort should be made to balance the social costs and benefits of wetland conservation/ development policies. Unfortunately, a substantial measure of uncertainty surrounds the specific technical linkages between wetlands and their functional and structural services. So an important data set, as far as any cost-benefit analysis is concerned, would seem to be in a rather rudimentary condition. Shabman and Bertelson (1979) have remarked that 'without knowledge of such "production functions" economic valuation cannot be successfully accomplished'. Just how severe the data deficiencies and the implications for policy analysis are will be examined in succeeding sections.

WETLAND FUNCTION AND STRUCTURE VALUES

The scientific search for a universally acceptable definition of the term 'wetland' has proved to be a long drawn out and somewhat arbitrary process. Since the term 'wetland' can be applied to any part of the continuum between aquatic and terrestrial environment, no single definition is likely to be completely adequate. But formal 'working' definitions and classification systems are required in order to form the basis for wetland resource inventories, which in turn play an indispensable role in any management plan. The most comprehensive classification system currently available (Cowardin *et al.*, 1979) is based on factors such as: the salinity and pH of wetlands; the form of characteristic vegetation and dominant plant species; the frequency and duration of wetland exposure, saturation and flooding; and the organic or mineral composition of characteristic soils. On this basis wetlands are defined as lands transitional between terrestrial and aquatic systems, where the water table is usually at or near the surface, or the land is covered by shallow water. The dominant factor is an excess of water. The degree of water permanence then determines the nature of soil development and the types of plant and animal communities living at the soil surface. Five wetland ecosystems are usually recognised: marine, estuarine, riverine, lacustrine and marsh/bog/swamp.

From an anthropocentric viewpoint all ecosystems can be classified in terms of their structural and functional aspects (Westman, 1985). Ecosystem structure is defined as the tangible items such as plants, animals, soil, air and water of which it is composed. Thus structural benefits (of instrumental value to humans) include fish, waterfowl, peat, timber reed and fur harvests as well as non-consumptive use benefits such as aesthetic appreciation, recreation and research or education. By contrast, ecosystem functions are encompassed by the dynamics of exchange of means of energy. The interaction between wetland hydrology and topology, saturated soil and emergent vegetation more or less determines the general characteristics and the significance of the processes that occur in any given wetland. These processes are subsequently responsible for the functional services – life support services, such as the assimilation of pollutants, cycling of nutrients and maintenance of the balance of gases in the air.

The Cowardin classification system (Cowardin *et al.*, 1979) is hierarchical and therefore assumes that not all wetlands possess equally valuable structural aspects or are likely to be equally productive in providing functional services. But ranking wetlands, in terms of conservation value, is complicated by scientific uncertainties surrounding the extent of current and future functional services provided by any given site. Furthermore, the assigned structural value of a given wetland area will be controversial given that conservation preferences can be based on a range of different ethical, religions, aesthetic or recreational values. The use of wetlands has become an issue that generates not just a public versus private interests and values conflict but also an intra-public interest conflict (for example recreational versus waste-water treatment usage).

Five basic wetland functions have been identified in the scientific literature.

(1) *Nutrient cycling and storage capabilities resulting in potential water quality improvement benefits* It has been argued that wetlands can provide low-cost sewage effluent disposal facilities. But it is not currently possible to predict accurately the waste-water treatment potential or to manage the wetland for optimum treatment efficiency. Little is known about long-term toxic material removal capacities and the ultimate impact on the health of the wetland ecosystem itself. Data from the Norfolk Broads, which have received long-term applications of waste-water, show decreased plant and animal species diversity (Moss, 1983).

(2) *Potential aquifer or groundwater recharge function* Not all wetlands possess this function and in many cases their recharge value relative to upland areas may be low;

(3) *Provision of a delay mechanism for the release of flood-waters* Again it is not possible to generalise because analytical techniques for predicting the magnitude of the flood control function are still rudimentary.

(4) *Buffer zones capable of reducing shoreline erosion are provided by salt marshes, dune complexes and mangrove forests* Artificial coastal protection measures, on the other hand, tend to be capital intensive and often incur heavy maintenance charges.

(5) *Ameliorating influences on local microclimates and a possible biospherical stabilisation role* The process of microbial decomposition encouraged within wetland ecosystems leads to storage or emissions of gaseous byproducts which may be important to global atmospheric stability (Journal of the Limnological Society of Southern Africa, 1983; Odum, 1979). The Gaia hypothesis put forward by Lovelock (1979) stated that 'the environment at the surface of the earth is actively homeostated by the biota for the benefit of the biota'. This scientific hypothesis implied that life profoundly modifies the environment and that this modification acts to stabilise the environment. If and when the hypothesis is ever conclusively proved, the process of evolution would have to

be interpreted as a punctuated affair, a step-wise evolution from statis through a period of rapid change over a relatively short period of time to a new statis. Lovelock has identified the 'core' regions of Gaia as 'those between latitudes 45° North and 45° South, including, in particular, the continental shelves and wetlands and the tropical forests and scrub lands'. The anaerobic microflora in marshes and wetlands contribute to the global supply of carbon. The rate of carbon burial adjusts automatically to regulate the concentration of oxygen, and essential elements are returned to the atmosphere. The essential Gaian message confirms that not all wetlands are equally valuable (in terms of this life support function) but until the uncertainties surrounding biospherical processes and the role of 'core' regions are reduced, exploitation and development of such areas is not recommended.

Some wetland types (such as saltmarshes) appear to represent very productive (in terms of primary production of biomass) ecosystems. Leith and Whittaker (1975) have estimated that wetlands as a whole produce 2.3 per cent of the world's net productivity, though they occupy only 0.4 per cent of the world's area. But some caution is necessary, since recent research has served to cast doubt on the validity of some of the data previously cited in the scientific literature. Saltmarsh ecosystems are also thought to generate more widespread beneficial impacts (in terms of exported particulate organic carbon) on surrounding coastal waters. Significant proportions of the plant material produced in situ may be washed by tides into nearby coastal waters, fuelling marine food levels. Many people are attracted to an environment that remains essentially untouched by man's presence. Wetlands represent such habitats yielding a variety of visual-cultural values including landscape contrast and diversity, as well as unique geological, biological or historic features (Nelson and Logan, 1984). Wetland flora and fauna often appear in lists of endangered and threatened species. Many 'relict' plants and animals are now mostly confined to wetland habitats.

Some wetlands are of particular scientific value and yield 'natural laboratory' service. Their relatively undisturbed state can provide important ecological baseline conditions which provide ideal sites for scientific study of ecosystem processes and succession. On the other hand, the 'semi-natural' European wet meadow wetlands have developed a characteristic collection of plants and animals because of human intervention and management. They can serve as templates for the study of plant population dynamics and ecosystem stability. Research into saltmarsh plants may aid the development of irrigation techniques in arid climates. The plants themselves also represent a genetic resource which may be used to develop 'superior' future crop varieties, using gene technology. Krutilla and Fisher (1975), and more recently Myers (1983), have stressed that the natural biota represent our reservoir of genetic information, which can have great actual and potential economic value. Finally, wetlands contain a diverse range of recreational opportunities. An Office of Technology Assessment Report notes that 19 of the 25 most visited Wildlife Refuges have substantial wetland components. These 19 refuges represent approximately 50 per cent of the total visitation to all US National Wildlife Refuge Units (US Office of Technology Assessment, 1984).

OPTION VALUES

A growing literature has suggested that non-use values should be counted as part of the total value of a natural resource such as a complex wetland. It has already been stressed that the full magnitude and extent of wetlands function and structure values have yet to be firmly established, but enough evidence has been accumulated to suggest that future use values will be positive and large. In this context option value can be interpreted as the effect of uncertainty on value, that is, an adjustment to convert the expected value of consumer surplus to an *ex ante* value to allow for uncertainty. Option value becomes significant to resource allocation problems when conditions of uncertainty as to both future demand and/or supply exist. Option value will be positive for risk-averse individuals demanding unique or irreplaceable natural environments. A number of studies have been undertaken to estimate option value empirically. Greenley et al. (1981) reported positive option value for recreation on the South Platte River, representing about 40 per cent of the reported consumer surplus of users. Desvousges et al. (1983) and Smith et al. (1983) also reported option values that were relatively large to consumer surplus. Walsh et al. (1984), among other researchers, have also reported large positive option values for wilderness areas, derived via contingent valuation studies. Critics of the contingent valuation method have concentrated their attention on the existence of biases claimed to be inherent to this technique (Bishop and Heberlein, 1979; Bishop *et al.*, 1983; Boyle *et al.*, 1985; Rowe and Chestnut, 1983).

The important question to ask in this context is how serious are these bias problems? Some, but not enough, empirical work has been directed at the question of the practical extent of the biases. There seems little doubt that biases have affected many of the studies undertaken so far, and further that too little attention has been paid to the question of the comparative validity of economic monetary value estimates derived from the alternative methods available (Seller *et al.*, 1985). Despite these shortcomings, however, it seems reasonable to conclude that option value is a real phenomenon and can be significantly positive.

It has also been argued that in cases where development of an environmental resource is irreversible then a quasi-option value exists. Freeman (1984) has argued that the models developed in the literature up to 1980 all produced a quasi-option value benefit to preserving a natural area or delaying its development, because of a common key feature. Quasi-option value was modelled as essentially the expected value of the information gained (produced merely by the passage of time) by delaying irreversible development decisions. Freeman, however, interprets quasi-option value as a neutral and not a preservation biased concept. He argued that small-scale development, stopping short of full implementation, in order to generate information about developmental investment costs, can reduce uncertainty and thereby yield development-related quasi-option value. In practice it is rather difficult to imagine cases such as those to which Freeman alludes. Some lower order wetlands, for example, could be manipulated to some extent in order say to test their waste assimilation and/or flood control properties. But in the majority of cases wetlands should not be intensively developed because of the interrelated nature of the functional and structural properties they possess and because of their overall high value as natural or semi-natural environments. As Fisher and Hanemann (1985) have recently emphasised, the value that may be discovered in some indigenous species will only be determined over time if the relevant habitats (which can be wetlands) are not developed, though they may need to be managed, and research is undertaken into the medicinal or other value of these species. In these cases, quasi-option value will be non-negative and will be equal to or greater than the unconditional value of information.

NATURAL WETLANDS AND SUBSTITUTABILITY

Given the scientific uncertainties that exist, it is not surprising that arguments over whether or not natural and semi-natural wetlands are reproducable and/or substitutable are not currently fully resolvable. Unique complex natural and some semi-natural wetlands are undoubtedly to all intents and purposes fixed in supply. While, within in a given area, other lower order wetlands may also be fixed in supply, this may not be as permanent a situation as that pertaining to the higher order wetlands. It may prove possible to augment the supply of lower order wetlands by constructing new artificial wetlands and/or by reclaiming, or more intensively managing, existing but degraded areas. Current marsh establishment technology can play a positive though limited role. The available technology is potentially useful for restoring degraded marsh areas, or for repairing small portions of extant marshes. However, European experience, based on attempts to restore complex semi-natural wetlands in both Britain and Holland, indicates that restoration is a protracted and expensive affair. Considerable restoration success has been achieved, for example, in small areas of the Norfolk Broads by completely sealing off a Broad from the rest of the wetland system which is heavily utilised by tourists and contains polluted water. Extensive use of this method in multiple use wetlands is, however, clearly not a practicable proposition.

It seems reasonable to conclude that substitute humanly created ecosystems do not fully replicate the lost ecosystem structure and functions; and that they do not yet represent guaranteed and permanent substitutes for sacrificed habitats. Race and Christie (1982), found that there were often substantial differences, especially in animal density and composition, between artificially created and natural or semi-natural wetlands. Lack of data on the development and stabilisation of man-made wetlands is such that marsh-creation cannot be regarded as in any sense an adequate mitigation strategy in the light of the ongoing wetland resource depletion trends.

After an evaluation of past wetland restoration projects in San Francisco Bay, Race (1985) concluded that 'Many of the projects never reached the level of success purported and others have been plagued by serious problems.' More intensive management of alternative, lower order or degraded areas of wetland, or construction of new wetlands, are not the only substitution possibilities. Increasingly stringent institutional rules covering recreational and other activities and improved effluent discharge standards could also have a role to play in some high value wetlands that are already exposed to multiple usage. Overall, it seems reasonable to regard the majority of wetlands as natural systems which, once destroyed, can at best be only partially and imperfectly replaced by man. Since most outright wetland development decisions are irreversible (on physical grounds or for reasons of practicality) then a strong case for wetland conservation can be made on both economic efficiency and intergenerational equity grounds. A safety margin approach to wetland development policy, based on safe minimum standards, has much to commend it in such circumstances.

Since not all wetlands are equally valuable in structural/functional terms, conservation strategies need to be tailored to suit the requirements of different sub-classes of wetlands. For unique irreplaceable and complex wetlands outright development should be precluded and any on-going usages strictly regulated via institutional rules. For a number of other intact, but less valuable, wetlands and/or already degraded areas, development activities might, in principle, take precedence. Development impacts in such wetlands may be reversible, if reversible is interpreted to mean restoration of part of the functions and structural content sufficient to permit resumption of, for example, basic recreational activities. Restoration may be accomplished via more intensive management, or more speculatively by the construction of completely new wetlands (Batie and Shabman, 1982). In practice, many of the developent schemes that have been proposed or undertaken in wetlands have not represented economically efficient resource allocations and/or were themselves substitutable. Overall, great caution is required, wetlands as a composite whole may play an important biospherical role. A large number of wetland sites are unique and/or high value irreplaceable assets for which strict conservation strategies are required. Preservation benefits are substantial for the whole wetlands class of natural environments.

PUBLIC DECISION-MAKING AND ENVIRONMENTAL VALUES

Environmental disputes, such as the potential conflict over ecology and amenity preservation in wetlands and agricultural improvement, involve clashes between values which have been variously described as fragile, qualitative, and ethical in nature and values that are more easily quantified in monetary terms, such as increases in productivity. The term 'value' can be interpreted as the objective quality of a thing itself, merit or intrinsic value. Alternatively, value can be expressed in terms of usefulness or utility. Value-in-exchange is expressed in terms of market prices and consumer preferences. Another economic concept, opportunity cost, also relates to value. Finally, there is the meaning attached to symbols such as liberty in society. Philosophers, scientists and environmentalists have been concerned with most of these interpretations of value. Economists, however, have concentrated on value as expressed via individual consumer preferences and on opportunity costs. Such preferences are compatible with the dominant philosophical doctrines in Western society, such as among others, individualism and utilitarianism.

As far as preservation values are concerned, the environmental economics literature has identified several possibilities of willingness to pay (WTP) for the preservation of unique environmental resources in addition to consumer surplus from, for example, actual recreation use. Total non-use satisfactions (preservation benefits) have been categorised into option demand, existence demand, and bequest demand (Krutilla, 1975; Weisbrod, 1964). It has already been argued that many conserved wetlands are likely to attract option value benefits. Existence value is the willingness to pay for the knowledge that a wetland is protected by some conservation strategy even though no recreation or other use is contemplated. A number of studies have indicated that existence value can be isolated empirically and that it is significantly positive (Mitchell and Carson, 1985; Walsh *et al.*, 1984). Existence value is related to the degree of uniqueness and reproductivity of the resource in question, but does not require that it be irreplaceable. Bequest value is defined as the WTP for the satisfaction derived from endowing future generations with unique and irreplaceable environmental resources. It therefore depends on uncertainty as to future generations' demand and/or supply for such resources.

Brown (1984) has recently surveyed the concept of value in resource allocation. He emphasised the distinction between held values, which are the basis of preferences, and assigned values which are the results of preferences. Value only occurs because of the interaction between a subject and an object and in terms of this explanation is not an intrinsic quality of anything. A given object can have a number of assigned values because of differences in the perception and held values of human valuators and different valuation contexts.

Economic value measures are in Brown's terms context specific assigned values and may therefore be inappropriate as the sole value measures for public resource allocation (Brown, 1984). Willingness to pay (WTP) or willingness to be compensated (WTBC) may have limited usefulness because of contextual problems. Wetland resources belong to a social group but the context of WTP or WTBC measures is usually a private not a social one.

The appropriateness of held values and the assumption that all individuals operate on the basis of a flat plane of subsitutable wants have been critically questioned by a minority of analysts (economists, moral philosophers and other social scientists) since the eighteenth century. Some analysts have doubted that held values are always consistent with welfare, in particular because of the influence of the process of socialisation. Existing social tastes and preferences are learned and will change in response to increased knowledge and education (Boulding 1970; Veblen, 1899). Wetland conservation values currently estimated through conventional economic analysis could well increase in the future as tastes and preferences evolve.

Ecocentric schools of thought have frequently called into question the preferences and behaviour of people as expressed in the workings of the economy. The suggestion is that such preferences and behaviour are not always in the interests of the individuals concerned or in the best interests of the environment. Preferences may be imperfectly related to human needs which are arranged hierarchically for each individual (Lutz and Lux, 1979). Some environmental amentities could be classified as either 'equity goods' or 'merit goods'. Individuals, it could be argued, have an inherent right to the former category of goods and would probably not pay enough for the latter category to suit society's collective needs. Social norms can be interpreted as principles of behaviour that ought to be followed. A survey conducted by Brown (1984) produced some results which can be interpreted to mean that there is a concept of environmental value which is different from real WTP and which comes to light when monetary responses are not called for and a social constituency is involved.

Some environmentalists seek to separate out private and public preferences. The former are largely self-interested preferences and the latter express what the individual believes is in the public interest or in the interest of a group or community to which he or she belongs.

Sagoff (1981) contends that private and public preferences belong to different logical categories. Public preferences do not involve desires or wants, but opinions or beliefs.

Undoubtedly, many environmentalists reject the economic calculus because they wish to change humanity's moral relationship with nature. Ecocentric ideologies seek to base environmental policy on ideals (social norms) that individuals accept as members of a community rather than exclusively on the preferences (measured by WTP) individuals reveal in markets. Social norms governing behaviour are enforced via collective pressure, although few are static over time or universally held. Some ecocentric positions place primary emphasis on a distinction between instrumental value (expressed via human held values) and intrinsic, non-preference related value. They therefore reject the view that if humans did not exist there would be no environmental value related to wetlands and other components of the biosphere in any meaningful sense of the term. The possibilities for, and the content of, an environmental ethic will be examined in greater detail in a later section. To date there has been little consensus on these issues. When, for example, wetland development and preservation values have come into conflict with each other, politicians have not had available to them an agreed environmental ethic to complement scientific and economic data.

WETLAND CONSERVATION VERSUS DEVELOPMENT VALUES

Batie and Mabbs-Zeno (1985) have recently argued that most of the previous efforts to provide information on the economic value of wetland functions and services (and therefore on conservation value) have been flawed by the use of inappropriate economic methods. Further, the forgone economic surplus value of these functions and services (lost when a natural wetland is developed) is a valid measure of value only if there are no wetlands substitutes. If there are practical and genuine substitutes then the value of the wetlands area will be the lesser of (a) the cost of the substitutes, or (b) the direct measure of natural wetland service value. It has already been shown, however, that although much of the scientific data covering the importance and extent of wetland functions and services as well as substitution possibilities is currently deficient, only a minority of lower order wetlands are substitutable. The valuation problem is further compounded by the difficulties encountered by economists when trying to place economic values on nonmarket services and by ethical arguments in favour of diverse ecosystems preservation.

Development relates to the extent that natural wetlands services are lost, so that development benefits are the opportunity costs of wetland conservation. A developed wetland area may yield intermediate services. For example, a location site for an industrial plant; or become a direct input into production, for example, drained and converted marshes producing increased crop output; or provide direct consumer services such as residential and recreational housing sites. The economic benefit of these development services are, however, dependent on the existence or lack of substitutes such as modified wetland development options or alternative development sites. Modified development plans may result in higher costs and/or a reduced service flow but offer the compensation of reduced natural services loss. The alternative development site must be capable of providing a 'similar' service to the infilled or otherwise developed wetland. Thus following Batie and Shabman's analysis, if there are no substitutes available the benefits of wetland development are equal to the change in economic surplus from the wetlands service. If substitutes are available then development benefit value is the difference between the economic surpluses earned with development taking place and the economic surpluses which would have been earned in the absence of development (Batie and Shabman, 1982).

It would seem that, given the scientific and methodological uncertainties involved, the best practicable measure currently available of the economic value of lower order and/or degraded natural wetlands is the cost of the least cost wetland substitute. As far as wetland development values are concerned the economic value is best represented by on-site returns. The latter proxy measure will be upwardly biased to the extent that alternatives to development do exist and the former measure also represents the upper maximum limit to natural wetland value. The magnitude of those biases is uncertain and will vary from case to case. As far as the majority of wetlands are concerned, there is enough evidence to suggest that they collectively represent unique and irreplaceable resources which generate significant preservation benefits and should therefore not be developed.

DETERMINATE COST-BENEFIT ANALYSIS VERSUS FIXED STANDARDS APPROACH

The potential facility to provide a common monetary measurement scale for diverse costs and benefits is of course the great attraction of the determinate economic cost-benefit approach to valuation. Nevertheless, research into the monetary valuation of environmental services is still in a state of flux and it is probably too early to tell how ultimately useful some of the experimental approaches being tested will be. Studies reported in the literature have made use of a range of valuation methods including: market prices, travel costs, land prices, replacement, alternative/substitute costs, hedonic prices and property values, contingent valuations via bidding games, unit-day values and related expenditures – in order to estimate natural wetland values.

The consensus view on the state of the art in wetlands valuation analysis is that it will remain deficient in terms of optimal management for the forseeable future (Batie and Shabman, 1982; Shabman *et al.*, 1979). If a determinate cost-benefit analysis tailored to the requirements of wetlands management is not currently feasible, the question becomes what interim conservation strategy and management guidelines ought to be adopted. In a pioneering work written in the 1960s, Ciriacy-Wantrup (1968) argued that the objectives and criteria of conservation decisions ought to be devised in a way which takes uncertainty (social and natural) explicitly into account. He suggested that this could be achieved by formulating the economic optimum in terms of minimising maximum possible losses. Public decision-making would be guided by a modified form of the minimax principle derived from game theory. The approach could be operationalised via the 'safe minimum standard (SMS) of conservation' concept.

Both Ciriacy-Wantrup (1968) and Bishop (1978) have argued that SMSs (related to biophysical and other quantifiable criteria) are required in order to safeguard against, in particular, irreversibilities in the loss of 'critical zone resources'. Thus a safe minimum population of, for example, an endangered wetland species should be maintained unless the social costs of doing so are unnacceptably high. The decision process concerned with determining the level at which social opportunity costs actually do become excessive will have to incorporate considerations of intergenerational equity and other ethical concerns along with economic analysis.

In the light of these uncertainties the wetlands policy approach adopted ought initially to be 'conservative' and should seek to conserve (to some extent) all wetlands regardless of rank. In combination they would represent the safe minimum standard which would be re-evaluated over time as and when social and natural uncertainties are reduced. For some lower order and/or degraded wetlands, potential development activities need to be carefully appraised and it is in this context that economic analysis has an important role to play. While unique wilderness wetlands should remain free of development activities (on economic efficiency, distributional equity and other ethical grounds) many of the semi-natural European wetlands present a more complex management problem. These areas are already subject to (and indeed were often formed because of) human management and exploitation. For these areas conservation will mean strict institutional rules to ameliorate potentially adverse environmental impacts generated by ongoing recreational and other activities.

DEVELOPMENT VALUES AS THE OPPORTUNITY COST OF WETLAND CONSERVATION

The argument for the adoption of the SMS is subject to the major caveat that its expected cost should not be deemed 'unacceptably' high. Clearly a range of concerns will impinge on this broad social decision but economic analysis can play a constructive role alongside other political and ethical considerations, in these inherently uncertain situations. Adopting a pragmatic approach, it seems reasonable to accept the assumption that the opportunity cost of unpriced wetland functions and structure can be estimated from the forgone income of potential development uses. In the USA a number of studies have been undertaken to estimate the opportunity cost of preserving coastal wetlands (Batie and Mabbs-Zeno, 1985; Batie and Shabman, 1982; Shabman and Bertelson, 1979). The analysis indicates that where alternatives to wetland development exist (on so-called fastland sites) then development values may not be very significant. On the other hand, provision of water access to a large group of homeowners via the development of small areas of wetland could yield significant social value, especially in areas where water access is limited.

In the UK, most of the semi-natural wetlands have been under pressure from agricultural conversion and land drainage schemes. The validity of the official appraisal analyses carried out by Water Authorities and Internal Drainage Boards, together with the economic value of wetland development, have been investigated in a number of studies (Bowers, 1983; Bowers and Black, 1984; Bowers and Cheshire, 1983; Turner et al., 1983). The broad conclusions of this work have been that the official literature suffers from serious technical deficiencies and that the majority of drainage and conversion schemes did not represent economically efficient investments. At the farm and scheme level, financially attractive arterial and field drainage investment returns have subsequently proved to be negative economic returns. This has been mainly due to the level of subsidy enjoyed by the agricultural industry within the EEC. Actual calculations of producer subsidy values are not straightforward, because of the complexity of the intervention measures pursued by producer countries (Bowers and Black, 1984).

The methodology used to appraise the net benefits of these conversion schemes in the UK has been subject to continuing debate and consequent refinement (Bowers, 1983; Penning-Rowsell and Chatterton, 1984; Turner, 1985). Both the rate of benefit uptake by farmers and the incremental fixed costs incurred, consequent upon a drainage and conversion scheme, have proved difficult to forecast accurately. The net present value of a given scheme should be estimated on the following basis:

$$PVNB = \sum_{t=0}^{t=n} \frac{GMI_t - C_t - Fd_{t-1} - FCI_t}{(1 + r)^t}$$

where GMI = increased gross margin value (economic prices)

C = arterial drainage, pumps, etc investment costs

Fd = field drainage investment costs, based on the area of land in the year before the crop output value is received

FCI = incremental fixed cost increases

r = discount rate

Some analysts (Penning-Rowsell and Chatterton, 1984) have included an additional flood protection benefit variable (d_t) which they define as 'the expected value of reduced crop damage in year t

experienced with the scheme'. This is not a valid procedure and amounts to double counting. However, (d_r) could conceivably be interpreted as reduced flood damage to assets (other than crops) on the farm, but its significance is difficult to assess. Bowers (1983) has, in any case, argued that (d_r) should be a negative variable since flood protection standards are not infinite. Flood losses could be greater in the 'post improvement' situation since the enterprises (mostly grazing) in the 'pre improvement' situation are not particularly vulnerable to flooding.

YARE BASIN FLOOD CONTROL PROJECT

During the 1970s the Anglian Water Authority in the UK put forward a flood control scheme for the Yare basin in Norfolk. It was argued by the Authority that the project and related land drainage works would generate a range of benefits. Among the benefits claimed were: potential gains in agricultural productivity (pasture to improved pasture or arable cultivation); increased levels of flood protection for rural and urban inhabitants; flood protection for environmental resources. On the costs side of the equation, however, the project was officially designated as environmentally benign. In fact the project had the potential to generate significant impacts, with possibly irreversible consequences for the surrounding wetland ecosystem and landscape (the Norfolk Broads).

Broadland is of considerable significance for wetland conservation. It contains three National Nature Reserves, two of which are included in the list of wetlands recognised by the British government under the Ramsar Convention. There are also a large number of sites of Special Scientific Interest (existing and pending) in the area. The marshes support important populations of birds and the marsh dykes (ditches) contain over a hundred different species of freshwater plants.

Navigation of the Yare river channel may also have been adversely affected. Both the case for development (build the barrier, on grounds of a positive net benefit, and allow consequent agricultural land conversion); and the case for preservation (build the barrier only if an adequate safeguarding programme for both ecological and landscape amenity resources is also accepted, or oppose the barrier's construction on grounds of environmental preservation and/or negative net economic benefits) were beset by a large measure of uncertainty. Many of the central variables, such as the rate and extent of arable conversion, flooding return periods, value of agricultural benefits, flood damage costs and environmental damage costs, were not quantifiable with any great precision.

The official cost-benefit analysis (Rendell *et al.*, 1978, 1983) contained a number of technical defects. These included: an over-rapid assumed rate of agricultural conversion of the grazing marshes; forecasted additional agricultural output priced incorrectly; crop yield data often not based on averages but on the highest yields theoretically attainable; an inadequate assessment of the environmental impacts of the scheme; unrealistic assumed conversion of acid sulphate soil areas (peat land); inadequate methods and techniques to assess the direct flood damage protection benefits in the urban area of Yarmouth; lack of sensitivity analysis on flood return periods (Bowers, 1983; Turner, 1983).

Table 9.1 summarises the main costs and benefits generated by the project and compares the official (RPT, 1983) estimates with those computed on the basis of an analysis which sought to correct for the benefits over-estimation listed above (Turner, 1983). The adjusted cost-benefit analysis predicts negative net present values, despite containing rather 'conservative' assumptions about the required producer subsidy equivalent adjustments for agricultural output. The barrier proposal was in fact abandoned in 1984, but considerable tracts of marsh have nevertheless still been drained and converted to arable crops, with the consequent loss of 'grade 1' landscape and other ecological assets.

ENVIRONMENTAL ETHICS

Users of policy-analytic techniques in advocacy situations are under constant pressure (aggravated by the institutional and legal contexts in which the techniques are used) to reduce the many dimensions of each problem to some common calculus to facilitate 'objective' comparison. There is therefore a tendency ' . . . to exclude values too widely diffused over space, or too incrementally affected over time, to be strongly championed by any single client of a policy analysis' (Sagoff, 1981). Thus the rights or interests of future generations and of non-human nature may be ignored. But at the same time, many analysts claim to have detected a growing sense of unease in industrialised societies about the current man and nature

Table 9.1 Project net present values: case (1) development scenario

	RPI estimates* (60-year horizon)	Other flood return periods 1 in 75 years	1 in 50 years	Adjusted estimates* (30-year horizon)	Other flood return periods 1 in 75 years	1 in 50 years
PV Total costs	£16.057m.			Total costs £15.657m.		
PV Benefits				PV Benefits		
Urban	£4m.–£5m.	£8m.–£9m.	£14m.–£15m.	£3m.–£4m.	£6m.–£7m.	£9m.–£10m.
Agricultural	£7m.–8m.			£2m.–£3m.		
Agricultural peat	£1.9m			0		
Environmental	£717 000			£0.1m.–£0.2m.		
Total	£13.6m.–£15.6m			£5.1m.–£7.2m.		
Net present value	–£2.5m.––£0.5m.	+£1.5m.–£2.5m.	+£7.5m.–£8.5m.	–£10.5m.––£8.5m.	–£7.5m.––£5.5m.	–£4.5m.––£2.5m.

* Flood return period = 1 in 100 yrs to 1 in 175 yrs for urban benefits; and 1 in 50 yrs for agricultural benefits.

Source: Turner, 1983.

relationship (the 'man-as-mere-resource paradigm'; Rolston, 1983) and the lack of normative insight into this relationship. These environmentalist arguments seem to be appealing to some kind of intuitive ethic, such that, humans ought not to over-exploit nature, but should protect its ongoing, holistic integrity.

Further indirect evidence about human valuations concerning non-human nature as well as the needs of future generations was highlighted earlier in the discussion about economic studies attempting to empirically measure option, existence and bequest values via WTP. Actual wetlands conservation/development policies then need to incorporate more adequately these underlying ethical value systems which are being adopted on an increasingly widespread basis in Western society.

There is little consensus among philosophers, however, as to whether this intuitive ethic can be given rational and theoretical support, or what the content of the ethic should be. A number of writers have suggested that traditional forms of ethical reasoning must be broadened or even abandoned. There must be an extension of the moral reference class beyond current individuals to cover the rights and interests of non-human nature (animals, plants, species and ecosystems) and/or future generations of humans.

THE RIGHTS OF FUTURE GENERATIONS

Philosophers are divided over the question of what, if any, are the current generation's obligations to future people. According to Kavka (1978), future people and contemporary strangers are worthy of broadly similar treatment. Thus the current generation has corresponding obligations in both cases. Both Kavka (1978) and Attfield (1983), among others, reject most of the general arguments that have been put forward in favour of giving less consideration to the future than to the present:

(1) because of the very temporal location of future people;
(2) ignorance of future people's wants and needs;
(3) because of the contingency of future people.

Their conclusion was, as long as some people will exist and will be in no relevant way unlike current right-holders, they are worthy of equal consideration. Further, whatever the uncertainty about the extent of future preferences, it is clear that basic needs will exist and will not be substantially different from contemporary ones. The satisfaction of these basic needs will be a prerequisite of the satisfaction of most of the other desires and interests of future people regardless of their uncertainty.

The contingency of future people argument refers to the fact that they may not exist at all and that the actual number depends in large measure upon current actions and decisions. Narveson (1978) supported a version of utilitarianism which holds that the current generation's duties are limited to assignable persons (plus duties of non-maleficence). Parfit (1976) put forward an argument which highlighted the distinction between 'possible' or potential people and future actual individuals who will exist at some subsequent time. If all 'possible' people have a right to life, or to other rights hypothetically, then environmental preservation will surely be at risk (Parfit's Paradox; see Broome's paper in this volume for further clarification). According to Parfit's argument no future person's rights are infringed by a policy of high consumption in the present generation and therefore rights of future generations are an inadequate basis for an environmental ethic. Narveson (1978) concluded, 'What we owe to future generations is neither Everything nor Nothing, but merely Something. And that something need not be the same for all, nor can its content be rationally estimated . . . . beyond the lifetime of the present youngest generation'.

However, do obligations to the future require knowledge of people's identity, since it seems fairly certain that there will be a human future? Attfield (1983) concluded that we can be nearly certain that there will be a great many future people and that once we accept their future existence as given, the contingency problem does not provide sufficient ground for subordinating their interests to those of existing contemporaries. He went on to advocate a variant of the 'Total Utility' version of utilitarianism, as the basis for a theory of normative ethics capable of supplying a coherent treatment of obligations to future generations. The current generation's obligation is then not to definite people but to ensure that human existence continues at a fairly high level of intrinsic value. Intrinsic value is best maximised by provision for everyone's basic needs. This requires equal provision for the needs of each generation, once population has stabilised.

Barry (1978) has stressed the fact of the asymmetry of power (lack of equity) between generations that do not overlap and has shown that if Hume's doctrine of the 'Circumstances of Justice' is accepted, then there are no relevant criteria of intergenerational justice. Hume's 'circumstances' are moderate scarcity, moderate selfishness and relative equality. But Barry concluded that while Hume's doctrine constitutes a sufficient condition for a society to have uniform rules of justice it is not a sufficient condition for the application of the concept of justice. Other circumstances, which it has been argued, give rise to obligations, such as reciprocal relationships within a community and entitlements to property (Nozick, 1974) are also not relevant in the intergenerational justice context. Attfield (1983) has argued, however, that there are good reasons for rejecting Hume's position and that general moral intuitions seem to go against the community and property entitlement arguments. It seems very doubtful that ethics based on concern (that is, Humean ethics) or on Passmore's concept of love (Passmore, 1974) offer a sufficient basis for environmental policy designed to take equity into account (Care, 1982).

A number of attempts have been made in the literature to utilise a contractarian approach in order to suggest criteria for intergenerational equity. In particular, Rawls's 'Theory of Justice' (Rawls, 1972) has, in amended form, been used as the basis for a number of theories of intergenerational equity (Page, 1977). But the case that can be made out for the formulation of a principle governing the just distribution and rate of resource usage over long periods of time, utilising the Rawlsian framework, is not totally convincing. The dual aspects of the theory – justice as rational cooperation (Hume) and justice as hypothetical universal assent (Kant) – conflict as soon as the analysis moves away from the self-contained society of contemporaries. Page's extension of the Rawls principles into the intergenerational equity context relies on the Kantian element of the theory (Page, 1977). But if all generations are represented in the original position then the parties could deduce how many generations there will be, even though this is one of the issues which is supposed to depend on their deliberations (Attfield, 1983). The representative parties must then know that some (not all) generations are represented and should not know the temporal location of those generations. Under these conditions, it has been argued, justice becomes essentially an agreement to pass on 'intact' an inheritance (environmental and economic goods and services) from one generation to the next. Both the rights of possible people and non-human species are, however, not catered for in any set of rules that would be arrived at in this Rawlsian framework.

Some analysts have argued that future generations will not require special treatment because they are almost bound to be better off than the current generation given their inherited enhanced stock of capital and knowledge. Much seems to depend on the true nature of the so-called 'environmental risk' situations (Page, 1978) that technologically advanced economies seem to generate. If global life-support systems are seriously impaired, future generations may have little opportunity to ameliorate or to adapt to their grossly polluted world.

Kavka (1978) has suggested that in terms of the resource base inheritance, each generation should leave 'enough and as good for others'. This 'Lockean standard' will involve policies to ensure the conservation of renewable resources, enhanced substitution technology and recycling innovation (Howe, 1979; Page, 1977; Pearce and Turner, 1984). Because of the current global inequities the Lockean standard will have to be the responsibility of future generations. The current generation would be justified in using up more than would otherwise be its fair share of resources in order to allow the developing economies to pass through the demographic transition and for world population to stabilise. Both Attfield (1983) and Sterba (1981) have argued that the current generation should determine a population level that is sustainable over time, one that is consistent with the requirement to provide for the basic needs of current and future people.

Kavka's approach is complementary to recent calls for 'justice as opportunity' (Barry, 1983; Page, 1983). What is proposed is that future generations are owed compensation for any reduction (due to the activities of the current generation) in their access to easily extracted and conveniently located natural resources. So the future's loss of productive potential must be compensated for if justice is to prevail. The current generation pays the compensation via improved technology and increased capital investment designed to offset the impacts of depletion, that is, a programme of 'sustainable' growth/ development (International Union for the Conservation of Nature (1980)).

THE RIGHTS AND INTERESTS OF NON-HUMAN NATURE

Regan (1981) has argued that an environmental ethic (referring to a comprehensive, coherent set of principles, obligations and value) must satisfy two conditions if it is to be defined as an ethic 'of the environment'. The two conditions are that it 'must hold that there are non-human beings which must have moral standing'; and secondly it 'must hold that the class of those beings which have moral standing includes but is larger than the class of conscious beings'. Moral standing can be ascribed to a being only if society morally ought to consider how it is affected by a given action or policy. Regan suggested that both conditions can only be fulfilled if non-human nature (conscious and non-conscious) is capable of being inherently valuable (that is, possesses intrinsic value). Any other ethic which lacks the above implication falls into a category Regan has labelled an ethic 'for the use of the environment'. Two important questions are raised by Regan's analysis. If inherent and not just instrumental natural value exists, what is it and how do we discover it? In other words, is it possible to justify judgements of inherent value? Secondly, is an ethic 'of the environment' necessary to protect the environment adequately or would an ethic 'for the use of the environment' offer sufficient safeguards?

Regan is pessimistic about ever resolving the problem of justifying intrinsic value in nature. Individual attitude surveys would be unreliable, but on the other hand, appeal to expert judgement only is open to the criticism of elitism. Other writers are less pessimistic and have argued their case on different metaethical grounds. Pluhar (1983), for instance, argues that Regan's position gives little ground for optimism because 'he has adopted the metaethical theory of non-naturalism, according to which, judgements of intrinsic value are assertions that non-natural ethical properties have instances in nature'. Not surprisingly, it seems very difficult to justify a view that requires actual instantiation on these nonsensuous intrinsic properties. Pluhar's position is nevertheless that a kind of justification is possible, on the basis of metaethical noncognitivism. In this approach, claims about intrinsic value are interpreted as attitudes of approval or recommendations for favourable treatment or regard. These ethical claims cannot be justified in the way in which factual claims can be. But it is conceivable that defensible ethical judgements might be arrived at by appealing to 'expert judgement'. Both Elliot (1982) and Rolston (1983) seem to have used this method in their defence of the existence of intrinsic value in wilderness areas.

If Regan's (1981) distinction between an anthropocentric and non-anthropocentric environmental ethic is correct, then a number of analysts have argued that the latter ethic is a sufficient but not a necessary condition for biospherical sustainability. Frankena (1979) has questioned the need for any radical environmental ethic on the grounds that an ethic which restricts moral standing solely to humans would still be sufficient to safeguard the basic integrity of the bio-sphere. His argument rests on the fact that nature yields a wide range of instrumental values and on the assumption that once this value is recognised, humans will so arrange matters that adequate environmental protection will be forthcoming. Nevertheless, Frankena is prepared to accept that all consciously sentient beings should have moral standing, a view that is shared by others such as Singer (1975, 1979) and Watson (1982).

An ethic restricted to the criterion of conscious sentience would still represent an extension of the preservation case. If some animals merit moral consideration then preservation of their habitats will also more often than not be justified. Value, according to this position, would still, however, depend on the possibility of its being perceived and enjoyed. On pragmatic grounds, arguments in favour of non-human individuals or collectivities, having interests and primary rights based on intrinsic value, are unlikely to make much headway in current policy-making circles. Watson (1982) has suggested that tactically the way forward for ecocentrists is to adopt the position advocated by Stone (1974). The suggestion was that nature can be assigned secondary rights, legal rights based on human interest in given entities, but not primary rights based on intrinsic value. Stone (1974) claimed further that humans themselves would be better off, that is, more 'complete' humans, if they adopted an 'environmental consciousness'.

Attfield (1983) is another writer who cannot accept completely the feasibility of an 'ethic of the environment' and in any case does not believe it to be necessary. He builds his ethical position from the traditions of stewardship and co-operation with nature which he finds evidence for from within the Judaeo-Christian tradition.

The robustness of the stewardship notion has been debated in the environmental literature. Black (1970) has made the case that me-diating mechanisms such as stewardship have become progressively weaker in modern societies. In the context of wetlands and agricul-tural development pressures the positive aspects of stewardship may not be able to resist the powerful short-term financial pressures for land-use change.

What is required, according to Attfield (1983), is an extended version of the ideology of stewardship. Such a position, he argues, can be described and defended in terms of human interests, alongside the interests of other creatures (sentient non-human animals and even non-sentient living creatures). Even if, as seems likely, the latter's moral significance is slight, it is as well to be aware of it, especially where large numbers of present or future organisms are in question. Goodpaster (1979) is in no doubt that all living things can have interests and are morally considerable. But the problem then becomes on what grounds it is possible to adjudicate in cases where human and non-human moral interests come into conflict. Goodpaster has observed that the determination of the scope and limits of moral consideration does not rigidly constrain views on the relative importance of one set of claims or interests over another. All life then, may have moral standing and possess intrinsic value, but this need not necessarily mean all life has equivalent moral significance.

Rodman (1977) has argued that the legal rights theories of Singer (1975) and Stone (1974) are still too strongly anthropocentric. From his viewpoint, humans degrade non-humans by 'giving' them rights on the basis of their inferior human status. Nevertheless, when interests conflict, difficult value comparisons will have to be made. Interspecies and animal–natural habitat conflicts as well as human interest conflicts will need to be equitably and practicably resolved (Taylor, 1983; Van De Veer, 1979).

Naess (1973) has outlined the principles of a suitable ecosophy for the 'deep' or radical ecocentric worldview. The central notion is 'biospherical egalitarianism in principle' (equality of species). The 'in principle' clause is inserted because 'any realistic praxis necessitates some killing, exploitation and suppression'. Singer (1975) has proposed a less radical position, a two-level theory of interests based on sentience and self-consciousness, which he called the 'Equality of Interests' principle. This principle has it that 'the interests of every being affected by an action are to be taken into account and given the same weight as the like interests of any other being'. Attfield (1983) has recently gone further and argued for an extended 'Singer Principle'. This is based on an amended 'two-factor egalitarianism theory', first proposed by Van De Veer (1979), which attempts to go beyond the sentience limitation.

Van De Veer's theory differentiates between the interests (basic, serious and peripheral) possessed by any creature's life. A Weighting Principle was suggested which ranks the interests of beings according to the complexity of their psychological capacities. For any given interspecies conflict of interests, morally permissible decision rules can be constructed on the basis of the category of interests at stake and the relative psychological capacities of the creatures. Attfield's qualification is that the more complex activities would be relevant only where their development or exercise is at stake.

SYSTEMS VALUE, LAND ETHICS AND THE GAIA HYPOTHESIS

Baird Callicott (1980), Clark (1983), Goodpaster (1974), Rodman (1977) and Rolston (1983) have all supported the argument that the class of morally considerable beings must extend to systems and not just individuals. The biosphere must be viewed holistically as either a community or as an organic whole. The anchor point for these positions is Leopold's Land Ethic (Leopold, 1949). Human life, however worthwhile, is of value only insofar as it preserves the sustainability of the biosphere. No individuals possess absolute intrinsic value, only relative value determined by their relative contribution to biosphere integrity.

Baird Callicott (1980) argued that the debate over animal liberation should be seen as triangular and not polar. The third force in the debate has been labelled the Land Ethic viewpoint. The ethical foundations of Leopold's 'Land Ethic' have been taken as the paradigm for this third general position. While only sentient animals are morally considerable according to the animal rights ethic, the land ethic encompasses plants as well as animals, and even soils and water. It also does not prohibit hunting, killing and eating of certain animal species. The *summum bonum* of the land ethic is the integrity, stability and beauty of the biotic community.

What Leopold seemed to be saying in ecological terms was that the characteristic structure of the ecosystem (its objective beauty) is vitally important to preserving its stability. But care is required in the exact interpretation the analyst places on the word 'stability'. The scientific literature should not be interpreted as saying that the more diverse an ecosystem is the more robust it is in dealing with outside interference. It is much more plausible to claim that the stability of an ecosystem is a function of its characteristic diversity (Hefferman, 1982).

Suitably modernised the Leopold maxim and its implied moral code of conduct could still carry some controversial consequences. Even relatively intensive agricultures would be morally suspect because of their threat to the integrity and stability of ecosystems. Hefferman suggested that the land ethic operate as a supplementary ethic alongside conventional ethics. Ecosystem good would have to be weighted along with human good in order to distinguish moral action. The range of 'critical' interest conflicts could be narrowed if a version of the Gaian notion proves acceptable. The land ethic is downgraded to a rule of conduct with exceptions. The combined influence of the Gaian notion and the 'weak' version of the land ethic might prove strong enough to re-orientate environmental policy along the lines necessary to guarantee an adequate inheritance for future generations.

THE GAIA HYPOTHESIS

This scientific hypothesis has been the subject of various interpretations within contemporary environmental ideologies. Clark (1983) has taken the Gaian notion of a self-regulatory biosphere as the basis for holistic ethical system very similar to the Baird Callicott (1980) interpretation of the land ethic. Clark's system attempts to accommodate the demands of both habitats and individual species. Clark argued that aside from moral respect for non-human arguments, there is what he termed a basic economic benefit to be derived from a 'natural' or 'wild' habitat. In Clark's view humans want and need a biosphere that can sustain itself without constant human effort. The Gaian notion fills that need and, although far from fragile, its mechanisms are not invulnerable. But humans are both part of nature and apart from nature. They should therefore not seek futile change but endeavour to intervene as constructively as possible. Clark cited as an example of constructive intervention in nature, the creation of the English countryside in the wake of the Enclosure Acts of the eighteenth century. It is this man-made landscape that is so prized by conservationists in the Norfolk Broadland. So it is not always necessary to have to appeal to the attributes of wilderness areas in order to find examples of beauty and balance. The main Gaian message, in this interpretation, is that it is not necessary to regard protection of the biosphere as a non-negotiable constraint. Not every particular ecosystem is necessary to the overall survival of the biosphere.

WETLANDS AND DEVELOPMENT: THE PARTNERSHIP ETHIC

Within the Gaian framework, and with Leopold's land ethic maxim (scientifically interpreted) as a general guide for macro policy decisions,

Ebenreck's 'partnership ethic' has much to commend it at the micro policy level (Ebenreck, 1983). This ethic is not conceived of in terms of rights language but instead is expressed as a theory of 'appropriate use'. Taking use to mean bringing into action or service, then it is legitimate to use nature as other humans are used or would be expected to be used. Both partners, humans and the land, are accorded 'intrinsic', if differing, values and the relationship becomes a mixture of respect and appropriate farmland use. It is not clear in Ebenreck's account what is exactly meant by 'intrinsic' yet differing values, although Attfield's (1983) stewardship ideology would fit the bill. Ebenreck concludes that with her approach it is possible to move past a principle of respect for land, couched in terms of wilderness or uniqueness, to a more general respect manifested by a kind of participation in community with land.

The setting aside of nature reserves is not precluded by this approach, while in other cases farmland would be 'used' on a sustainable basis. Favoured farming practices would include, mixed farming units and on-farm wastes recycling. At the national policy level, price-support systems would need to be reorientated (Bowers and Cheshire, 1983). Wetlands could be protected via the provision of amenity subsidies to farmers, or partnership payments could be made in order to ensure that sustainable cropping and husbandry practices could be combined with adequate conservation measures.

In Broadland, the so-called 'Broads Grazing Marsh Conservation Scheme' was initiated in 1985. This is a three-year, jointly funded, UK Countryside Commission and Ministry of Agriculture, Fisheries and Food experiment. The aim is to protect traditional practices by paying landowners or sitting tenants £50 per acre to maintain livestock management on certain terms. Over 90 per cent of the 150 or so farmers involved have indicated their support.

PROSPECTS FOR A 'WEAK ANTHROPOCENTIC' ENVIRONMENTAL ETHIC

From this viewpoint human alteration of the environment is regarded as inevitable but not necessarily destructive. The biosphere is not a static but a dynamic mechanism, in which humans can and should participate on a sustainable basis. It does not seem necessary to regard protection of the entire biosphere as a rigid constraint. If this were to be the case there is a risk of the sanctification of nature or of natural principles. Other dangers to be guarded against include too sharp a separation of environmental policy from human rights and social justice, and potentially reactionary eco-imperative thinking in which morality is determined uniquely by natural morality.

The ideology of stewardship (Attfield, 1983) can be extended to cover the interests of non-human species, although the concept of intrinsic value in nature remains a controversial one. Norton (1982a, b) remains pessimistic about efforts to formulate a coherent environmental ethic as long as the usual individualistic basis for interests and rights is retained. He believes that these interests and rights do not provide a comprehensive and theoretically sound support for the intuitive idea that the ongoing, holistic integrity of nature ought to be preserved. Regan's (1981) distinction between an ethic of the environment and for the use of the environment has been seen by many writers as the central issue in the debate. But Norton (1984) has argued that non-anthropocentrism (belief that non-human entities have intrinsic value independent of human value) is not the only adequate basis for a truely environmental ethic. For Norton, the individualism versus nonindividualism dichotomy is the crucial issue if a distinctive environmental ethic is to be constructed. A successful environmental ethic cannot be individualistic in the way that conventional ethical systems are.

In order to explore the question of what should count as a human interest, Norton (1984) suggested a distinction between felt preferences, any desire or need that can at least temporarily be sated by some specifiable experience of that individual and a considered preference expressed after careful deliberation, including a judgement that the desire or need is consistent with a rationally adopted worldview. According to Norton it may be possible to distinguish felt preferences from considered preferences when there are convincing arguments that the former are inconsistent with part of a world view that seems to be rational and worthy of support. This latter preference concept appears to be similar to Sagoff's public preference referred to in an earlier section. Using these two preference concepts, Norton (1984) went on to distinguish 'strong anthropocentrism' (based on value arrived at via felt human preferences) and 'weak anthropocentrism' (in which value is influenced by ideals which exist as part of a worldview essential to the determination of considered preferences).

Because 'weak anthropocentrism' recognises that felt preferences can be rational or not, it provides a basis for criticisms of value systems which conform to the exploitative 'nature-as-a-mere-resource' paradigm. 'Weak anthropocentrism' can encompass the notion of sustainability and also makes possible appeals to the value of experiences of natural objects and undisturbed places in human value formation. So nature provides for the satisfaction of fixed and often consumptive values, but also becomes an important source of inspiration in value formation. 'Weak anthropocentrism' can provide for an ethic based not on intrinsic value in nature but on non-individualism. All value is found in human loci, but value is not restricted to satisfactions of felt preferences of human individuals.

Norton's (1984) approach includes references to what he has called generalised obligations, that is, obligations of the current generation to maintain a stable flow of resources into the indefinite future, in order to ensure ongoing human life, rather than meeting individual requirements. Norton is at pains to stress that resource base stability should not be interpreted as ecological stability, which remains an open and controversial question. Nevertheless, he is confident that management rules for particular ecological conditions can be validly derived. It would therefore appear that the 'safe minimum standards' approach to wetlands management policy fits into the 'weakly anthropocentric' category; as do the 'Lockean Standard' and 'Justice as Opportunity' approaches to intergenerational equity.

References

Attfield, R. (1983), *The Ethics of Environmental Concern* (Oxford: Basil Blackwell).

Baird Callicott, J. (1980), *Animal Liberation: A Triangular Affair, Environmental Ethics*, vol. 2 (1).

Barry, B. (1978), 'Circumstances of Justice and Future Generations', in R. I. Sikora and B. Barry (eds), *Obligations to Future Generations* (Philadelphia: Temple University Press).

Barry, B. (1983), 'Intergenerational Justice in Energy Policy', in P. G. Brown and D. MacLean (eds), *Energy and the Future* (Totowa, New Jersey: Rowman & Littlefield).

Batie, S. S. and C. C. Mabbs-Zeno (1985), 'Opportunity Costs of Preserving Coastal Wetlands: A Case Study of a Recreational Housing Development', *Land Economics*, vol. 61 (1).

Batie, S. S. and L. A. Shabman (1982), 'Estimating the Economic Value of Wetlands: Principles, Methods and Limitations', *Coastal Zone Management Journal*, vol. 10 (3).

Bishop, R. C. (1978), 'Endangered Species and Uncertainty: The Economics of a Safe Minimum Standard', *American Journal of Agricultural Economics*, vol. 60 (1).

Bishop, R. C. and T. A. Heberlein (1979), 'Measuring Values of Extra Market Goods: Are Indirect Measures Biased?', *American Journal of Agricultural Economics*, vol. 61 (5).

Bishop, R. C., T. A. Heberlein and M. J. Kealy (1983), 'Contingent Valuation of Environmental Assets: Comparisons with a Simulated Market', *Natural Resources Journal*, vol. 23 (3).

Black, J. (1970), *The Dominion of Man: The Search for Ecological Responsibility* (Edinburgh: John Black).

Boulding, K. E. (1970), *Economics as a Science* (New York: McGraw-Hill).

Bowers, J. K. (1983), 'Cost-benefit Analysis of Wetland Drainage', *Environment and Planning A*, vol. 15 (2).

Bowers, J. K. and C. J. Black (1984), 'The Level of Protection of U.K. Agriculture', *Oxford Bulletin of Economics and Statistics*, vol. 4 (4).

Bowers, J. K. and P. Cheshire (1983), *Agriculture, The Countryside and Land Use: An Economic Critique* (London: Methuen).

Boyle, K. J., R. C. Bishop and M. P. Welsh (1985), 'Starting Point Bias in Contingent Valuation Bidding Games', *Land Economics*, vol. 61 (2).

Brown, T. C. (1984), 'The Concept of Value in Resource Allocation', *Land Economics*, vol. 60 (3).

Care, N. S. (1982), 'Future Generations, Public Policy and the Motivation Problem', *Environmental Ethics*, vol. 4 (3).

Ciriacy-Wantrup, S. V. (1968), *Resource Conservation: Economics and Policies* (Berkeley: University of California Press).

Clark, S. R. L. (1983), 'Gaia and the Forms of Life', in R. Elliot and A. Gare (eds), *Environmental Philosophy* (St. Lucia: University of Queensland Press).

Clawson, M. (1980), 'Wilderness as One of Many Land Uses', *Idaho Law Review*, vol. 16 (3).

Cowardin, L. M., V. Carter, F. C. Golet and E. T. La Rue *Classification of Wetlands and Deepwater Habitats of the United States* (FWS/OBS–79/31, Washington DC: US Fish and Wildlife Service).

Desvousges, W. H., V. K. Smith and M. P. McGivney (1983), *A Comparison of Alternative Approaches for Estimating Recreation and Related Benefits of Water Quality Improvements* (Washington DC: US EPA, EPA–230–05–83–001).

Ebenreck, S. (1983), 'A Partnership Farmland Ethic', *Environmental Ethics*, vol. 5 (1).

Elliot, R. (1982), 'Faking Nature', *Inquiry*, vol. 25 (1). (For a further debate see D. Mannison, 'Nature May Be of No Value', *Inquiry*, vol. 26 (2) (1983): and R. Elliot, 'The Value of Wild Nature', *Inquiry*, vol. 26 (2) (1983).)

Fisher, A. C. and W. M. Hanemann (1985), 'Endangered Species: The Economics of Irreversible Damage', in N. Myers and N. S. Magaris (eds), *Economics of Ecosystem Management* (Dordrecht: Dr. W. Junk Publishers).

Frankena, W. K. (1979), 'Ethics and the Environment', in K. E. Goodpaster and K. M. Sayre (eds), *Ethics and Problems of the Twenty First Century*

(Notre Dame and London: University of Notre Dame Press).

Freeman, A. M. (1984), 'The Quasi-Option Value of Irreversible Development'. *Journal of Environmental Economics and Management*, vol. 11 (3).

Goodpaster, K. E. (1979), 'From Egoism to Environmentalism', in K. E. Goodpaster and K. M. Sayre (eds), *Ethics and Problems of the Twenty First Century* (Notre Dame and London: University of Notre Dame Press).

Greenley, D. A., R. G. Walsh and R. A. Young (1981), 'Option Value: Empirical Evidence From a Case Study of Recreation and Water Quality', *Quarterly Journal of Economics*, vol. 95 (4).

Hefferman, J. D. (1982), 'The Land Ethic: A Critical Appraisal'. *Environmental Ethics*, vol. 4 (3).

Howe, C. (1979), *Natural Resource Economics* (Chichester: John Wiley).

International Union for the Conservation of Nature (1980), *World Conservation Strategy* (Geneva: International Union for the Conservation of Nature).

Journal of the Limnological Society of Southern Africa (1983), Special Issue: Wetlands, vol. 9 (2).

Kavka, G. (1978), 'The Futurity Problem', in R. I. Sikora and B. Barry (eds), *Obligations to Future Generations* (Philadelphia: Temple University Press).

Krutilla, J. V. (1967), 'Conservation Reconsidered', *American Economic Review*, vol. 57 (3).

Krutilla, J. V. and A. C. Fisher (1975), *The Economics of Natural Environments* (Baltimore: Johns Hopkins University Press).

Lecomber, R. (1975), *Economic Growth Versus the Environment* (London: Macmillan).

Lecomber, R. (1978), 'Social Costs and the National Accounts', in D. W. Pearce (ed.), *The Valuation of Social Costs* (London: Allen & Unwin).

Leith, H. and R. H. Whittaker (1975), *The Primary Production of the Biosphere* (New York: Springer-Verlag).

Leopold, A. (1949), *A Sand County Almanac* (New York: Oxford University Press).

Long, S. P. and C. F. Mason (1983), *Saltmarsh Ecology* (Glasgow and London: Blackie).

Lovelock, J. E. (1979), *Gaia: A New Look at Life on Earth* (Oxford University Press).

Lutz, M. and K. Lux (1979), *The Challenge of Humanistic Economics* (New York: Benjamin Cummings).

Maltby, E. and R. E. Turner (1983), 'Wetlands of the World', *Geographical Magazine*, vol. 55.

Mishan, E. J. (1982), 'The New Controversy about the Rationale of Economic Evaluation', *Journal of Economic Issues*, vol. 16 (1).

Mitchell, R. C. and R. T. Carson (1985), 'Option Value: Empirical Evidence from a Case Study of Recreation and Water Quality: Comment', *Quarterly Journal of Economics*, vol. 99 (1).

Moss, B. (1983), 'The Norfolk Broadland: Experiments in the Restoration of a Complex Wetland', *Biology Review*, vol. 58 (4).

Myers, N. (1983), *A Wealth of Wild Species* (Boulder, Colorado: Westview Press).

Naess, A. (1973), 'The Shallow and the Deep, Long-Range Ecology Movement: a Summary', *Inquiry*, vol. 16 (1).

Narveson, J. (1978), 'Future People and Us', in R. I. Sikora, and B. Barry (eds), *Obligations to Future Generations* (Philadelphia: Temple University Press).

Nelson, R. W. and W. J. Logan (1984), 'Policy on Wetland Impact Mitigation', *Environmental International*, vol. 10 (1).

Norton, B. G. (1982a), 'Environmental Ethics and the Rights of Future Generations', *Environmental Ethics*, vol. 4 (4).

Norton, B. G. (1982b), 'Environmental Ethics and Nonhuman Rights', *Environmental Ethics*, vol. 4 (1).

Norton, B. G. (1984), 'Environmental Ethics and Weak Anthropocentrims', *Environmental Ethics*, vol. 6 (2).

Nozick, R. (1974), *Anarchy, State, and Utopia* (Oxford: Basil Blackwell).

Odum, E. P. (1979), 'The Value of Wetlands: a Hierarchical Approach', in P. E. Greeson, P. E. Clark and J. R. Clark *Wetland Functions and Values: The State of our Understanding* (Minneapolis: American Water Resources Association).

O'Riordan, T. and R. K. Turner (1983), *An Annotated Reader in Environmental Planning and Management* (Oxford: Pergamon).

Page, T. (1977), *Conservation and Efficiency* (Baltimore: Johns Hopkins University Press).

Page, T. (1978), 'A General View of Toxic Chemicals and Similar Risks', *Ecology Law Quarterly*, vol. 7 (2).

Page, T. (1983), 'Intergenerational Justice as Opportunity', in P. G. Brown and D. Maclean (eds), *Energy and the Future* (Totowa, New Jersey: Rowman Littlefield).

Parfit, D. (1976), 'Rights, Interests and Possible People', in S. Gorovitz *et al.* (eds), *Moral Problems in Medicine* (Englewood Cliffs, New Jersey, 1976). (See also D. Parfit (1982) 'Future Generations: Further Problems', *Philosophy and Public Affairs*, vol. 11 (2) (1982)).

Passmore, J. (1974), *Man's Responsibility for Nature* (London: Duckworth).

Pearce, D. W. and R. K. Turner (1984), 'The Economic Evaluation of Low and Non-Waste Technologies', *Resources and Conservation*, vol. 11 (1).

Penning-Rowsell, E. C. and J. B. Chatterton (1984), 'Gauging the Economic Viability of Agricultural Land Drainage Schemes', *Journal of the Institution of Water Engineering and Scientists*, vol. 38 (2).

Pluhar, E. B. (1983), 'The Justification of an Environmental Ethic', *Environmental Ethic*, vol. 5 (1).

Porter, R. C. (1982), 'The New Approach to Wilderness Preservation through Benefit Cost Analysis', *Journal of Environmental Economics and Management*, vol. 9 (1).

Race, M. S. (1985), 'Critique of Present Wetlands Mitigation Policies in the United States Based on an Analysis of Past Restoration Projects in San Francisco Bay', *Environmental Management*, vol. 9 (1).

Race, M. S. and D. R. Christie (1982), 'Coastal Zone Development: Mitigation, Marsh Creation and Decision-Making', *Environmental Management Journal*, vol. 6 (4).

Rawls, J. (1972), *A Theory of Justice* (Oxford University Press).

Regan, T. (1981), 'On the Nature and Possibility of an Environmental Ethic', *Environmental Ethics*, vol. 3 (1).

Rendell, Palmer and Tritton (1978), *Yare Basin Flood Control Study*, 3 vols (Southwark Street, London: Rendell, Palmer and Tritton).

Rendell, Palmer and Tritton, *Anglian Water's Yare Basin Flood Control Project, Cost-Benefit Analysis* (Southwark Street, London: Rendell, Palmer and Tritton).

Rodman, J. (1977), 'The Liberation of Nature', *Inquiry*, vol. 20 (1).

Rolston, H. (1983), 'Values Gone Wild', *Inquiry*, vol. 26 (1).

Rowe, R. D. and L. G. Chestnut (1983), 'Valuing Environmental Commodities: Revisited', *Land Economics*, vol. 59 (4).

Sagoff, M. (1981), 'Economic Theory and Environmental Law', *Michigan Law Review*, vol. 79 (7).

Seller, C., J. R. Stoll and J. Chavas (1985), 'Validation of Empirical Measures of Welfare Change: A Comparison of Nonmarket Techniques', *Land Economics*, vol. 61 (2).

Shabman, L., S. Batie and C. Mabbs-Zeno (1979), 'The Economics of Wetland Preservation in Virginia', *Journal of the North Eastern Agricultural Economics Council*, vol. 8 (2).

Shabman, L. and M. K. Bertelson (1979), 'The Use of Development Value Estimates for Coastal Wetland Permit Decisions', *Land Economics*, vol. 55 (2).

Simon, J. (1982), 'Are We Losing our Farmland?', *Public Interest*, vol. 67 (Spring).

Simon, J. and Kahn, H. (eds) (1984), *Resourceful Earth* (Oxford: Basil Blackwell).

Singer, P. (1975), *Animal Liberation* (New York Review Press).

Singer, P. (1979), 'Not for Humans Only: The Place of Nonhumans in Environmental Issues', in K. E. Goodpaster and K. M. Sayes (eds), *Ethics and Problems of the Twenty First Century* (Notre Dame and London: University of Notre Dame Press).

Smith, V. K., W. H. Desvousges and A. Fisher (1983), 'Estimates of the Option Values for Water Quality Improvements', *Economic Letters*, vol. 13 (2).

Sterba, J. P. (1981), 'The Welfare Rights of Distant People and Future Generations: Moral Side-Constraints on Social Policy', *Social Theory and Practice*, vol. 7 (1).

Stone, C. D. (1974), *Should Trees Have Standing?* (Los Altro, California: William Kaufmann).

Taylor, P. W. (1983), 'In Defence of Biocentrism', *Environmental Ethics*, vol. 5 (3).

Turner, R. K. (1983), *An Economic Approach to Environmental Management: Incorporating A Review of Anglian Water's Yare Basin Flood Control Study* (Colegate, Norwich: Broads Authority).

Turner, R. K. (1985), 'Land Evaluation: Financial, Economic and Ecological Approaches', *Soil Survey and Land Evaluation*, vol. 5 (2).

Turner, R. K., D. Dent and R. D. Hey (1983), 'Valuation of the Environmental Impact of Wetland Flood Protection and Drainage Schemes', *Environment and Planning A*, vol. 15 (4).

US Office of Technology Assessment, *Wetlands their Use and Regulation* (Washington DC: US Government Printing Office).

Van, De Veer, D. (1979), 'Interspecific Justice', *Inquiry*, vol. 22.

Veblen, T. (1899), *The Theory of the Leisure Class* (London: Macmillan).

Walsh, R. G., J. B. Loomis and R. A. Gillman (1984), 'Valuing Option, Existence and Bequest Demands for Wilderness', *Land Economics*, vol. 60 (1).

Watson, R. A. (1982), 'Comment: Interests, Rights and Self-Consciousness', *Environmental Ethics*, vol. 4 (3).

Weisbrod, B. A. (1964), 'Collective-Consumption Services of Individual–Consumption Goods', *Quarterly Journal of Economics*, vol. 78 (3).

Westman, W. E. (1985), *Ecology, Impact Assessment, and Environmental Planning* (Chichester: Wiley).

10 Farm Incomes and the Benefits of Environmental Protection

John Bowers

The past few years have seen increasing recognition that post-war agricultural expansion in the UK under the aegis of agricultural support policies has incurred considerable social costs. These costs have taken a number of forms. On the one hand there have been the classic negative externalities of pollution, posing new problems for the theory and practice of pollution control because of the plethora of polluters and the wide area of land over which pollution has taken place. On the other there have been problems of the under-provision of public goods provided jointly with agricultural output. The reduction in landscape diversity, accessibility of agricultural land and reduced suitability for recreational activities fall under this head, as does the reduction in ecological diversity of the farmed environment appearing as loss of various types of semi-natural habitats and their associated plant and animal populations. The elements of agricultural change that have been identified as causing these costs have been increased intensity of land-use, involving a substitution of bought inputs (machinery and chemicals) for the services of land, specialisation and a shift in crop production from grass to arable.[1] What factors have brought about these changes is only partially understood. Most commentators have emphasised the importance of the agricultural support package, but whether it is possible to attribute specific aspects of agricultural change to specific elements of policy is doubtful. The climate of opinion engendered by a commitment of successive governments to farm income support has no doubt played a part, while the existence of price guarantees has reduced uncertainty by placing a floor under producer prices. The changes identified above have been objectives of policy-makers who have sought to achieve them by an integrated system of research, exhortation, advice and financial incentives. Thus a factor which might otherwise be thought of as an exogenous contributor to agricultural development, technical progress, is patently not so. Its pace and direction is to an unknown degree an artefact of the support system.

The problem as described is one of market failure in agriculture. The level of output is above the social optimum because decision-makers have not taken account of externalities. The production function of public goods and the structure of agricultural output is also socially sub-optimal, environmental damage having resulted from intensive use of land and socially excessive use of chemical and capital inputs. It might be thought that to determine the optimum level and structure of agricultural output and the socially efficient techniques of producing that output requires an assessment of the social cost of agricultural expansion. But if this is so then we have serious practical difficulties and arguably a theoretical problem. In the current state of knowledge it is possible within limits to describe the environmental changes brought about by modern agriculture and, within limits, to model the physical processes which bring them about, but we are very far from being able to value these changes. Available techniques for doing so are underdeveloped and are all open to a variety of objections, both theoretical and practical. Yet the rate of habitat loss is such that action cannot wait on progress in this field, since the losses to the natural environment at least are essentially irreversible.[2] I propose to consider the validity of the view that for rational decision-making it is necessary to obtain some measure of the benefits of environmental protection to compare with the costs in terms of lost production and reduced farm incomes from measures to safeguard or restore natural environments.

Assume that there exists a set of negative environmental effects (destruction of wildlife habitats or whatever) that occur if farmers use certain production techniques that are available to them. Other 'efficient' techniques exist that do not carry these negative externalities. By an 'efficient' technique I mean one that would be the lowest cost means of production for some set of positive input prices. These statements suffice if we think of agricultural output as one single product. If we allow for a range of products to be produced on the farm then some modifications are required. There exists in this case a set of product mixes and input combinations which do not have the postulated negative environmental effects and which would maximise farm incomes for some set of positive product and input prices.

This assumption about the nature of the environmental problem may well be wrong. The 'environmentally safe' production techniques, or combinations of techniques and product mixes, may be technologically obsolete and hence 'inefficient', that is, there may be no set of prices at which they would maximise farm incomes or minimise costs. This is the problem of irreversibility of technology. In this case if we can identify some point in the past, a 'golden age', when these environmentally safe techniques (product mixes) were in use, then replicating the price structure prevailing at that time will not take us back to environmental safety. An obvious approach to testing the issue would be to examine the change in the price set. If the price structure has not altered since this golden age, or has altered in ways that favour environmentally sound production, then the environmentally sound production techniques must have become inefficient as a consequence of technical progress.

The negative environmental effects are external diseconomies because society derives utility from the existence of these environments and hence is made worse off by their destruction. For simplicity assume that farmers are indifferent to their environments in this regard: their welfare is unaffected by the matter. Finally assume that at the current set of prices, profit-maximising farmers choose techniques/production mixes which carry the negative environmental effects. We then have a number of cases.

Case A

No agricultural subsidies. Perfect competition prevails, markets continuously clear.

We then have a variant of the classic externalities problem. If bargaining between farmers and consumers (the Coase solution to externalities) is precluded, say by transactions costs, the externality can best be eliminated by the imposition of a set of Pigovian taxes on producers. If bargaining is technically possible then the Pigovian taxes would need to be accompanied by a comparable set of subsidies on those who suffer from the externality in order to avoid production being driven below the social optimum as a result of bargaining. The combination of Pigovian taxes and subsidies yields no revenue to the government but distributes all the social gain to those who suffer the external diseconomy. If bargaining is technically impossible and taxes alone are imposed, the government has revenue which it may spend either to compensate the farmers for their loss of welfare or to supplement the welfare of consumers, for example, by the creation of nature reserves. The choice depends on the government's distributional objectives.

In principle the externality may also be eliminated by paying the subsidy without the tax. As well as raising the familiar problem of finding the revenue in a neutral way, the nature of the environmental goods involved does not make subsidies to consumers a feasible proposition.

The position is more complex if the environmentally sound technique/product mix is inefficient as defined above. Essentially the environmental effects are 'bads' produced jointly with the agricultural goods. There are two possibilities to be considered.

In Figure 10.1 we show the isoquants for producing a given output of an agricultural product, 'Q_o', before ($Q_o{}^0$) and after ($Q_o{}^1$) technical progress. The technical progress has been input 'B' augmenting in the Hicksian sense so that, for a given input price ratio, point 'O' on '$Q_o{}^0$' is chosen before technical progress and point 'P' on '$Q_o{}^1$' after technical progress; 'P' entailing both a higher ratio of 'B/A' and absolutely more of input 'B' than point 'O'. Input 'B' is an environmental 'bad', input 'A' environmentally neutral. In this case the Pigovian tax solution is appropriate. The use of input 'B' is taxed so as to move the farmer to point 'R' on '$Q_o{}^1$', thus restoring environmental quality to its level prior to technical progress.

Figure 10.1

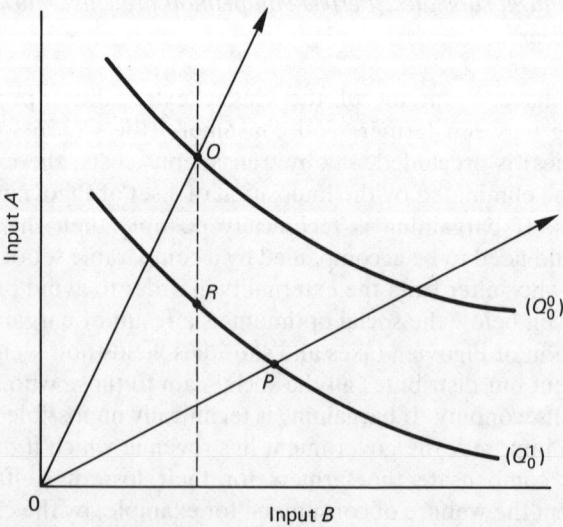

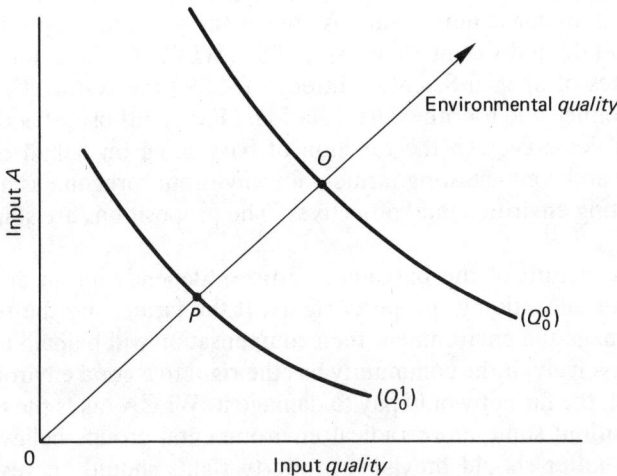

Figure 10.2

In Figure 10.2 technical progress is Hicks-neutral so that at a given input price ratio the same input ratio is chosen at '*P*' on 'Q_o^1' as at '*O*' on 'Q_o^0'. But in this case the production function of environmental quality entails the use of both '*A*' and '*B*' in the fixed proportions indicated by the slope of the line passing through '*P*' and '*Q*'. If output 'Q_o' is market-determined, environmental quality can only be maintained by subsidising inputs or raising the output price received by farmers supplying the desired environmental quality. In other words, the ratio of output prices to input prices must be raised.

A two-tier pricing system thus has to be operated with the output prices (or input prices) varying with the technique used. We are faced with a form of the classic public goods problem appearing, in this case, as a problem of policing. The farmer has the incentive to free ride: to accept the subsidies available to the users of the inefficient technique, but in fact to use the efficient one.

With the inefficient technique, the social decision rule is the basic cost-benefit one. Because the environmentally sound technique is inefficient, conservation has a social cost. With the socially optimum price set (that is, the 'Pigovian' solution where price equals marginal social cost), environmental conservation is worthwhile if total social benefit is greater than social cost. Intra-marginal benefits matter because conceptually we have moved from an auction market problem to an investment decision.

If the barrier to bargaining is transactions cost, the alternative approach to a solution is to create an agency or agencies to bargain on behalf of consumers. I suppose this is the solution adopted under the Wildlife and Countryside Act, 1981 (WLCA), where for scheduled sites of Special Scientific Interest (SSSIs) the Nature Conservancy Council and for other sites, National Park Authorities and Local Authorities are given the function of bargaining on behalf of consumers and compensating farmers for any profit foregone as a result of meeting environmental objectives. The propositions are standard:

(1) The nature of the bargaining process depends on an arbitrary prior allocation of property rights. If the farmer has the right to damage the environment then compensation will be paid to him; conversely, if the community has the right to a good environment then the farmer would pay to damage it. WLCA takes the former position: some more radical environmental groups believe that the latter should prevail – property rights should be vested in society.

(2) Given an allocation of property rights, bargaining will result in a shift to the social optimum. The division of the resulting social surplus, however, is indeterminate. If we assume property rights lie with the farmer, then the minimum payment he will accept for changing his techniques/product mix is the sum that will leave him no worse off than he was to start with. The maximum that the consumers will be prepared to pay is the addition to social benefit that results from the move, thus leaving them no worse off. With bilateral bargaining, any division between the parties of the difference between these two magnitudes is a feasible outcome. The 'imposed' Pigovian tax solution gives the surplus to the consumer.

The WLCA gives property rights to the farmers but the financial guidelines published under the Act suggest a solution where the farmer is just compensated, that is, where the resulting surplus is given to the consumers. This might be thought a reasonable compromise and an equitable outcome, and indeed would be such if case 'A' applied. It does not apply, however, since agricultural subsidies are being paid.[3]

Plainly, the evaluation of environmental benefits and costs is central to rational decision-making under this case 'A'. If farmers are not subsidised, WLCA would appear to provide a basis for such valuation. Also, since if the bodies that are charged with negotiating on the consumers' behalf are willing to pay compensation equal to the net income forgone by the farmer as a result of conservation, and society votes the funds that enables them to do so, one might conclude that society values the benefits from conservation at least at the value of the additional revenue forgone. A social optimum would result from this process under two conditions: either with some means of enforcing agreements when society's agents are willing just to compensate farmers – and the condition exists for SSSIs through the Nature Conservancy's powers of compulsory purchase,[4] but not for other types of sites – or where the agents are permitted to bargain freely over payments above this necessary level up to their estimate of the social value of conserving the site. The difference between the two cases would be in terms of the distribution of the social surplus.

The argument so far has ignored the question of irreversibilities. As various writers have shown,[5] in the presence of irreversibilities with uncertainty as to future value of alternative land-use practices, more conservative investment decision criteria will apply. This may be approximated by the incorporation of an option value into the calculation of marginal social cost of agricultural improvements, although while empirical work is proceeding, at present there is no satisfactory practical means of calculating that option value.[6] In these circumstances an option value will presumably also exist for the private decision-maker, the farmer, but the social and private option values will not typically be equal for two reasons. First, the public goods aspect of the environmental benefit means that the farmer would not anticipate converting a possible future higher social valuation of good environment into revenue. His private valuation, in other words, would be lower than society's because of non-excludability and non-rivalness. Second, because of Pigou's 'defective telescopic faculty', his time horizon for decision-making will be shorter than that of society. On the other hand, of course, a decision that is irreversible for a short time horizon may not be so for a longer one.

We now consider how the argument is modified by the presence of agricultural subsidies. If lump-sum transfers are unfeasible, one can quite reasonably prefer a distributionally superior but inefficient allocation to an efficient allocation with an undesirable distribution. Observation of such choices would give contours on a social welfare function if one could find indices to measure distribution and allocative efficiency. That such choices can in principle be made supplies the logical basis for the social welfare function postulate.[7]

Agricultural policy is such a case of the sacrifice of allocative efficiency for distributional objectives. The output price and input subsidy system is neither by intention nor effect a correction of market distortions. Rather it is designed to maintain or enhance farm incomes above the levels that the unfettered market would provide. Within this overall income objective, considerations of resource allocation appear to affect the thinking of policy-makers. Incentives for farm amalgamations and increased capital intensity are aimed at ensuring that agricultural production is technically efficient, but such efforts are liable to fall foul of the theory of second-best. Once the constraint on farm incomes is imposed, the second-best optimum may not involve choice of technique which maximises capital intensity and output per acre or per man. It has been argued that this is indeed so. British agriculture is over-capitalised and the negative environmental effects are symptoms of resource misallocation.[8] It is sometimes argued also that agricultural protection is designed to yield another externality: security of supply. Since I have considered this argument at length elsewhere, and rejected it,[9] nothing more will be said here.

If agricultural support is provided for reasons of income distribution and society wishes to change the system then logically this is either because it has produced unforeseen allocative losses which tip the balance, or distributional values have changed, or both. We thus move to the second case.

Case B

Society is supporting farm incomes on distributional grounds. A number of alternative diagnoses of the problem may then be considered.

(1) The environmental effects were unforeseen consequences of agricultural support. While it wishes to eliminate these externalities, society's commitment to farm income support is unimpaired.
(2) Society's priorities have altered. The significance it attaches to a sound environment has risen and its commitment to farm income support has fallen in priority.

(3) 'Social Thatcherism'. Subsidies are seen as undesirable *per se* but it is recognised that where farmers are providing something of value to society, which from its nature (as a public good: note the extent to which environmental benefits *are* public goods in the technical sense needs consideration) is not paid for, then they should be compensated for this service.

(4) Society no longer wishes to support farm incomes but is prepared to pay for a sound environment.

(1) is the most straightforward case. If the environmentally sound product mix/techniques can be identified, then the prices may be set to achieve them. The resulting income levels may need adjusting either through direct subventions or, if it does not result in further shifts in product mix/techniques away from the environmentally desirable, by adjustments of the price set. This would probably mean a change in the types of inputs that receive subsidy – for example, labour instead of capital. If the environmentally sound techniques/product mixes are inefficient, problems of incentives and policing are as discussed above. This case is the one implied by the view that, 'if we are going to subsidise agriculture we might at least ensure that we get the type of agriculture that we want'. In this case there is no need to attempt a valuation of environmental benefits, although an implicit minimum valuation is given by the net cost of income support with environmental protection, that is, net compared to the cost without a sound environment. It is not clear that such a minimum sum would be positive even allowing for the opportunity cost of forgone output.

(2) has been deliberately phrased in an imprecise manner and its implications depend on further interpretations. I suppose that in general it implies that if shifting to environmentally sound production through adjusting the price set results in falling agricultural incomes, then the question of whether compensatory income adjustment should be undertaken is a matter for debate. Compensation may not be universal nor complete. Only those farmers whose income is judged inadequate when farming in the approved manner would have an entitlement to compensation. Again, this view could accord with a recent popular view that 'some farmers have become millionaires from agricultural subsidies while poor farmers receive practically nothing'. If environmentally sound techniques are inefficient, of course, then payments will have to be made (and policed) regardless of income levels. Again, there is no pressing need to value environmental benefits in formulating policy.

I define view (3) as implying that the social surplus generated from environmental protection, and which may not be recouped by the producer through the market (by privatising conservation), should accrue to the producer. Property rights are assigned to him and he should receive what the providers of environmental goods are prepared to pay. In this case the benefits of a sound environment need to be assessed. Prices are set by 'market forces' and a mechanism devised for compensation to be paid to those who choose to conserve the environment. This in fact is best achieved by eliminating subsidy and permitting society's agents to bargain freely over compensation for safeguarding environments.

Case B(4) is, *de facto*, the alternative to B(3). Prices can be set to marginal social cost as in the unsubsidised state and payments made and so on, if desired techniques are inefficient. Measurements of benefits are thus required. The alternative would be to set market prices and to compensate farmers for income forgone in choosing techniques/product mixes which retain environmental benefits. Since there is no profit (but no loss) involved in conservation, some method of enforcing conservation (such as the WLCA) is necessary. In this latter case again, there would be no need to measure conservation benefits since the surplus is assigned to society. This is the enforced minimum compensation variant discussed above.

My conclusion is that at least it is not obvious that environmental protection, in the limited way it has been defined, requires an assessment of its social value in a situation where agriculture is subsidised. With a free market and no subsidies, optimal decision-making clearly requires an assessment of environmental benefits, both marginal and total, although these valuations may be implied from actions that society is making through the democratic process to sanction support and pay for it. But we do not have a free market. The situation is rather, in my judgement, somewhere between cases B(1) and B(2). We do not therefore need to cost environmental damage in order to decide whether to contain or eliminate it. We do of course need to know what sorts of agricultural technology and structure will protect the environment in any event, and what sort of policy package can bring about this structure. But as a research agenda, this is a practical one.

Notes

1. The process has been described and analysed in J. K. Bowers and P. Cheshire, *Agriculture, the Countryside and Land-Use* (London: Methuen, 1983). For the loss of semi-natural habitat see Nature Conservancy Council, *Nature Conservation in Great Britain* (London, 1984). For other aspects of social costs, see Countryside Commission *New Agricultural Landscapes: Issues, Objectives and Action* (London, 1977).
2. In the current state of knowledge this appears to be the case for many types of semi-natural habitat which are effectively destroyed by agricultural change. If, for example, species-rich grassland, ancient woodland, or heather-moorland are brought under the plough, then the time-scale in which they can be restored is very long. However, the possibility of technical progress in habitat creation should not be discounted. Species extinction is the extreme case, where irreversibility is, with current knowledge, absolute, and the social benefits of species diversity completely obscure. A case can be made for the view that environmental pollution is also an irreversible process.
3. A substantial proportion of compensation payments made under the Act are payments in lieu of agricultural subsidies. See J. K. Bowers, 'Compensation payments under the Wildlife and Countryside Act', Appendix 11 of House of Commons Session 1984–5. This first Report from the Environment Committee. *Operation and Effectiveness of Part II of the Wildlife and Countryside Act*, vol. II, pp. 326–8.
4. NCC in fact rarely exercise these powers because of a strong belief in the need for voluntary agreement. They presumably recognise problems of policing where conservation is dependent on a continuation of some form of agriculture.
5. For a survey of the literature see Anthony C. Fisher, *Resource and Environmental Economics*, Cambridge Surveys of Economic Literature (Cambridge: 1981) ch. 5.
6. For an appraisal, see J. K. Bowers and C. A. Nash, 'Environmental Effects in Cost-Benefit Analysis: a review', in R. K. Turner (ed.), *Environmental Economics Issues: Sustainability, Resource Conservation and Pollution Control*, Economic and Social Research Council, 1986, forthcoming.
7. Strictly speaking, such observations would give insight only to personal social welfare functions. Aggregation remains problematical under the Arrow impossibility theorem, unless one accepts the views of the new social contract theorists that, when determined in the correct manner, personal SWF's will be identical. See, for example, J. C. Harsanyi, 'Cardinal Welfare, Individualistic Ethos and Interpersonal Comparisons of Utility', *Journal of Political Economy*, 63 (1955), pp. 309–21.
8. Bowers and Cheshire, *Agriculture, the Countryside and Land-Use*, ch. 6.
9. Bowers and Cheshire, ch. 7.

11 Policies towards Natural Resources and Investment in International Trade

Alistair Ulph and David Ulph

INTRODUCTION

In his book *The Economics of Natural Resources*, Richard Lecomber analysed carefully the many reasons why actual markets may be inadequate for allocating exhaustible natural resources over time – for example, common property problems, imperfect competition, absence of markets for dealing with risk. Central to the book, however, is the notion that natural resources are assets, and that a key source of biases in the rate of resource utilisation will be distortions in asset markets – markets for translating forgone consumption today into assets such as physical or human capital to produce higher consumption in the future.

Important though this message is, Richard's book, like much of the resources literature of the 1970s (for example, Dasgupta and Heal, 1979), treats the depletion problem from the perspective of a closed economy. For some questions such a perspective is useful, but since the publication of *The Economics of Natural Resources*, there has been increasing attention paid to the fact that natural resources (predominantly energy resources such as oil, and, of growing importance, coal and gas) are internationally traded. This awareness reflects partly the fact that endowments of some natural resources are distributed geographically quite asymmetrically. More importantly it arises from the realisation that this asymmetry is often accompanied by another asymmetry in endowments of other forms of assets – physical capital and technical skills. As a result, some of the issues in the North–South debate are posed in terms of trade between resource-rich capital-poor countries of the South and the resource-poor, capital-rich countries of the North.

This North–South perspective adds a crucial new dimension to the resource depletion problem – whose interests should be served in deciding on resource depletion rates, those of the resource exporters or those of the resource importers? Different patterns of resource depletion may have very different implications for the distribution of wealth between resource-rich and resource-poor countries, and since there is no world government to implement a wealth redistribution policy, the struggle over shares of world wealth will take the form of countries attempting to alter terms of trade in their favour. While Lecomber (p. 88) is, perhaps rightly, sceptical about the ability of individual producers and consumers to exert market power in resource markets, it is more probable that such power could be effectively exploited by governments via their distortionary trade policies.

While there is now a considerable literature on imperfect competition and international trade, what makes the analysis of the exploitation of market power in the context of exhaustible resources of particular interest is the crucial role that time plays in all exhaustible resource problems. As the conventional view emphasises, resources have to be used up now in order to be converted into other assets for production of future consumption. This means that resource exporters need to think not only about what they are getting now for their resources, but also about what they will get in the future. What gives this problem added bite is that the resource exporters may find it impossible to secure future consumption solely by investing in their domestic economies – they have to invest abroad. This means that resource importers can respond to attempts to distort current terms of trade in favour of resource exporters by affecting the future rate of return on surpluses invested abroad. Analysing the possibilities for the exploitation of market power by both resource importers and resource exporters is complicated by the fact that these are not isolated markets but highly interrelated. Thus the traditional analysis of exhaustible resource extraction emphasises the crucial role of interest rates on the extraction decisions, and hence resource prices. In turn there are two sources of influence of resource prices on interest rates. Firstly because capital and resources are both inputs to production, the demand for investment and hence the interest rate must be influenced by resource prices. Secondly the transfers of wealth between importers and exporters as resource prices change will, in general, alter the aggregate propensity to save and hence the supply of investible funds. Thus, in addition to the close interaction one would expect between markets for resources and other assets, there is the interaction due to attempts by traders to distort terms of trade in both markets.

All of this suggests a number of questions that need to be answered: recognising that changing resource prices may affect returns to capital – how ought resource exporters to take account of this in their pricing policies? If resource importers can affect the rate of return on funds invested by resource exporters overseas, should they seek to do so, and if so in what direction? How do the answers to these questions change if we consider them simultaneously – that is, what policies should resource importers and resource exporters pursue if resource exporters are distorting the resource market while resource importers are distorting the capital market?

Developments in the resource economics literature since the late 1970s have involved the attempt by economists to build models which could throw some light on such issues, and in this paper we shall sketch out a simple model which shows what kind of analysis one needs to conduct, and the kind of results that emerge. It should be clear from the foregoing discussion that what is needed to answer the questions posed is a dynamic general equilibrium model of trade with multiple distortions, and it should be equally clear that it would be difficult to build such a model at any reasonable level of generality and expect to use it to answer unambiguously all the questions posed. Inevitably, the models presented here are going to seem rather special, and they should be thought of as first steps in a complicated programme of research, rather than as the end product of such a programme. In particular, the models will focus on a single resource exporter and a single resource importer, so we shall have nothing to say about competition between different resource exporters, or between different resource importers; we shall also assume that there are perfect future markets, although some of the concerns of resource exporters probably arise precisely from the absence of mechanisms for making future commitments. Both these factors complicate the analysis substantially, and for a survey which pays more attention to these issues, see Lewis and Ulph (1985).

The structure of this paper is as follows. The next section provides a very brief literature survey, and in the third section we spell out the basic model to be used in this paper. We then use the model to ask how should resource exporters modify their policies if resource prices affect rates of return on capital. The penultimate section turns to the question of the desirability of resource importers affecting rates of return on funds invested abroad, while in the final section we put both parts together to look at a model with distortions in both resource and capital markets. To give a sense of concreteness to the analysis, we shall throughout refer to the resource as oil, although we do not pretend that the analysis to follow is a realistic description of the operation of the oil market.

A BRIEF LITERATURE SURVEY

As already noted, to address the issues we are interested in, what is required is a fully specified general equilibrium model of trade involving both resources and capital which takes account of all the interactions between these markets – that is, higher oil prices will affect the demand for physical capital since both capital and oil are inputs in the production process, while changes in interest rates will affect the optimal rate of depletion of oil. Earlier analyses had missed out important effects by either ignoring the possibility of trade in capital (for example, Kemp and Long, 1980; Vousden, 1974), by considering only a single country (for example, Aarrestad, 1978; Dasgupta *et al.*, 1978), or by taking a static framework (Calvo and Findlay, 1978; Chichilnisky, 1981).

The earliest fully specified models of trade in resources and capital were the papers by Chiarella (1980) and Dixit (1981). The former paper presented an infinite horizon model with savings behaviour characterised by optimisation; however, it was concerned primarily with characterising the notion of competitive equilibrium in such a model, and did not address trade policy issues. Dixit's paper was the first to focus on trade policy in a properly specified dynamic general equilibrium trade model. His model is a two-period one, which allows for many resource importing and exporting countries, but looks at trade policy in terms of deviations from a competitive equilibrium. An important theme of Dixit's paper is that different resource exporters (or importers) may have quite different attitudes to say, an export tax on oil, because the resulting effects on other (intertemporal) prices may affect their welfare in different ways (due to differences in their level of industrialisation, for example). However, in Dixit's model, saving behaviour is not explicitly derived from intertemporal utility maximisation.

Following on from Dixit's paper were two papers which tried to derive more explicit trade policy recommendations. In Marion and Svensson's paper (1983), the Dixit paper was specialised to just two countries, one a resource importer and one a resource exporter, with quite strong assumptions on production (for example, the resource/exporter can produce only the resource). They carried out quite detailed trade policy analysis for the resource importing country; however, they did so under the assumption that oil prices were fixed, so that policy was directed primarily to affecting the supply of financial capital from the surpluses earned by the resource exporter. They found that the resource importer would benefit from taxing interest payments on funds invested by the resource exporter in the resource importing country. This confirms simple partial analysis; if the elasticity of supply of net saving to an oil importing country is positive, then taxing interest payments should drive down the world interest rate leading to welfare losses for the net creditor and welfare gains to the debtor.

However, this does not allow for the full general equilibrium effects of trade policies such as an interest rate tax. Standard arguments from the resource depletion literature suggest that by driving down the world interest rate the interest rate tax will lead to resource exporters investing in resources-in-the-ground thus driving up the current oil price, though lowering future oil prices. This makes the welfare impact on the resource importer ambiguous. As van Wijnbergen (1983) has shown in extending the Marion and Svensson analysis to allow for endogenous oil price determination, the application of recent work on optimal tariffs with complementarity shows that it may sometimes be in the interests of the resource importers to subsidise interest rates, even if they are initially net debtors.

The problem with this analysis is that it rests on the assumption that oil prices are determined in competitive markets. Now, of course, there are questions about how far OPEC has been responsible for raising oil prices (for example, Griffin and Teece, 1982). But it seems incongruous in an analysis which takes seriously the possibility of oil importers collectively exercising market power in the capital market, not also to admit the possibility that the resource exporters also exercise market power in the resource market.

In a related paper (Ulph and Ulph, 1981) we explored some of the issues of modelling imperfect competition in the oil and capital markets, when each side is optimising given its perceived demand curve. However, that paper used infinite horizon models, and it was difficult to do more than characterise the nature of the various equilibria (assuming different combinations of market power in the two markets). In this paper we adopt the two-period framework common to Dixit, Marion and Svensson and van Wijnbergen. We use this model to examine optimal policies for a resource exporter, then, in a later section we derive the Marion and Svensson and van Wijnbergen results, but with some generalisations; finally we shall reexamine the arguments for an interest rate tax by the resource importing country, but allowing for oil prices to be determined endogenously by a monopoly supplier of oil.

THE MODEL

As we emphasised in the introduction, there is a balance between building a model sufficiently rich to capture all the interesting interactions between oil and capital markets and tractability in terms of deriving specific policy conclusions, and we have employed about the simplest model capable of demonstrating the interaction effects of interest. We use the two-good, two-country model employed by Marion and Svensson (1983), van Wijnbergen (1983) and Ulph and Ulph (1981), among others. The two goods are oil, an exhaustible resource, and a produced good, which can be used for either consumption or investment. Of the two countries, the resource importer, called Industria, is assumed to have no oil, but is capable of producing the other good using oil and capital (labour can be though of as entering the model in uninteresting ways). To focus on the need for the resource exporter, called Arabia, to invest abroad, we make an extreme assumption of limited domestic absorption capacity by supposing that while Arabia is endowed with the world's supply of oil, for reasons of topography or whatever it is completely incapable, now and in the future, of producing the other good, so must look to foreign trade and investment for its current and future consumption. The production of oil will require the produced good as inputs. Finally we restrict ourselves to only two time periods, and assume that stocks of oil are sufficiently small that exhaustion will always take place. We now spell out the details assuming no distortions in trade.

Technology in Industria is represented by the two production functions

$$X_1 = F_1(M_1)$$
$$X_2 = F_2(M_2, I) \tag{1}$$

where X_t is output in period t, M_t is input of oil in period t, I is the addition to the initial capital stock made in period 1 and available for use in period 2 (the level of the initial capital stock is implicit in the forms of F_1 and F_2).

We take the spot price of output in each period to be 1, and the spot (world) prices of oil to be q_1 and q_2 respectively and denote by δ the world discount factor. From all this we derive the *inverse* demand functions for oil in Industria as

$$q_1(M_1) \equiv F_{1M}(M_1) \tag{2}$$

$$q_2(M_2, \delta) \equiv F_{2M}(M_2, I(\delta, M_2)) \tag{3}$$

where in (3) we employ the investment demand function $I(\delta, M_2)$ defined by the condition

$$\delta F_{2I}(M_2, I(\delta, M_2)) \equiv 1 \tag{4}$$

From (2) and (3) we can also derive the marginal revenue functions

$$MR_1(M_1) \equiv \frac{d}{dM_1}(M_1 q_1)(M_1))$$
$$MR_2(M_2 \delta) \equiv \frac{\partial}{\partial M_2}(M_2 q_2(M_2, \delta)) \tag{5}$$

To complete the specification of Industria's behaviour, we need to say something about their choice of present and future consumption, and we do this in two (equivalent) ways. Directly, we assume that consumers in Industria can be represented by a single household which lives for two periods with life-time utility function $U(C_1, C_2)$. Letting W denote Industria's life-time wealth, where

$$W = F_1(M_1) + \delta F_2(M_2, I) - q_1 M_1 - \delta q_2 M_2 - I) \tag{6}$$

then maximisation of U subject to

$$C_1 + \delta C_2 \leq W$$

will lead to uncompensated demand functions for consumption in each period $C_1(\delta, W)$, $C_2(\delta, W)$. Alternatively, letting $E(1, \delta, U)$ represent Industria's expenditure function, we can derive *compensated* consumption demand functions $D_1(\delta, U)$, $D_2(\delta, U)$ for periods 1 and 2.

Turn now to Arabia. There is a stock of oil S and to extract each unit of oil requires the input of k units of the produced good, where k is independent of both the current stock of oil and flow rate of extraction. Under no trade distortions, oil depletion policy in Arabia will satisfy the usual Hotelling condition.

$$q_1 - k = \delta(q_2 - k) \tag{7}$$

Finally, we adopt a similar approach to modelling consumption preferences in Arabia as we applied to Industria. Let

$$Z = (q_1 - k)M_1 + \delta(q_2 - k)M_2 \tag{8}$$

denote Arabia's wealth (in the no distortion case), and assuming that Arabia has a utility function $V(X_1, X_2)$ for current and future consumption, we would derive uncompensated consumption demand functions $X_1(\delta, Z)$, $X_2(\delta, Z)$. Alternatively, we can employ the compensated demands, $Y_1(\delta, V)$, $Y_2(\delta, V)$.

We can now put all this together. A no-distortion trade equilibrium, or simply a competitive equilibrium, consists of prices δ, q_1, q_2, or equivalently δ, M_1, M_2, that satisfy

$$C_1(\delta, W) + X_1(\delta, Z) + I(\delta, M_2) + kM_1 = F_1(M_1) \tag{9}$$

$$C_2(\delta, W) + X_2(\delta, Z) + kM_2 = F_2(M_2, I(\delta, M_2)) \tag{10}$$

$$q_1(M_2) - k = \delta(q_2(M_2\delta) - k) \tag{11}$$

$$M_1 + (M_2) - S \tag{12}$$

$$Z = (q_1(M_1) - k)M_1 + \delta(q_2(M_2, \delta) - k))M_2 \tag{13}$$

Equations (9) to (13) determine δ, M_1, M_2, Z, W. (9) and (10) are the equations for clearing the goods markets in periods 1 and 2; (11) and (12) are the equations for determining oil market equilibrium while (13) is the budget condition for Arabia (the corresponding equation for Industria (6) is redundant by Walras Law).

If there were mechanisms for international lump-sum wealth transfers then we could also characterise the utility possibility frontier for the world economy implicitly as follows:

$$D_1(\delta, U) + Y_1(\delta, V) + I(\delta, M_2) + kM_1 = F_1(M_1) \tag{14}$$

$$D_2(\delta, U) + Y_2(\delta, V) + kM_2 = F_2(M_2, I(\delta, M_2)) \tag{15}$$

$$q_2(M_2) - k = \delta(q_1(M_2, \delta) - k) \tag{16}$$

$$M_1 + M_2 = S \tag{17}$$

Equations (14) to (17) will allow us to solve for δ, M_1, M_2 and U for any value of V, and so by varying V we could map out the utility possibility frontier for the world economy (using the equivalence between Pareto efficient allocations and competitive equilibria).

Of course, there is no world government to implement lump-sum transfers between countries, yet the two countries will have a strong incentive to alter the distribution of wealth in their favour by exploiting their market power. What policies they might employ to do this, and whether they will in fact succeed will be discussed in the following sections.

In all this discussion we need to know the properties of the demand function for oil and capital, and the details can be found in Appendix A. Essentially these amount to guaranteeing that the demand functions are well behaved – that is, they display negative own-price effects and diminishing marginal revenue. However, we have emphasised the importance of one form of interaction between the oil and capital market and that is that these demands are interrelated, so we need to say something about the cross-price effect. Neither theory nor empirical evidence gives any guidance on what sign these cross-price effects should take, and in our general model we shall leave them unsigned. One special case that has been used, for example, by van Wijnbergen (1983), is what we call the *separable case*, where the cross-price effects are assumed to be zero, and at various stages in the subsequent analysis we shall invoke the separability assumption to show how it simplifies the results one is able to derive.

EXERCISING MARKET POWER BY ARABIA

The question we focus on here is what should Arabia's policy be if it tries to influence terms of trade in its favour, and in particular how should policy differ from the usual 'partial' analysis of oil pricing. We can obtain the usual partial analysis by assuming that Arabia acts as what we called elsewhere (Ulph and Ulph, 1981) a 'naïve monopolist', that is, it acts as a price-taker in the capital market, so it takes δ as given.

With δ taken as given Arabia's problem is to choose X_1, X_2, M_1, M_2 to maximise $V(X_1, X_2)$ subject to

$$X_1 + \delta X_2 = M_1(q_1(M_1 - k) + \delta M_2(q_2(M_2, \delta) - k)$$

and

$$M_1 + M_2 = S$$

As is well known, with δ given, we can immediately separate Arabia's accumulation decision:

Choose X_1, X_2 to max $V(X_1, X_2)$ subject to

$$X_1 + \delta(X_2) = Z$$

from its production decision:

Choose M_1, M_2 to maximise

$$Z = M_1(q_1(M_1) - k) + \delta M_2(q_2(M_2, \delta) - k) \text{ subject to}$$

$$M_1 + M_2 = S \tag{18}$$

The solution of (18) is the usual Hotelling condition

$$MR_1(M_1) - k = \delta(MR_2(M_2, \delta) - k) \tag{19}$$

The determination of full equilibrium then is given by replacing the competitive supply condition (11) with (19) and solving (9), (10), (12), (13) and (19).

Since (19) is part of a system of general equilibrium equations, the comparison of the monopoly equilibrium with the competition equilibrium is considerably more complex. In the first place there will typically be a different value of δ in the competitive equilibrium and in the monopoly equilibrium. Moreover, in general the demand (and hence marginal revenue) curves for oil will depend on δ, and hence will be shifted by the general equilibrium effects of oil prices on the capital market. Finally these demand and marginal revenue curves are full general equilibrium demand curves: thus, one might think of the demand for oil as depending on oil prices, other factor prices and output; the effect of changes in oil prices on output is assumed to be taken account of by Arabia. Of course the second effect can be ignored if we impose the *separability assumption* – then the second period marginal revenue curve can be thought of as a simple partial equilibrium curve, independent of other aspects of the economy. However, the first effect will still remain.

Now Arabia is being naïve in two, slightly different, respects. First it is acting as if there was no effect from its oil pricing policy on other prices (in particular δ) in the economy. This implies in particular that if it pursues the policy implicit in (19) there is no guarantee that it will actually be better off than in the competitive equilibrium. Second, as a consequence of its price-taking behaviour in the capital market, Arabia is acting only in the oil market, and not simultaneously in the oil and capital markets. We can deal with these two points separately. Suppose now that we have what we shall call a *restricted monopolist*. By this we shall mean that Arabia recognises that its operations in the oil market have implications for prices elsewhere in the economy, but it restricts itself only to operations in the oil market, so there is some limitation on the policy instruments available to it. (This is meant to reflect the fact that in a world where each of our two countries will be a block of countries, it may be possible for a coalition of countries to agree policy on only a rather small subset of all possible economic policy instruments.) In effect then, the move from naive monopoly to restricted monopoly is like the move from Nash equilibrium to Stackelberg equilibrium: instead of taking the policy of Industria (that is, δ) as given, Arabia is taking as given the schedule relating Industria's choice of δ to its own policy choice. What policy would a restricted monopolist pursue?

Rather than thinking of oil prices as Arabia's policy instruments, we shall take the policy instrument available to Arabia as first period oil production M_1. For any value of M_1 we can determine M_2, δ, V and W from

$$C_1(\delta, W) + Y_1(\delta, V) + I(\delta, M_2) + kM_1 = F_1(M_1) \tag{20}$$

$$C_2(\delta, W) + Y_2(\delta, V) + kM_2 = F_2(M_2, I(\delta, M_2)) \tag{21}$$

$$M_1 + M_2 = S \tag{22}$$

$$W = F_1(M_1) - I(\delta, M_2) + \delta F_2(M_2, I(\delta, M_2)) -$$
$$- q_1(M_1)M_1 - \delta q_2(M_2, \delta)M_2 \qquad (23)$$

we can then ask what value of M_1 will lead to the maximum value of V as determined by (20)–(23), and we show in Appendix B that the optimal depletion policy for Arabia is now characterised by the rule

$$(MR_1 - k) - \delta(MR_2 - k) = \delta'[F_2 - C_2 - q_2M_2] - \delta'\delta M_2 q_{2\delta} \qquad (24)$$

where δ' is the general equilibrium effect of a change in M_1 on the discount rate, and $q_{2\delta}$ is the cross-price effect of a change in the discount rate on the (inverse) demand for oil.

This is a rather nice result. It tells us that if $\delta' = 0$, so that changing oil depletion policy has no effect (in the general equilibrium sense) on the discount rate, then the RHS of (24) will be 0, and the 'naïve' Hotelling rule is optimal. Deviations from that rule are only required if $\delta' \neq 0$, and will reflect two considerations. The first term reflects the 'wealth effect' that changes in δ have on Arabia, since $(F_2 - C_2 - q_2M_2)$ is the amount of resources transferred from Industria to Arabia in the second period; the second term of on the RHS of (24) reflects the effect of variations in δ on the demand for second period of oil. Under the separability assumption, this term would vanish for second period oil. To give the problem some interest, we assume that $F_2 - C_2 - q_2M_2$ is positive, so Arabia is lending to Industria in period *1*, but there is nothing in our model which would allow us to sign δ' or $q_{2\delta}$ unambiguously. Nevertheless (24) is useful in that it tells us which features are likely to be crucial in determining the direction and extent to which oil pricing should deviate from the usual partial analysis.

The pricing rule in (24) is for a *restricted monopolist*, one who recognises that what he does to oil prices will affect other prices (in particular rates of return on capital) in the world economy and therefore needs to take that into account when he sets oil prices. However, he does not draw the other conclusion, that if he can influence rates of return *indirectly* through oil prices, then he should also seek to offset any adverse effects on rates of return by also acting directly on the capital market. Thus if the move from competitive to monopolistic oil prices (in the partial model) caused rates of return to fall, harming the oil exporter, he can offset this not just by moderating his oil depletion policy, but also by moderating his overseas investment policy. Put more simply, in our model, the resource exporter is also the sole exporter of savings, so he has monopoly power in the market for both oil and funds, and should seek to exploit his power in *both* markets simultaneously. This could be done by, for example, taxing the flow of interest payments coming into Arabia; this would discourage lending abroad, and hopefully drive up the world rate of return. A monopolist who operates simultaneously in the oil and international capital markets we call a *full monopolist*, and we conclude this section by looking briefly at how the full monopolist policy differs from the naïve and restricted monopolist.

Suppose then that δ denotes the discount rate employed by Industria and let $\varrho = \delta + \tau$ denote the discount rate used in Arabia, where τ captures the distortion imposed by Arabia taxing interest payments made by Industria. Then the policy instruments for Arabia are now M_1 and τ and we can simply modify equations (20) and (21) by replacing $Y_1(\delta, V)$, $Y_2(\delta, V)$ with $Y_1(\varrho, V)$ and $Y_2(\varrho, V)$ respectively. Call the modified equations (20)' and (21)', then for any choice of M_1 and τ (20)', (21)' (22) and (23) determine M_2, δ, V and W, so we can now ask which values of M_1 and τ maximise V. Appendix B shows that the optimal choice of τ and M_1 can be characterised as follows. (For simplicity we confine ourselves to the case where the separability assumption is imposed).

The optimal distortion in the capital market, τ, is given (implicitly) by

$$\tau \left[\frac{1}{\delta\delta'} - D_{2\delta} \right] = [F_2 - q_2 M_2 - C_2][1 + \tau C_{2w}] \tag{25}$$

where δ' is now the slope of the inverse demand function for capital (where the 'price' is the discount factor, and so $\delta' > 0$), and $D_{2\delta}$ is the effect of an increase in δ on the compensated demand for second period competition in Industria, and therefore $D_{2\delta}$ is negative. Since we are considering the case where $F_2 - q_2 M_2 - C_2 > 0$, (25) could only yield a negative value for τ if we had $\tau < -1/C_{2w} < -1$, which would make $\varrho < 0$, and this seems implausible; so (25) says that for plausible cases we must have $\tau > 0$, so that at the optimum Arabia would tax interest payments earned on investments abroad.

The rule characterising optimal depletion in the oil market now becomes

$$(MR_1 - k) - (\delta + \tau)(MR_2 - k) = \tau[(1 - \delta C_{2w}) \\ (q_2 - MR_2) \\ + C_{2w}(q_1 - MR_1)] \tag{26}$$

From the reasonable supposition that $0 < C_{2w} < 1$, $0 < \delta < 1$, (26) tells us that the optimal departure from the naïve Hotelling rule for oil depletion (using Arabia's discount factor to discount oil wealth), will involve having marginal revenue *higher* in the final period than the naïve rule would suggest (even allowing for the fact that Arabia is using a higher discount factor than in the naïve case). This has the rather important implication that once one assumes that Arabia takes full account of the interactions between the oil and capital markets, and *acts* in all markets, we get a pricing rule which would have the effect of *raising* prices in the first period (relative to the partial Hotelling rule).

EXERCISING MARKET POWER BY INDUSTRIA

In the previous section we gave a fairly full analysis of the exercise of market power by resource exporters, given various assumptions about how they take account of the link between resource and capital markets. We turn now to Industria. For reasons of space we shall not duplicate all the analysis of the previous section, but focus on only the case of Industria acting as a naïve monopsonist in the market for funds (that is, it takes as given world oil prices), and as a restricted monopsonist in the market for funds (where it takes account of the fact that its policies in the capital market will affect the price it pays for oil). In both cases oil prices will be determined competitively. The first case corresponds to the analysis conducted by Marion and Svensson (1983), the second to the analysis by van Wijnbergen (1983). Our model is rather more general then van Wijnbergen's, in that we do not impose the separability assumption.

We begin with the Marion and Svensson analysis or, in our terminology, the naïve monopsonist in the market for international capital. Let $p = \delta + \tau$ denote the discount factor employed by Arabia; then Arabia chooses X_1, X_2, M_1, M_2 to maximise $V(X_1, X_2)$ subject to $X_1 + \varrho X_2 = M_1(q_1 - k) + \varrho M_2(q_2 - k)$, and $M_1 + M_2 = S$, where ϱ, q_1, q_2 are taken as given; this will yield oil supply functions, and more importantly, a supply of investible funds function $L = L(\varrho, q_1, q_2)$, where L denotes the amount of capital Arabia is prepared to lend Industria in period 1. Let us say something briefly about $L(\varrho, q_1, q_2)$. For values of ϱ for which $(q_1 - k) > \varrho(q_2 - k)$, Arabia in maximising oil wealth will set $M_1 = S$, $M_2 = 0$, so that throughout this range of values of ϱ, oil wealth is independent of ϱ and is earned all in the first period. Clearly for such ϱ, $L > 0$. Moreover, assuming that the substitution effect dominates the wealth effect, we will have $\frac{\delta L}{\delta \varrho} < 0$;

clearly when $(q_1 - k) < \varrho(q_2 - k)$, we must have $L < 0$, and by choosing M_1 and M_2 so that Arabia consumes its income in both periods where $(q_1 - k) = \varrho(q_2 - k)$, we shall think of L falling smoothly to 0 as ϱ rises to the breakeven level. For economy of notation, since Industria also takes q_1, q_2 as given we shall henceforth suppress the dependency of $L(\cdot)$ on q_1 and q_2. It will be more useful in what follows to work with the function $B(\varrho) = L(\varrho)/\varrho$. $B(\varrho)$ denotes what Industria has to repay Arabia in period 2 give that it borrows $L(\varrho)$ in period 1.

To complete the specification of Industria's problem, let

$$\psi_1 = \max_{M_1} F(M_1) - q_1 M_1, \quad \psi_2(I) = \max F_2(M_2, I) - q_2 M_2$$

denote the restricted profit functions for Industria given oil prices q_1, q_2 and investment level I, where, again, for notational simplicity the dependence of ψ_1 and ψ_2 on q_1 and q_2 respectively has been suppressed. Then with Industria acting competitively in the oil market, but facing a lending schedule that responds to the discount factor, Industria's problem can be formulated as the choice of C_1, C_2 I, and ϱ to maximise $U(C_1, C_2)$ subject to

$$C_1 + I = \psi_1 + \varrho B(\varrho) \tag{27}$$

$$C_2 = \psi_2(I) - B(\varrho) \tag{28}$$

Recalling that δ is the discount factor employed domestically by Industria the first order conditions are readily shown to be

$$\frac{\frac{\delta u}{\delta C_2}}{\frac{\delta u}{\delta C_1}} = \delta = \frac{1}{\psi_2}(I) \tag{29}$$

$$\delta = \varrho + \frac{B(\varrho)}{B'(\varrho)} \tag{30}$$

Equation (29) expresses the usual equality between consumption and production rates of interest at an optimum in Industria, while (30) is the condition for the optimal tax on investible funds. Assuming as we have throughout, that $B(\varrho) > 0$ at the optimum, then $B'(\varrho) < 0$ guarantees that Industria faces a lower discount rate than Arabia –

that is, Industria has a witholding tax on interest payments to Arabia. As in the previous section, the naïve monopsony model simply confirms the usual partial argument in favour of an interest rate tax.

We turn now to the restricted monopsony model, essentially that of van Wijnbergen (1983). If q_1 and q_2 were genuinely independent of ϱ, then starting from a solution where both M_1 and M_2 are positive small variations in ϱ would induce discontinuous changes in M_1 and M_2 as Arabia dumped all its oil in one period or another. Industria would therefore quickly learn that oil prices would have to adjust following any change in ϱ, and in the restricted monopsony case Industria does indeed recognise this interdependence, though it continues to use interest rate taxes as its sole instrument of policy. Would it now be desirable to tax interest payment to Arabia?

To answer this we set up our model in a way that is the exact analogue of that employed for the restricted monopolist in oil. It will be simplest to do this using the separability assumption of production. Thus we have

$$D_1(\varrho - \tau, U) + X_1(\varrho, z) + I(\varrho - \tau) + kM_1 = F_1(M_1) \tag{31}$$

$$D_2(\varrho - \tau, U) + X_2(\varrho, z) + kM_2 = F_2(M_2, I(\varrho - \tau)) \tag{32}$$

$$M_1 + M_2 = S \tag{33}$$

$$Z = (q_1(M_1) - k) M_1 + \varrho(q_2(M_2) - k)M_2 \tag{34}$$

$$q_1(M_1) - k = \varrho(q_2(M_2) - k) \tag{35}$$

For any given value of τ we can solve (31)–(35) for ϱ, U, Z, M_1, M_2, and, in line with the rest of the literature in this area we do not ask what is the optimal value of τ, but rather what would be the optimal direction for moving from a system of no capital market distortion; and we ask whether a small tax on interest payment would cause welfare in Industria to rise or fall. If we let ΔU denote the effect on Industria's welfare of a small tax on interest payments, then we show in Appendix B that

$$\Delta U = p' \left\{ X_2 - (q_2 - k)M_2 \right) + \frac{q_2 - k}{q_1' + \varrho q_2'} \left[q_1 - MR_1 \right] - \varrho(q_2 - MR_2) \right\} \tag{36}$$

Assuming that $\varrho' > 0$ the first term on the RHS of (36) is just the term $B(\varrho)$ in equation (30) – so as long as Arabia is a lender to Industria in period 1, this term will make it desirable for Industria to impose the interest rate tax. The second term comprises three factors; $q_2 - k$ is clearly non-negative, while, given our assumptions, the denominator $q_1' + \varrho q_2'$ will be negative; the term $(q_1 - MR_1) - \varrho(q_2 - MR_2)$, which we shall denote as H, can be written as $q_1/\varepsilon_1 - \varrho q_2/\varepsilon_2$ where ε_1 and ε_2 are the absolute values of the own price elasticities of oil demand in the two periods. As is well known (Stiglitz, 1976), there will be one special case where H is zero – when there are constant elasticities of demand ($\varepsilon_1 = \varepsilon_2 = \varepsilon$) and zero cost of production of oil (so the competitive rule is $q_1 = \varrho q_2$). In general, for competitive oil markets H can be written as $k(1 - \varrho)/\varepsilon_1 + \varrho q_2(1/\varepsilon_1 - 1/\varepsilon_2)$, so if the elasticities of demand are roughly equal, we would expect H to be positive. However, the sign of H must be presumed to be ambiguous in general. The upshot is that the second term in the bracket in the RHS of (36) can take either sign, but will be negative if the oil demand elasticities turn out to be equal in the two periods.

Thus, as van Wijnbergen, 1983 showed, once Industria takes account of the effect of driving down the world interest rate on the price of oil, there is no longer a presumption in favour of taxing interest payments – it could pay to *subsidise* them.

It is possible to extend the analysis for Industria to consider naïve and restricted monopsony behaviour in the oil market, and the exercise of full monopsony power in the oil and capital markets. However, lack of space prevents us covering this – for further analysis see Ulph and Ulph (1981) and Lewis and Ulph (1985). To complete this paper, we want to turn to what we believe to be the more interesting question, and one not usually addressed – the analysis of equilibrium when both countries seek to exercise market power.

EXERCISE OF MARKET POWER BY BOTH COUNTRIES

Modelling the simultaneous exercise of market power by Industria and Arabia is a rather tricky matter. Recall that in the full monopoly case, we said that giving Arabia power to affect the world price of oil and the world discount rate gave it effective control over Industria's investment and consumption policies. Clearly if Industria does not passively allow Arabia to do this, we have to say what each country believes the response of its rival will be to its policies. Traditionally, this involves making one of two sets of assumptions. The first is that each country takes as *given* the policy instruments of its rival (that is, it assumes no retaliation); in game theoretic terms, the countries act in a Nash fashion. Each country would thus take as given the *tariffs* set by the other country (if it took the world *prices* set by its rival it would be acting competitively) and we would look for a equilibrium in tariff rates. The other approach often found is to make one player *anticipate* the response of its trading rivals, so that, in game theoretic terms, one country acts as a Stackelberg leader. These distinctions between Nash and Stackelberg equilibrium are familiar from the industrial economics literature.

We shall round off this paper by giving a simple version of a Stackelberg model. Specifically, let us take the model of the previous section, in which Industria sought to exercise monopsony power in the capital market, and ask whether it will be desirable for Industria to impose an interest rate tax if Arabia is exercising monopoly power in the oil market. Thus we shall suppose that Arabia is acting like a *naïve monopolist* in the oil market – it takes as given the world discount rate, and sets oil prices according to the usual partial Hotelling rule for a monopolist. Industria acts as a *restricted monopsonist* in the capital market – it recognises that any interest rate tax it imposes will affect the price for oil it has to face, although now the rule for pricing oil will be the monopolistic one, not the competitive one. How does the existence of monopoly power in the oil market affect the analysis of the previous section on the desirability of Industria imposing a small tax or subsidy on interest payments to Arabia?

For simplicity, and lack of space, we confine attention again to the case of separability in production. The analysis then involves a simple modification of that carried out in the previous section. In equations (31)–(35), we replace the competitive oil pricing rule (35) with the naïve monopoly pricing rule

$$MR_1(M_1) - k = \varrho(MR_2(M_2) - k) \tag{37}$$

Then equations (31), (32), (33), (34) and (37) allow us to solve for ϱ, U, Z, M_1, M_2 for any value of τ. As in the previous section, we want to evaluate the effect on Industria's welfare, U, of introducing a small tax, on interest payments to Arabia. We show in Appendix B that the effect of Industria's welfare, Δu, can be expressed as

$$\Delta u = \varrho'\{(X_2 - (q_2 - k)M_2 \quad + \quad \frac{MR_2 - k}{MR_1' + \varrho MR_2}$$
$$[(q_1 - MR_1) - \varrho(q_2 - MR_2)]\} \tag{38}$$

By comparison with (36), we can see that the effect of switching from competitive to monopolistic oil markets is to change the factor multiplying H in the RHS bracket from $q_2 - k/q_1' + \varrho q_2'$ to $MR_2 - k/MR_1' + \varrho MR_2'$; given our assumptions on the nature of the factor demand equations, this change does not alter the fact that this factor will be negative. With monopolistic oil pricing the term H can be written as

$$H = \frac{k(1 - \varrho)}{\varepsilon_1^{-1}} + \varrho MR_2 \left[\frac{1}{\varepsilon_1^{-1}} - \frac{1}{\varepsilon_2^{-1}} \right]$$

which will be positive when the demand elasticities in the two periods differ only slightly. The broad qualitative conclusions about the inability to determine the desirability of taxing or subsidising interest payments by Industria carries over from the case of competitive to monopolistic oil pricing; indeed for the Stiglitz case where $H = 0$ (38), (36) and (30) are essentially identical, and it is always desirable to tax interest payments.

Although the qualitative features of the rules (38) and (36) are similar, it is clearly possible that because of the different quantities involved in the terms in the RHS brackets of (36) and (38) one rule could recommend taxing interest rates, while the other recommended a subsidy. We have not found it possible to say in general whether competitive or monopolistic markets for oil are more likely to warrant subsidies or taxes on interest payments from Industria to Arabia.

CONCLUSIONS

Resource economists have long recognised that since natural resources are one of the many assets with which economies are endowed, any distortions in the market for assets will have important implications for the rate at which natural resources are exploited. This concern is reflected in the work of Richard Lecomber. However, this view sees the link between asset markets and resource markets as unidirectional – from asset markets to resource markets. Of course, resource economists were aware that in a general equilibrium sense resource depletion and the accumulation of other assets would be determined simultaneously, hence the importance attached to the degree of substitutability between resource and capital in the models of economic growth with exhaustible resources that were an important focus of the literature in the middle 1970s.

Recent developments in resource economics have given added emphasis to the link between resource and capital markets, in particular the analysis of models of international trade with exhaustible resources. For countries which are richly endowed with natural resources will often need to use transactions in international asset markets to transfer resource rents earned in one period into purchases of consumption or investment goods in other periods. Since resources are often concentrated geographically, attempts by countries to exploit market power in resource markets will have implications for asset markets, both because usual general equilibrium trade considerations suggest that distortions in resources markets will affect the interest rates at which international credit will be made available, and because, recognising this interaction, countries will take distorting actions in the market for credit as well.

This paper has used a simple two-country, two-period trade model to show how such interactions between the resource and capital markets can be modelled, and some of the implications that follow. We have emphasised an important distinction between the case where countries *recognise* that their actions in one market affect international prices (including interest rates) in other markets, and the case where countries not only recognise these spillover effects, but try to offset or exploit them by acting simultaneously in all markets. In the former case, we can characterise the rule that agents should follow when they recognise the spillover effect, and these rules usually involve a generalisation of the familiar partial equilibrium analyses that would be appropriate were such spillover effects ignored (or not present). But not surprisingly, given this general equilibria feature of the model, it is not easy to interpret these rules in a simple way, so that, as we have seen, the partial rule that it would pay a borrower to tax interest payments in order to drive down world interest rates can be reversed into an argument for subsidies once one takes into account the effect such a change in interest rates would have for resource prices. Results are stronger when we turn to the second case – when countries take action in all markets. As we have seen, this leads to the usual partial result being confirmed and indeed reinforced – so that a resource exporter who also supplies foreign credit should both tax interest payments and use a pricing rule for resources which is more monopolistic than the usual partial rule, that is, it leads to higher current prices at the expense of lower future price.

Much of the literature has focused on the actions of only one country, and in this paper we have sketched out one special case where countries simultaneously exert market power. Since each country acts in only one market the ambiguity of the first case discussed above remains.

The model we have used is very special, and it would be desirable to extend the analysis of Dixit (1981) to consider trading policies when there are many resource exporters and resource importers. Thus, we should like to consider what happens for example when some resource exporters are borrowers in early period and others are lenders. However, this remains for further work; what we hope to have done is to give an indication of the kind of work some resource economists have been doing since the publication of *The Economics of Natural Resources*, and the way this work deepens the need to study the link between resource and asset markets identified by Richard Lecomber.

APPENDIX A: PROPERTIES OF DEMAND FUNCTIONS FOR OIL AND CAPITAL

Assuming that F_1 is strictly concave, we have that q_{1M} is a decreasing function of M_1. Whether $MR_1(M_1)$ is a decreasing function of M_1 depends on the third derivative of F_1, about which we have little intuition, so we shall simply assume that $MR_1(M_1)$ is 'well-behaved' and is a strictly decreasing function of M_1.
For $q_2(M_2, \delta)$ we have

$$q_2(M_2, \delta) = F_{2M2}(M_2, I(\delta, M_2))$$

$$\delta F_{2I}[M_2, I(\delta M_2)] = 1$$

Dropping time subscripts, temporarily, we then have

$$q_M = F_{MM} + F_{MI}I_M \tag{A1}$$

$$\delta[F_{I_M} + F_{II}I_M] = 0 \tag{A2}$$

Solving out for I_M from (A1) we get

$$q_M = \frac{F_{MM}F_{II} - (F_{MI})^2}{F_{II}} \tag{A3}$$

So if F is strictly concave the numerator will be positive, the denominator negative, and so demand for oil in the second period will also be downward sloping.

To analyse the effect of the discount factor on the demand for second-period oil, we have

$$q_\delta = F_{MI} \cdot I_\delta \tag{A4}$$

$$F_I + \delta F_{II} \cdot I_\delta = 0 \tag{A5}$$

Since $F_I > 0$, $F_{II} < 0$ (A5) implies $I_\delta > 0$, so (A4) says that

$$\text{sign} = q_\delta = F_{MI} = \text{sign } I_M \text{ from (3).}$$

As in the first period case, the derivatives of $MR_2(M_2, \delta)$ involve third-order derivatives of F_2, and as in the first case, we shall assume that the signs of the marginal revenue partial derivatives are the same as of the inverse demand derivatives; that is, we assume that

$$\text{sign } \frac{\partial MR_2}{\partial M_2} = \text{sign} \frac{\partial q_2}{\partial M_2} = -ve$$

and

$$\text{sign } \frac{\partial M_2}{\partial \delta} = \text{sign} \frac{\partial q_2}{\partial \delta} = \text{sign } F_{MI}.$$

We have as yet said nothing about the sign of F_{MI}, for the simple reason that there are no restrictions from theory that can be imposed on this. As noted in the text, we shall usually leave this unsigned but shall on occasion invoke the *separability assumption* that $F_{MI} = 0$, so there are no cross-price effects between oil and capital demands.

APPENDIX B: DERIVATION OF RESULTS

(I) Restricted monopolist

Totally differentiate (20)–(23) with respect to M_1, and we obtain

$$C_{1\delta} \cdot \delta' + C_{1w}W' + Y_{1\delta}\delta' + Y_{1v}V' + I_\delta\delta' + I_M M_2' + k = F'_1 \quad \text{(B1)}$$

$$C_{2\delta} \cdot \delta' + C_{2w}W' + Y_{2\delta} \cdot \delta' + Y_{2v} \cdot V' + kM_2'$$

$$= F_{2M}M_2' + F_{2I}(I_\delta\delta' + I_M M2') \quad \text{(B2)}$$

$$1 + M_2' = 0 \quad \text{(B3)}$$

$$\begin{aligned}
W' = {} & F_1' - I_\delta \cdot \delta' - I_{M2} \cdot M_2' - MR_1 - \delta MR_2(M_2\delta)M_2' \\
& - \delta' q_2(M_2,\delta)\, M_2 - \delta M_2 q_{2\delta} \cdot \delta + \delta' + \delta F_{2M}M_2' \\
& + \delta' F_2(M_2\delta) + \delta F_{2I}(I_\delta \cdot \delta' + I_M \cdot M_2')
\end{aligned} \quad \text{(B4)}$$

Multiply (B2) by δ and add to (B1), use (B3) and the fact that $\delta F_{2I} = 1$, $C_{1w} + \delta C_{2w} = 1$, $C_{1\delta} + \delta C_{2\delta} + C_2 = 0$, $Y_{1\delta} + \delta Y_{2\delta} = 0$, $V_1(Y_{1v} + \delta Y_{2v}) = 1 \cdot$ where $V_1 = \partial v/\partial X_1$, $q_1 = F_1'$, $q_2 = F_{2M}$, to get

$$-C_2 \cdot \delta' + W' + V'/V_2 = (q_1 - k) - \delta(q_2 - k) \quad \text{(B5)}$$

Similarly, one can simplify (B4), insert the resulting expression for W' into (B5), and by collecting terms and noting that at an optimum $V' = 0$, we obtain the condition for optimal depletion by Arabia to be

$$(MR_1 - k) - \delta(MR_2 - k) = \delta'[F_2 - C_2 - q_2M_2] - \delta'\delta M_2 q_{2\delta} \quad \text{(B6)}$$

(II) Full monopolist

In the text we talked of Arabia using the natural instruments of an extraction policy and an interest tax. It is easier to characterise the optimum if we work directly in terms of quantities so we will think of Arabia choosing M_1 (and hence M_2 given the stock constraint) and the level of investment I. It will also simplify matters without losing too much of the essence of the problem if we impose the separability condition. Accordingly, we can now use the inverse investment demand equation $\delta = \delta(I)$, expressing the domestic discount rate in

Industria as a function of the level of investment (recalling that we are now imposing separability). Then given a choice of M_1 and I, Arabia knows that its current and future consumption are given by

$$X_1 = F_1(M_1) - kM_1 - I - C_1(\delta(I), W) \tag{B7}$$

$$X_2 = F_2(M_2, I) - kM_2 - C_2(\delta(I), W) \tag{B8}$$

where

$$W = F_1(M_1) + \delta(I)F_2(M_2, I) - q_1(M_1)M_1 \\ -\delta(I)q_2(M_2)M_2 - I \tag{B9}$$

Choosing M_1, I to maximise $V(X_1, X_2)$ would yield first order conditions

$$\frac{\partial V}{\partial X_1} \cdot \frac{\partial X_1}{\partial M_1} + \frac{\partial V}{\partial X_2} \cdot \frac{\partial X_2}{\partial M_1} = 0 \tag{B10}$$

$$\frac{\partial V}{\partial X_1} \cdot \frac{\partial X_1}{\partial I} + \frac{\partial V}{\partial X_2} \cdot \frac{\partial X_2}{\partial I} = 0 \tag{B11}$$

or

$$\frac{\partial X_1}{\partial M_1} + (\delta + \tau) \frac{\partial X_2}{\partial M_1} = 0 \tag{B12}$$

$$\frac{\partial X_1}{\partial I} + (\partial + \tau) \frac{\partial X_2}{\partial I} = 0 \tag{B13}$$

where $\delta + \tau = \partial V/\partial X_2 / \partial v / OX_2 = \varrho$ is the discount rate used by Arabia.

Carrying out the differentiations involved and simplifying yields

$$[MR_1 - k] - \delta[MR_2 - k] + \tau \frac{\partial X_2}{\partial M_1} = 0 \tag{B14}$$

$$- \delta'[F_2 - C_2 - q_2M_2] = \tau \frac{\partial X_2}{\partial I} = 0 \tag{B15}$$

where

$$\frac{\partial X_2}{\partial M_1} = - \left[\{q_2 - k\} + C_{2w}\{(q_1 - MR_1) - \delta(q_2 - MR_2)\}\right] \quad \text{(B16)}$$

$$\frac{\partial X_2}{\partial I} = 1/\delta - \delta' C_{2\delta} - \delta' C_{2w}\{F_2 - q_2 M_2\} \quad \text{(B17)}$$

and

$$\delta' = \frac{d\delta(I)}{dI} = \frac{-F_{2II}}{[F_{2I}]^2} > 0$$

in the market for funds, τ. From (B17), (B15) can be rewritten as

$$\tau \left[\frac{1}{\delta\delta'} - D_{2\delta} \right] = [F_2 - q_2 M_2 - C_2] [1 + \tau C_{2w}] \quad \text{(B18)}$$

Using (B16) we can rewrite (B14) as

$$\begin{aligned}
&(MR_1 - k) - (\delta + \tau)(MR_2 - k) \\
&= \tau[(1 - \delta C_{2w})(q_2 - MR_2) + C_{2w}(q_1 - MR_1)]
\end{aligned} \quad \text{(B19)}$$

Equations (B18) and (B19) correspond to equations (25) and (26) in the text.

(III) Restricted monopoly

Totally differentiate (31) and (32) to obtain

$$\begin{aligned}
&D_{1\delta}(\varrho' - 1) + D_{1u}U' + X_{1\varrho}\varrho' + X_{1z}Z' + I_\delta (\varrho' - 1) \\
&+ kM_1' = F_I'M_I
\end{aligned} \quad \text{(B20)}$$

$$\begin{aligned}
&D_{2\delta}(\varrho' - 1) + D_{2u}u' + X_{2\varrho}\varrho' + X_{2z}Z' + kM_2' \\
&= F_{2M}M_2' + F_{2I}I_\delta(\varrho' - 1)
\end{aligned} \quad \text{(B21)}$$

Multiply (B21) by ϱ and add to (B20), use the same simplification that was used in section B(I) and we obtain

$$\frac{u'}{u_1} - X_2 p' + z' = (q_1 - k)M_1' + \varrho[q_2 - k]M_2' \quad \text{(B22)}$$

From (33) $M_1' + M_2' = 0$ while differentiating (34) yields

$$Z' = (MR_1-k)M_1' + \varrho(MR_2-k)M_2' + \varrho'(q_2-k)M_2 \tag{B23}$$

Inserting (B23) into (B22) and rearranging we get

$$\frac{u'}{u_1} = \varrho'(X_2 - (q_2-k)M_2) + M_1' [(q_1 - MR_1) \\ -\varrho(q_2 - MR_2)] \tag{B24}$$

Finally, differentiate (35) to get

$$M_1'(q_1'+\varrho q_2') = \varrho' (q_2-k) \tag{B25}$$

Putting this into (B24) we get

$$\frac{u'}{u_1} = \varrho'\{(X_2-(q_2-k)M_2) + \frac{(q_2-k)}{q_1'+\varrho q_2'} \\ [(q_1 - MR_1) - \varrho(q_2 - MR_2)] \tag{B26}$$

We can always assume that U is chosen so that $U = 1$, so $\Delta U = \frac{u'}{u_1}$, and (B26) then gives equation (36) in the text.

(IV) Stackelberg model

Since equations (31)–(34) are common to the fifth and sixth sections of the text, the analysis of section III of this Appendix applies up to (B24). When we differentiate (37), rather than (35) we then get

$$M_1'(MR_1'+\varrho MR_2') = \varrho(MR_2-k) \tag{B27}$$

and putting (B27) into (B25) gives

$$\Delta U = \varrho'\{(X_2-q_2-k)M_2\} + \frac{MR_2 - k}{MR_1' + \varrho MR_2'} \\ [\{(q - MR) - \varrho(q - MR_2)\}] \tag{B28}$$

which is equation (38) in the text.

References

Aarrestad, J. (1978), 'Optimal Savings and Exhaustible Resource Extraction in an Open Economy', *Journal of Economic Theory*, 19, pp. 163–79.
Calvo, G. and R. Findlay (1978), 'On the Optimal Acquisition of Foreign

Capital through Investment of Oil Export Revenues', *Journal of International Economics*, 8, pp. 513–24.

Chiarella, C. (1980), 'Trade between Resource-Poor and Resource-Rich Economies as a Differential Game', in M. Kemp and N. Long (eds), *Exhaustible Resources, Optimality and Trade* (Amsterdam: North-Holland).

Chichilnisky, G. (1981), 'Oil Prices, Industrial Prices and Output: a General Equilibrium Macro Analysis', mimeo, University of Essex.

Dasgupta, P., R. Eastwood and G. Heal (1978), 'Resource Management in a Trading Economy', *Quarterly Journal of Economics*, 92, pp. 287–305.

Dasgupta, P. and G. Heal (1979), *Economic Theory and Exhaustible Resources* (Cambridge University Press).

Dixit, A. (1981), 'A Model of Trade in Oil and Capital', Discussion Papers in Economics, no. 16, Princeton University.

Griffin, J. and D. Teece (1982), *OPEC Behaviour and World Oil Prices* (George Allen & Unwin).

Kemp, M. and N. Long (eds) (1980), *Exhaustible Resources, Optimality and Trade* (Amsterdam: North Holland) Essays 16, 17, 18.

Lecomber, R. (1979), *The Economics of Natural Resources* (London: Macmillan).

Lewis, T. and A. Ulph (1985), 'A Survey of Game Theoretic Models of Trade and Exhaustible Resources', mimeo, University of British Columbia.

Marion, N. and L. Svensson (1983), 'World Equilibrium with Oil Price Increases: an Intertemporal Analysis', *Oxford Economic Papers*.

Stiglitz, J. (1976), 'Monopoly and the Rate of Extraction of Exhaustible Resources', *American Economic Review*, no 66.

Ulph, A. and D. Ulph (1981), 'International Monopoly – Monopoly Power over Oil and Capital', Discussion Paper no. 8116, University of Southampton.

Van Wijnbergen, S. (1983), 'Taxation of International Capital Flows, the Intertemporal Terms of Trade, and the Real Price of Oil', *Oxford Economic Papers*.

Vousden, N. (1974), 'International Trade and Exhaustible Resources; A Theoretical Model', *International Economic Review*, 15, pp. 149–67.

Index